# Weatherhead Center
## FOR INTERNATIONAL AFFAIRS
### HARVARD UNIVERSITY

*Celebrating Fifty Years*
*1958–2008*

Dearest Jerry,

Looking forward to yet
another one of your lectures,
this time @ the Center for
International Affairs.

With Warm Regards.

Musaed N. Al-Saleh
Harvard 19th Nov. 09'

# In Theory and in Practice

Harvard's Center for International Affairs,
1958–1983

**David C. Atkinson**

Published by Harvard University
Weatherhead Center for International Affairs
Distributed by Harvard University Press
Cambridge, Massachusetts and London

Designed by Vern Associates, Inc., Newburyport, Massachusetts
  www.vernassoc.com

ISBN: 978-0-674-02777-0


Library of Congress Cataloging-in-Publication Data

Atkinson, David C., 1975–
  In theory and in practice: Harvard's Center for International Affairs, 1958-1983 /
David C. Atkinson.
    p.  cm.
  Includes bibliographical references and index.
  ISBN 978-0-674-02777-0 (pbk.)
1. Weatherhead Center for International Affairs.  2.  International
relations—Research.  3. International relations—Study and teaching.  I. Title.
JZ1234.A85 2007
  327.071'1744—dc22
                        2007032157

*Photo credits*
Bowie: Harvard University Archives, call # UAV 605, Professor in Action Series,
  F2440 frame 8
Members 1959–60: Harvard University
Yoshino, Soemarman, Il Kwon Chung, & Pandit: Harvard University Archives,
  call # UAV 605Box 97 frame #25 GP 78
Schelling: Harvard University Archives, call # UAV 605.270.5p Box 7, frame 14a
Mason: Martha Stewart
Kissinger: Center for International Affairs, Harvard University
Lee Kuan Yew & Vernon: Center for International Affairs, Harvard University
Huntington: Harvard University Archives, call # UAV 605, Professors in Action Series,
  Huntington, frame 11a
Brown: Harvard University Archives, call # UAV 605.468.3p se 296#18a
CFIA library: Harvard University Archives, call # UAV 605.295.7p Box 7
Brzezinski: Harvard University News Office
Brown & Huntington: Center for International Affairs, Harvard University
Putnam, Huntington, Vernon, Bowie, Nye, & Dominguez: Martha Stewart
Center group photo 2006–07: Martha Stewart

# Contents

# Dedication

*To the thousands of men and women of the Weatherhead Center for International Affairs who have contributed their intellecutal gifts and their good will to extending the frontiers of knowledge and benefiting humankind.*

# Foreword

THE CENTER FOR INTERNATIONAL AFFAIRS (NOW THE WEATHERHEAD Center for International Affairs) has one of the most interesting histories of any research center of its kind. Founded near the height of the cold war, the Center was originally conceived as an institution that fosters interdisciplinary research about some of the most important foreign policy and global issues of the day. Its four founders—Robert R. Bowie (law), Henry A. Kissinger (government), Edward S. Mason (political economy), and Thomas C. Schelling (economics)— were pioneers in their fields and personalities on the national and world stages. The history of the CFIA reflects both their intellectual leadership and the evolution of thinking in international affairs and the social sciences, as well as views about the proper relationship between the two.

The purpose of this volume is to explore, reflect upon, and celebrate the first twenty-five years of the Center. Establishing the Center was a major entrepreneurial undertaking, for in 1958 some people could not understand the need for a research center devoted to "international affairs"; after all, Harvard had a Russian Research Center, what more was there to know about the world? Much, as it turns out, and as these pages reveal. The Center has always been concerned with a world in perpetual motion; as Robert Bowie, the founding Center Director put it, "The Center must continue to innovate, or its subject matter will elude its grasp." Over the years assessed in this volume, attention shifted from warfighting to arms control and deterrence theory; from the internal developments of individual European countries to the broader development and meaning of the "Atlantic community"; and from the rebuilding of Europe to broader questions of development and "modernization" worldwide. The recent past has of course brought new challenges to our understanding of international issues, but the past can also illuminate our path as we attempt to meet these challenges in the future.

Another interesting theme in the history of the Center is the relationship between the world of scholarship and the world of practice. This volume reminds us of the purpose for which the CFIA was founded: to foster basic research on important policy issues of the day. Certainly, the early intellectual leadership of the Center came from individuals with an intimate connection with the policy-making world. The Center was also meant to be a place where practitioners could come to invest in and draw on the Center's intellectual capital. The Vietnam era highlighted the complexities and difficulties of such a relationship. Basic social science research itself has become in many cases less readily accessible to policy makers. And of course, the institutional landscape at Harvard has changed; the WCFIA is not the only center of learning and research relevant to policy studies. Still, rigorous policy-relevant research animates the intellectual life of the Center today, though with a tone and emphasis much different from that of our first decade.

This volume is the result of the careful scholarship, dedication, and endeavors of David C. Atkinson. Basing his work almost exclusively on primary sources, David has stitched together the history of the CFIA from the Center's archives, photo collection, publications collection, and most valuable of all, face-to-face interviews with many of the CFIA's early affiliates and staff members. David is to be thanked for helping to bring the history of the Center alive to a new generation of scholars and practitioners.

Certainly, there is much more to say about the institution whose leadership I have inherited. After the period covered in this volume, numerous institutional challenges of an intellectual, bureaucratic, and financial nature were shouldered very responsibly by Center Directors Joseph Nye, Robert Putnam, and Jorge I. Domínguez. My colleague, Jorge I. Domínguez, deserves special recognition and appreciation from not only me but also at least two generations of scholars. For over a decade, under his energetic and sensitive leadership the Center established wise norms of governance, extended faculty membership far beyond the Faculty of Arts and Sciences to almost every Harvard professional school, and became worthy of the generous endowment gift of Albert and Celia Weatherhead to the University, which guarantees the financial health of the center far into the future. Indeed, these more recent years surely deserve their own analysis, but we will not begin to understand fully the lessons they have to teach us until more distance comes between our work today and those years' considerable accomplishments. The next twenty-five years will provide as much of a challenge to our understanding of international affairs and our ability to craft wise policy advice as the first twenty-five years of the Center's existence. Thankfully, we will be able to put those challenges in perspective with the help of this volume.

*Beth A. Simmons*
*Center Director*
*Cambridge, Massachusetts*
*July 2007*

# Preface

MOST FACULTY, FELLOWS, STUDENTS, AND STAFF WHO HAVE BEEN affiliated with the Weatherhead Center for International Affairs (WCFIA) over the years probably have some notion of the Center's rich history. That history is everywhere one cares to look, from the photographs of former associates that line the walls at 1737 Cambridge Street, to the eponymous Bowie-Vernon room. Yet much of this history may seem static upon first glance; black and white photographs, bookcases of Center-sponsored publications, and the plain, text-only covers of its early annual reports offer no immediate insights into the institution's extraordinary fifty-year history. As the Center prepares to commemorate that half century, however, it seemed to be an opportune time to dust off these ostensibly bland artifacts and delve more deeply into the Center's past.

What one finds, in contrast, is a vivid and remarkable institution, one that has grappled with the most important questions affecting the world in which we live. The Center has made enduring contributions to international affairs scholarship in the fields of defense policy and arms control, development and modernization, and transatlantic relations, among countless others. The Center has provided an intellectual space in which scholars of all disciplines have ruminated, collaborated, and disagreed on topics as varied as exchange-rate parity and Israeli-Palestinian relations. Through its Fellows Program, the Center has housed hundreds of diplomats, military officers, media professionals, and scholars from countries around the world, who have in turn enriched the scholarship of both the Center's faculty and the Harvard community as a whole. Insights generated in CFIA seminars, conferences, and conversations have resonated in Washington, D.C. as well as in capitals throughout the world.

Two years ago, as this fiftieth anniversary approached, I was asked by then–associate director, Steven Bloomfield, if I would be willing to write a history of the Center for International Affairs (as the WCFIA was known before the 1998 endowment gift of Albert and Celia Weatherhead). Having been a staff member at the WCFIA from 2000 to 2002, I left that position to begin a Ph.D. in history at Boston University, and Steve felt I would be suited to undertake this study. With the support of Jorge I. Domínguez and James A. Cooney—at that time the Center Director and Executive Director, respectively—I accepted this exciting, if not a little daunting, challenge. Our collective thoughts turned immediately toward my writing an intellectual and institutional history, long on analysis and short of celebration. I was asked to carry out a robust research project with high academic promise—and particularly to pursue a series of face-to-face interviews with many quite fortunately long-lived individuals who dedicated much of their professional lives to the Center and who would offer their reflections with both pride and perspicacity.

Together, we decided that the first twenty-five years of the CFIA's history were the most compelling, and as such this is a story of the Center's founding and maturation, which took place during a period of international tension and flux. The intellectual and institutional context of the CFIA's development during these formative years was particularly interesting, and the Center's research output was energetic, profuse, and in many cases pioneering. We developed a simple outline of the trends of which I should be broadly aware, and I set off to work, with offers of subsequent guidance, if necessary, but with an expectation among us all that I would seek the truth about the Center's history mostly on my own, wherever it led me. I can't say that I never looked back, but after our initial discussions, with this encouragement, I looked forward.

While it was obvious that there was an absorbing and important story to be told, locating source materials represented one of the most challenging aspects of reconstructing the Center's history. Relatively little in the way of administrative material has survived the Center's three institutional moves (to Coolidge Hall in 1979, to 1033 Massachusetts Avenue in 2002, and back to the new CGIS complex in 2005). Another challenge was also immediately evident. In an academic research institution such as the CFIA, much of what transpired took place during discussions among faculty members in seminar rooms, or informal conversations in offices and hallways. Thus, a great deal of what made the Center as productive as it was—dialogue and debate—went unrecorded. To be sure, these conversations often manifested themselves in the books and articles produced by Center associates, but it is nevertheless impossible to accurately trace the numerous influences that inform scholarly arguments and analysis.

Nevertheless, a number of sources were available that brought the Center's history into sharper relief. I was fortunate to have the work of a Harvard College student, Mara Allison Guagliardo, whose 1996 senior thesis on the CFIA provided innumerable insights and references that helped guide my research. In addition, despite the apparent destruction of many documents from the founding period, a small amount of historically important material was retained, most of which pertained to founding the Center and recruiting the Center Director. These documents are now located in the Harvard University Depository. On a larger scale, the Harvard University Archives (HUA) has a number of collections that relate to the CFIA. These include the minutes of the Harvard-MIT Joint Arms Control Seminar, and the records of the Development Advisory Service, both of which proved invaluable to my research, and this material informs much of the narrative in Chapters Five and Six. In addition, the HUA holds a number of related collections upon which I drew heavily, including the protests of the late 1960s and documents relating to the foundation of the CFIA dating from the early 1950s.

The Center's annual reports, compiled by successive Center Directors, were of inestimable value to my research. They recorded the CFIA's activities in every detail—often interpretive as well as descriptive—and through them it was possible to trace the major developments, scholarly contributions, and administrative issues faced by the Center over the first twenty-five years. Of course, the hundreds of books, articles, and working papers produced by Center associates over the quarter century under review also represent an unparalleled resource. In the confines of this study it was possible to discuss only a small number of the most significant studies conducted during this period, but through its scholarly output alone one is able to obtain a portrait of the Center's extraordinary productivity and contributions to scholarship. The Harvard *Crimson* also proved to be a helpful resource, especially with regard to the upheavals of the Vietnam era and the relationship between Harvard students and the CFIA in that period.

Farther afield, the Institute Archives at MIT yielded important documents relating to the Harvard-MIT Joint Arms Control Seminar. The Papers of Bernald Feld and the Papers of Max Millikan were especially helpful. In addition, since members of the CFIA were often active participants in the policy debates of the period, the John F. Kennedy Presidential Library proved to be a valuable source of information regarding CFIA scholars and their scholarship during the Kennedy administration.

The most interesting and rewarding insights into the Center's history, however, came through interviews with current and former faculty and research associates of the CFIA. They provided an incomparable source of information, new lines of enquiry, and answers to questions I hadn't thought to ask. The Center was—and is—after all, nothing without the community of scholars and practitioners that filled its offices and seminar rooms. I owe each of these interviewees my gratitude for being so generous with their time and for sharing their recollections of the Center.

I would also like to express my sincere thanks to Steven Bloomfield, Jorge I. Domínguez, and James A. Cooney for providing me with the opportunity to undertake this project, and for their continued support throughout the research and writing of this book. Steve has been especially helpful in guiding this publication and his encouragement and support has been invaluable to me. My special thanks also go to Amanda Pearson for her outstanding editorial work and good humor. Without her steady influence and careful attention this would have been a much more difficult process, and a far less enjoyable one. Robert R. Bowie, Karl Kaiser, Jorge I. Domínguez, Beth A. Simmons, and Steven Bloomfield all read the manuscript, and their comments and corrections were gratefully received and exceptionally helpful. I would like to acknowledge Robert Bowie in particular for his judicious and astute reading of the manuscript; his clarifications and suggestions were greatly appreciated. Responsibility for any remaining errors of fact and interpretation, of course, rests entirely with me.

My thanks also go to the archivists and staff of the Harvard University Archives, the John F. Kennedy Presidential Library, and the MIT Archives, who helped me to navigate the process of locating sources and were indispensable in obtaining the necessary permissions. In particular I would like to express my gratitude to Barbara Meloni, Michelle Gachette, Kyle DeCicco-Carey, Robin McElheny, and Megan Sniffin-Marinoff of the HUA, all of whom were gracious and kind in their assistance throughout the manuscript preparation. Barbara Meloni and Michelle Gachette deserve special praise for their constant goodwill and helpfulness.

Finally, I would like to thank Charity Tabol, my wife and best friend, who has been a continuous source of support, love, and patience over the last two years while this book was being researched and written.

*David C. Atkinson*
*July 2007*

# Editor's Note

THE EDITORIAL AND PRODUCTION PROCESS FOR THIS BOOK BEGAN in August 2006. Early on, I suggested that the Weatherhead Center be the sole publisher of David Atkinson's manuscript because the Center wanted, ideally, to start distributing the book at the November 2007 Fellows Program reunion conference. This condensed publication schedule required that we embrace the challenge of completing the project in-house. I am therefore grateful to a number of people for their help with various aspects of this book.

It is fortunate that David Atkinson and I have been friends for years, but more so that he blends extraordinary writing talent and scholarship with humor and a gift for clever banter. One Harvard College undergraduate, Henry Walters, was also a blessing. He was the ideal editorial assistant: required little guidance; had tremendous follow-through (even after leaving campus for Ireland); and was thoughtful, earnest, and bright. "When all is said and done, we're each on our own with language. In this most collaborative of human endeavors," wrote longtime editor Barbara Walraaf, "consensus at any level is rare." Inspired to reach consensus on over two hundred pages, we communed in an office—writer, editor, and editorial assistant—to hash out language, tinker with style alternatives, and challenge each other on "best fixes." At the end of these collaborative sessions, Weatherhead Center staff member Katherine Brady enthusiastically provided thorough proofreading of the appendices and notes.

Henry Tom, executive editor of Social Sciences at the Johns Hopkins University Press, generously shared his extensive knowledge of both academic presses in general and the scope of this project in particular.

Sara Davis at Harvard University Press provided rapid responses to my numerous questions about book distribution processes and Library of Congress cataloging procedures.

Peter Katz, Assistant University Attorney at Harvard's Office of the General Counsel, combined wit with concise advice on issues of copyright and permissions.

At Harvard University Archives, Michelle Gachette was indispensable in helping us wade through copious amounts of information regarding the Center for International Affairs. When Henry Walters and I located several photographs that were "not for circulation," Associate University Archivist Robyn McElheny helped steer us to the right place (ultimately the Harvard News Office). Both were eager supporters of our efforts to gain access to relevant, restricted records so that we could use these images to complement the manuscript.

Guiding a book from acquisition through publication often represents far more than the months it took to manage the project. As such, the publication of *In Theory and in Practice* affords me the opportunity to record my great appreciation for two colleagues who have influenced my professional life for the past nine years. Former Center Director Jorge I. Domínguez not only hired me at the Center but also encouraged me to give editing a shot—with one of his books, no less. The Center's current Executive Director, Steven B. Bloomfield, is a wise mentor for many of us; if there were more people like Steve in the world, surely it would be a more kind and gracious place in which to live and work. His unflappable encouragement in the face of chaotic deadlines has been invaluable, as have been his friendship and trust.

*Amanda Pearson*
*August 2007*

# One

# The Founding of the Center for International Affairs

IN THE FALL OF 1958, HARVARD UNIVERSITY INAUGURATED A NEW research institution devoted to the study of international relations. This new center was the culmination of five years of cautious but deliberate contemplation by Harvard faculty members and administrators. It also represented a watershed in the study of international affairs at a university that for the most part had eschewed efforts to institute the research and teaching of what some considered to be, at best, a dubious academic discipline, and at worst, akin to reading the daily newspaper. Notwithstanding Harvard's initial reticence, the Center for International Affairs (CFIA) has endured for half a century and ultimately has grown into the largest international affairs research center in the Faculty of Arts and Sciences (FAS).

The issues facing those who study international affairs have changed significantly in the past fifty years, and consequently the Center has adapted its program; the Center is constantly evolving to meet the practical and intellectual challenges engendered by the fluidity and instability of the international state system. The core tenets of the Center's mission, however, have largely remained the same: the development and dissemination of fundamental research on long-range problems of international relations. Furthermore, the position of the Center as an integral component of Harvard University's commitment to the study of international affairs has been assured by the quality and importance of its scholarship. The broader significance of the research conducted under the auspices of the Center over the last fifty years is equally remarkable, and the contributions of Center associates remain among the keystones of international relations theory.[1]

## Harvard and International Affairs

International issues began to shape the University curriculum at the turn of the twentieth century in conjunction with the increasing political and economic interests of the United States in world affairs. As a 1960 FAS report to the Ford Foundation opined: "Harvard's commitment in international affairs is both very old and very new. Learning has no automatic boundary signs, and at least since the early days of Eliot we have had a working concern for international matters . . . Yet plainly it is this new level of national involvement . . . that has been the prime mover in Harvard's commitment to international studies."[2] According to the report's authors, the first glimmer of interest in international affairs at the University inevitably followed the emergence of the United States as a world power after the United States' acquired a colonial empire in the aftermath of the Spanish-American War in 1898. American participation and experience in both World War I and World War II provided a further impetus to include international affairs in the curriculum. The present epoch, they speculated, heralded a far more durable and concerted commitment to the discipline:

> At each stage, the level of the University's activity has been many times
> multiplied: the research interest of a few faculty members in 1910 becomes part
> of the course catalogue after World War I; the dramatic temporary involvements
> of many in World War II are now being strongly developed into institutional
> activity of a lasting sort . . . it is thus not something tacked onto Harvard; it <u>is</u>
> [emphasis in the original] Harvard, as much as any other part of our work, and
> in some fields this great subject of international affairs is now the cutting edge
> of all we do.[3]

The process by which the University would finally institute a research center dedicated to the study of international affairs began in earnest in 1954, and it reveals much about the attitudes and expectations of the Harvard faculty and administration.

## The Scholar and Government Service

In addition to these stimuli from within the University, the CFIA also emerged in large part as a response to the exigencies of U.S. foreign policy, which by the middle of the 1950s had become increasingly complex and fraught with potential danger. Indeed, throughout American history periods of upheaval and transformation have almost invariably provided the catalyst for the increased involvement of the scholar in public policy appraisal and formulation, engendering the mobilization of the nation's intellectual capital and expediting the application of knowledge and expertise to matters of strategy and method. During World War I, for example, Woodrow Wilson—a scholar in his own right—established a panel of academic experts known as "The Inquiry" in order to investigate wartime and postwar political and economic problems.[4] Later, the Great Depression and the New Deal extended the scope of the federal government throughout all aspects of American political and economic life, employing the considerable intellectual talent of the beleaguered nation in an attempt to overcome the challenges of mass unemployment, inadequate social services, and shattered financial institutions.

World War II, however, represented the apotheosis of the scholar in government service up to this point. "[WW II] influenced certain academic concepts," argues V.R. Cardozier, "the aims of education, the introduction of new programs and curricula, the measurement of learning, the nature of teaching, administration, and changes in the campus culture."[5] The magnitude of the struggle required an unprecedented subordination of the nation's intellectual resources to technological research and social-scientific investigation—of which the Manhattan Project was only the most significant, and perhaps most successful, example. Accordingly, the U.S. Office of Education Wartime Commission embarked upon a campaign to mobilize the nation's educational institutions, from elementary schools to private universities, "in order that the student body may prepare itself to meet the demands of the armed forces, industry, and community service."[6] Without question, World War II engendered profound and far-reaching changes in the relationship between the American government and academia, changes that would continue to resonate throughout the postwar years.

During the cold war the imperatives of American foreign policy vis-à-vis the Soviet Union facilitated, and arguably necessitated, yet another unprecedented consolidation of the bond between American academics and their government. In many instances, this increased association of the scholar and the foreign policy maker during the 1950s and 1960s engendered a productive and constructive relationship. "This is the age of the expert," averred Henry Rowen in 1964, then deputy assistant secretary of defense and a former research associate of the CFIA, "experts are valuable."[7] Indeed, in myriad ways—from government consultation to scientific research, from game theory to modernization theory—some scholars underwent a fundamental politicization during the formative years of the cold war and others became an integral part of the foreign policy apparatus. Nevertheless, the nexus between the government and academia could just as often be fractious and divisive; tensions reached acute levels during the ideological maelstrom of the McCarthy era and again during the broader political and social dislocations of the Vietnam era.

The foundation of the Center for International Affairs took place against the backdrop of this dramatic intensification of the relationship between the U.S. government and the American academy. While the rancor of McCarthy's bitter investigations still disturbed some members of the American academy, especially those who had been subjected to his vitriol, by 1958 the relationship between power and intellect continued to solidify in the midst of the ongoing confrontation between the United States and the Soviet Union. In this context, Harvard was but one of an increasing number of American universities to recognize the need for a deeper understanding of the forces that shaped the international system in a postwar era characterized by tension and disharmony.

In addition to the exigencies of American foreign policy, the pivotal role of America's foremost philanthropic foundations in facilitating the relationship between power and intellect cannot be underestimated. "The Carnegie, Ford, and Rockefeller foundations have consistently supported the major aims of United States foreign policy," notes Edward H. Berman, "while simultaneously helping to construct an intellectual framework supportive of that policy's major tenets."[8] In most cases, these foundations provided the necessary financial capital, and, in some instances, even the intellectual stimulus to establish and expand academic efforts in the study of international affairs; foundations also provided a crucial catalyst for the growth of internationally oriented programs of research and instruction at a plethora of American academic institutions. Whereas in 1945 only a small number of American universities had programs in international affairs, by 1965 "international-affairs and area-studies programs were entrenched in major university centers from New York to California," largely owing to a massive infusion of money from the major foundations.[9]

Despite these potent stimuli, Harvard University remained somewhat restrained in regard to creating an avowed program of scholarship in international affairs. This reluctance was due to a wide variety of institutional and intellectual concerns. Some Harvard faculty members resisted such a program as an inappropriate field for academic analysis—"international affairs," they felt, was best suited for journalists and pundits rather than academics. In addition, sentimental but understandable notions of tradition coupled with fears of intellectual faddism permeated the Harvard hierarchy, and further inhibited the development of the discipline at the University.

## The Behavioral Sciences at Harvard, 1954

As founding Center Director Robert R. Bowie noted in the first annual report of the CFIA in 1960, the stimulus to establish the Center derived from the work of two faculty committees that were convened in 1954 and 1956, respectively.[10] The development of the first committee was motivated by an invitation from the Ford Foundation, which approached Harvard in 1953 with a proposal to fund a study on the behavioral sciences at the University. This offer culminated in *The Behavioral Sciences at Harvard*, a searching report that contained the initial recommendation to establish a "Center for International Studies" at the University. Consequently, in early 1956 the dean of the Faculty of Arts and Sciences, McGeorge Bundy, assembled a small group of faculty members in an effort to implement the recommendations of the 1954 Faculty Committee, which resulted in yet another faculty report, this time devoted exclusively to the creation of a new research center.[11] In addition to providing the institutional and intellectual genesis of what would eventually become the CFIA, these reports also afford an unparalleled glimpse into the academic culture of Harvard in the mid-1950s, especially as it relates to the study of international affairs.

As part of its efforts to promote academic interest in the behavioral sciences following World War II, in August 1950 the Ford Foundation sent to a number of colleges and universities a speculative memorandum soliciting proposals for academic research programs in the behavioral sciences, which included disciplines as varied as anthropology, history, psychology, and government. In the estimation of the Ford Foundation, there was a widespread "concern to increase our scientific knowledge of factors which influence or determine human conduct," coupled with a concomitant need to "extend the utilization of such knowledge for the maximum benefit of individuals and society."[12] In the realm of foreign affairs, this anxiety was perceived to be just as acute: "In the international scene there is no less need of such knowledge; with it we will be better equipped to deal with either peace or war."[13] Not surprisingly, the Ford Foundation affirmed that the nation's universities were particularly well equipped to nurture comprehensive research in the behavioral sciences, which incorporated a wide range of academic disciplines. Therefore, in the absence

5

at most American universities of an extant intellectual and administrative infrastructure that could be expected to cultivate the behavioral sciences, the Ford Foundation proposed to dispense grants for developing personnel and improving the conditions and facilities for effective research rather than for supporting specific research projects.[14] This would be the beginning of a sustained effort by the Ford Foundation to stimulate interest in the study of the behavioral sciences.

Three years later Ford expanded its efforts and began to solicit proposals from fifteen major universities (including Harvard), of which five would ultimately be chosen for a more extensive self-study project in the behavioral sciences.[15] As part of the Ford proposal, internal committees at each chosen institution conducted yearlong investigations (with the support of external visiting committees) on the state of the behavioral sciences at each university. The investigations culminated in published reports that assessed the strengths and weaknesses of the behavioral sciences and proposed recommendations for future strategies and improvements. According to the Ford Foundation, "the reports should thus be workable planning documents for the improvement of scientific study of human behavior at the institution for a period of about five years."[16] In response to the Ford Foundation's proposal, Harvard assembled an illustrious interdepartmental committee to prepare an application. The committee comprised relevant department chairs and directors, including then-designate chair of the Department of Government, McGeorge Bundy, and dean of the Graduate School of Public Administration (GSPA), Edward S. Mason, both of whom would play an important role in establishing the CFIA. This committee not only embraced but expanded the Ford Foundation's mandate by enlarging its scope in order to prepare a broad strategic plan for the next *ten* years of development.[17]

It is certainly likely that Harvard would have contemplated a center for the study of international affairs without the prompting of the Ford Foundation's behavioral sciences study, but this review afforded the University a unique opportunity to engage in a wide-ranging and systematic evaluation of Harvard's academic programs in the variegated disciplines pertaining to the study of human behavior. This in turn provided an opportunity for the faculty and administration to articulate their concerns and desires for the future of the behavioral sciences at the University, a process that ultimately led to the founding of the CFIA.

Despite their enthusiasm for implementing the Ford Foundation's proposal, the 1954 Faculty Committee was cognizant of the challenges posed by such an undertaking. Even during the application stage, they felt compelled to allude to the inevitable tension between "further strengthening what may be already strong versus filling in gaps."[18] In addition, the committee expressed a certain degree of skepticism toward interdisciplinary work: "Our inquiry should be on guard against deceptive glitter in this concept and should give due weight to the conservation of values contributed by the individual scholar who recoils from externally imposed pressures for cooperation or committee work."[19] The committee's application also articulated an undercurrent of reticence about the efficacy of "elaborate organization for research," deriving in large part from "the Harvard tradition that it is men rather than organizational mechanisms which fundamentally count."[20]

These qualms seemingly augured an unenthusiastic University-wide response to the Ford Foundation's proposals. Indeed, Harvard's final report of June 1954 amply expressed and supported such reservations. Nevertheless, the resulting study explored the broad spectrum of Harvard's activities in the behavioral sciences and probed the organization, substance, customs, and mind-set of the relevant departments and schools through extensive and anonymous interviews with a randomly selected cross section of individual faculty members. Ultimately, the fourteen-member 1954 Faculty Committee sought to "evaluate strengths and weaknesses in the fields of the behavioral sciences at this university, to appraise needs, and to look forward to the future."[21] The report provides a unique perspective on the institutional and intellectual milieu of Harvard University during the 1950s, and affords an unparalleled insight into the intellectual context within which the CFIA was established.

## Transcending Tradition

The authors of the report cited two basic issues that, in their judgment, needed to be addressed before the behavioral sciences could mature at the University—issues that would have an important bearing on the eventual foundation of the CFIA. First, the report alluded to a certain degree of institutional inertia, fostered by a commitment to Harvard's traditions and heritage, which in turn tended to inhibit the support of completely new research agendas: "Harvard has a responsibility not only to venture into the new and uncharted, but also to preserve the best already existing in its heritage from many generations of scholarship."[22] Of particular relevance to the establishment of new research centers, the authors remarked, "as compared to some universities, Harvard has been intentionally conservative with respect to setting up interdisciplinary degree programs and research institutes."[23] Such conservatism, according to the report, prevented the dilution of Harvard's traditionally high standards of research and precluded the possibility of imprudently hiring inexperienced and untried faculty. While the committee endorsed this cautious approach, they made several recommendations that were intended to strike new ground at the University and to consolidate and augment Harvard's extant institutional and organizational strengths. It was in this context that a "Center for International Studies" was proposed, which in the view of the committee would bolster a variety of existing work in several departments of Harvard College.

## Interdisciplinary Skeptics

The second major issue that the committee sought to address concerned the real and perceived obstacles that impeded academic endeavors in the Faculty of Arts and Sciences and the University's professional schools. "What are some of the strains that develop in life at Harvard and how can they be reduced?"[24] Again, the implications of this investigation provide insight into the potential scholarly and institutional impediments to creating an institution like the CFIA at Harvard. Perhaps most importantly, the committee highlighted reluctance among some faculty members to engage in interdisciplinary and collaborative research projects. This lack of enthusiasm was particularly evident in the Departments of Government, History, and to a lesser extent Economics— departments from which most of the faculty and researchers of a prospective Center for International Studies would be drawn.

Such reservations were particularly sensitive in the Government Department. In a memorandum containing draft recommendations that was submitted to the committee, for example, the Department of Government suggested a number of possibilities for future research. In addition, however, they also alluded to possible obstacles, including a general disinclination toward large-scale collaborative research. "Our custom of individual work," department chair V. O. Key protested, "comes from no particular antipathy toward multiple-person operation but largely from the type of problems we try to cope with."[25]

Key and his colleagues were far from myopic where the future was concerned, however, and, significantly, they listed as their first recommendation "the development of additional strength in the field of international relations."[26] Nevertheless, the department felt that it was not enough to simply augment the discipline by hiring new faculty. Indeed, they reasoned that the problem was "more fundamentally one of rethinking the proper method, substance, and organization of the field." This concern would become a recurring motif throughout exploratory discussions pertaining to the creation of a new research center devoted to international affairs. In short, the Department of Government believed that the discipline lacked the appropriate intellectual foundation and coherence to warrant the immediate diversion of funds and talent.[27]

One solution advanced by the Government Department was to establish a new research seminar that focused on issues of "Political Behavior in International Relations." Such a seminar would bring together faculty and graduate students interested in issues of international relations in order to "appraise the current state of theoretical and empirical work in the field and to make recommendations on the organization of courses, research methods, and a program of substantive research for the future." While the recommendations stopped short of suggesting the creation of a research center per se, they did propose that such a seminar could both sponsor research in international relations and provide funds for fellowships and publications. This in turn would address some of the more fundamental concerns expressed by the faculty about the lack of a scholarly keystone for the development of the field. In fact, the department's most pressing need, it estimated, were funds to support both the seminar and its research agenda.

## The Intersection of Research and Policy Making

Another issue raised throughout the course of the behavioral sciences study that had important implications for the creation of the CFIA was the constitution of an appropriate relationship between the researcher and the policy maker. The report revealed that there was a certain degree of tension at Harvard between abstract, theoretical scholarship, and applied policy-oriented scholarship. "The proper degree of concern with professional application of knowledge is subject to much discussion," admitted the committee, "but some acceptance of practical responsibilities to the world outside Harvard seems noncontroversial."[28] Indeed, according to the report, "the aim of guiding policy must compete with the aim of advancement of knowledge for its own sake, but it competes vigorously and powerfully."[29] This tension was certainly exacerbated by the cold war, which unquestionably facilitated the increased interdependence of the scholar and the statesman, an association that was alternately mutually beneficial and downright discordant.

The proliferation of research centers and think tanks that probed questions of perceived national importance, often sustained by government funding, blurred the distinction between independent scholastic inquiry and officially mandated investigation. Many scholars wrestled with the professional and ethical dilemmas of increased interaction with government agencies and

9

intelligence services. As one former faculty member of the Harvard History Department, Arthur M. Schlesinger, would later write, no doubt speaking from experience, there was:

> *a certain—and understandable—skepticism on the part of intellectuals about the uses to which power seeks to put intellect. Most of the time power wants the intellectual not at all as an intellectual—that is as a man with a critical and speculative interest in general ideas—but rather as a technician, as a man who can perform specified intellectual services.* [30]

The liaison between government and the academy would become increasingly strained as the 1960s wore on, but in the context of the CFIA's founding in 1957–58, predating as it did the tumult and friction generated by the Vietnam War and bolstered by the remarkable mobilization of the nation's intellectual resources during World War II, the connection was healthy and robust.

After assessing the University's strengths in the behavioral sciences, as well as the challenges that it faced, the report eventually highlighted the state of the field of international affairs at Harvard. The diagnosis was positive, but the prognosis was ambiguous: "Despite difficulties and dissatisfactions which we shall report shortly, the study of international affairs is actively pursued at Harvard."This was a somewhat accurate assessment, at least modestly so in the classroom, since the report calculated eight courses on international politics and foreign policy in the Department of Government, and five in other relevant departments. [31] Looking forward, however, "our survey indicated considerable dissatisfaction and uncertainty as to promising paths of development." [32] Again, what appeared to be lacking in the view of interested faculty was any clear intellectual or institutional framework within which research in international affairs could be systematically and comprehensively encouraged, undertaken, and improved. Indeed, the discipline was frequently derided as simply "a branch of current events," or "commentaries on yesterday's *Times*" in the words of two faculty members. [33] Those engaged in the field were apparently well aware of this attitude—and perhaps even shared it themselves—but there appeared to be few available remedies, since the study of international affairs was in many ways still perceived to be in its infancy and had yet to mature into a rigorous academic discipline.

Such concerns, however, did not diminish the potential significance of the field. According to the report, "the problem seems to be to give a solid intellectual structure to the field in terms of guiding ideas and appropriate subject matter. Its practical importance and the demands for instruction in it are greater than its intellectual resources readily meet."[34] Clearly, any attempt to establish a research center with a mandate for international affairs would have to address these institutional and intellectual concerns.

## Harvard Considers Establishing a New Center

The question of the establishment of a dedicated Center for International Studies warranted a separate discussion in the report. Significantly, the committee considered the broad parameters of international affairs to be a field of study that was deeply enmeshed in the traditional scope of enquiry of economics, political science, history, psychology, sociology, and anthropology rather than a separate discipline. "The advancement of knowledge in this area is not likely to be fostered by treating international relations as a self-contained science." Instead, the report adjudged, "what is required is an intensive application of skills in all the behavioral sciences to the problems and configuration of relationships that are particularly germane to this field."[35]

With the notable exception of the Law School, Harvard's devotion of resources, personnel, and research to the field of international affairs was deficient. Within the Faculty of Arts and Sciences, the committee reported "an awareness of neglected opportunities and a disposition to do what can be done to improve the situation." The principal issue was a lack of interested, qualified scholars, and a dearth of facilities and resources with which to support them. It was in this context that the committee proposed "the establishment of a Center for International Studies, modelled [sic] after the Russian Research Center, and financed by a long-term foundation grant" in order to "provide such a rallying point." Not only would the proposed center provide a focus for like-minded scholars in the field, but it would also engender "a climate in which the mutual stimulus of co-workers engaged in both separate and common enterprises would come into play," and possibly attract new faculty and researchers to Harvard.[36] This center was also expected to enrich the teaching mission of the University, and facilitate connections with analogous enterprises at Harvard and the broader academic community in Cambridge and beyond.[37] With these justifications in mind, the committee submitted the recommendation that the new center be established, and proposed that the University undertake to procure foundation support in order to finance the project.[38]

Despite the final recommendations of the committee, the external visiting committee, which was appointed jointly by the Ford Foundation and Harvard, expressed skepticism about the extent to which a separate research center was

11

necessary.[39] One reservation conveyed by the visiting committee pertained to the possible redundancy of a Center for International Studies in view of the extant Russian Research Center at Harvard. Although the visiting committee acknowledged the success of the Russian Research Center and agreed that it provided a possible model, they nonetheless speculated whether a separate Center for International Studies might create "undesirable duplication" that would seriously question its justification.[40] Putting their hesitations aside, the visiting committee ultimately approved the establishment of a Center for International Studies, which would be constituted in one of two ways: Either the new center would absorb the Russian Research Center, or the activities of the Russian Research Center would be enlarged to accommodate a broader research agenda.

12

The visiting committee's reservations are instructive in that they reflect (perhaps unsurprisingly) a narrow conception of the nature of international relations in the mid-1950s. They implicitly assumed that the purview of any research center dedicated to research in foreign affairs would necessarily focus on the bipolar competition between the United States and the Soviet Union. With the aid of a grant from the Carnegie Corporation, the Russian Research Center was established in 1948 with a mandate to "enlarge and deepen intellectual understanding as to how the Soviet system works, with special reference to determining factors in the international actions and policies of the Soviet Union."[41] It would remain to be seen whether the prospective new Center for International Studies would reflect the visiting committee's concern over the potential for redundancy by focusing primarily on issues relating to the U.S.-Soviet conflict, or whether its leadership would strike a new, distinctive course and fashion a much broader conception of what constituted international relations.

### Implementation: The 1956 Faculty Committee and a New Center for International Affairs

The question of whether or not to accept the recommendation of *The Behavioral Sciences at Harvard* report to fill the lacuna of international relations at the University now fell to an ad hoc committee established by FAS Dean McGeorge Bundy. Despite his participation in the Ford Foundation study, only three years earlier Bundy had expressed his view to the skeptical chair of the Department of Government, V. O. Key: "I feel quite certain that we are not likely to go into the business of 'institutes of international politics.'"[42] Nevertheless, Bundy would become one of the catalysts for developing such a "business" at Harvard University. Indeed, the Center's founding director, Robert Bowie, recalls "Bundy was really the spark plug," and credits him with providing the intellectual and institutional stimulus for the eventual establishment of the Center for International Affairs.[43]

The 1956 Faculty Committee unreservedly endorsed the recommendation of the 1954 report, and proceeded to outline their conception of the Center's role and research agenda. A Center for International Studies ought to be established to provide the institutional focus for the study of international affairs that Harvard lacked, despite the range of research and teaching that comprised the field. "Such a Center," they envisaged, "would be designed to bring together the existing resources of the University, and to supplement these resources for both training and research purposes." The Center as they conceived it would train both scholars and practitioners, from the United States and abroad, as well as provide a program of postgraduate training for future practitioners. In order to accomplish these goals, the Center was expected to engage in "the organization and support of research, including interdisciplinary research," which would in turn enhance the value and effectiveness of the training program.[44]

In terms of a substantive program for the new center, the committee suggested the establishment of several large-scale research projects, under the direction of designated faculty members. In turn, these professors would then recruit a number of senior research associates from either within Harvard or other institutions. Significantly, in addition to academic researchers and advanced graduate students, "mature public servants of scholarly proclivities" might be appointed to join the major research programs.[45]

## Defining the Scope of Center Research and Training

This speculative research agenda was also intended to exploit and augment the strengths and interests of current members of the Harvard faculty. The committee outlined what they perceived to be the possible purview of the Center, placing particular emphasis on issues of "economic development and social and political change" in addition to matters of "defense organization and political-military strategy." These fields were seen as being of fundamental importance, presumably because of both their centrality to the waging of the cold war and their value to the policy-making community in Washington. In addition, the committee also advocated the inclusion of several broad—and arguably principally academic—programs on diplomatic history, the theory and practice of international relations, methods of international organization, and comparative government.[46]

In conjunction with the major research programs, it was expected that the Center would also conduct a range of training initiatives for three distinct constituencies: Ph.D. candidates and postdoctoral scholars, mid-career practitioners, and masters-level students. First, there would be provisions for the training of Ph.D. candidates and postdoctoral-level scholars in the field of international affairs, largely in conjunction with the research programs directed by senior faculty members and the relevant academic departments. Second, during one academic year practitioners from the United States and abroad would be invited to sample a range of courses pertinent to their area of responsibility or interest.[47] In this category, it was expected that U.S. Foreign Service Officers, along with officials from various other U.S. agencies, would most likely take advantage of the opportunities of the Center and the University. Finally, the Center would also host masters-level students interested in careers in international relations, although such students would take courses offered by the academic departments.[48]

The committee envisaged that this enterprise would be the responsibility of a director, who would be a member of the faculty working in conjunction with an interdepartmental committee under the aegis of the Faculty of Arts and Sciences, although the Graduate School of Public Administration would oversee all training programs. In addition to designated library facilities devoted to materials on international affairs, the committee also recognized the need for physical space, but they did not indicate whether this space already existed in Harvard's real estate holdings. Finally, it was determined that outside sources of funding would constitute the bulk of the Center's operating budget, although the committee was reluctant to comment further until a more comprehensive plan was formulated.[49] The committee was adamant, however, that "If a venture of this magnitude is to be launched with a hope of continuity, it is obviously desirable that it be given support for an extended period, if possible for not less than ten years at the start."[50] It was now left to Dean Bundy to disseminate this plan, assess University-wide interest in the idea of a Center for International Studies, and install a director, whose responsibility it would be to refine and implement the committee's recommendations.[51]

## Leadership: The Search for a Center Director

The search for a director got underway almost immediately, and Bundy turned not to a current member of the Harvard faculty, but rather to Robert Richardson Bowie, a graduate of Harvard Law School and the then director of the Policy Planning Staff at the U.S. Department of State. By 1956, Bowie had already accumulated an impressive resume of government service, and had been involved in some of the seminal moments of postwar international relations. In the immediate aftermath of World War II, he had served as an assistant to General Lucius Clay, who commanded the military occupation in the U.S. zone of Germany. In 1946, Bowie joined the faculty of the Harvard Law School, specializing in antitrust law, where he would remain until May 1953, with the exception of a brief return to Germany from 1950 to 1952, where he worked closely with the U.S. high commissioner to Germany, John J. McCloy, as his legal advisor. In fact, it was at the urging of McCloy that the recently inaugurated Eisenhower administration invited Bowie to lead the Policy Planning Staff at the State Department, where he also served as assistant secretary of state for planning from December 1955 to his resignation on May 16, 1957.[52]

In the spring of 1956, following Harvard's decision to establish the Center for International Affairs, Bowie recalls that he was visited by a committee from the University and urged to accept the leadership role of the new center. Although the offer was an attractive one, Bowie was reluctant to leave the government at that time, but intimated that he would be more amenable to their offer the following year, if they were willing to wait.[53]

Bowie remembers being subject to a number of factors when contemplating the offer to become the director of the CFIA. For one thing, he felt he would have to leave the State Department, in large part due to the burden that his job placed upon his family, particularly since his two young children were approaching school age. Just as compelling, however, was the opportunity to engage in the strategic, long-term analysis of foreign affairs: "The idea of presiding over a university effort to shed light on these subjects appealed to me."[54] His interest in questions relating to the conduct and formulation of foreign policy had been stimulated during his years of government service, and, not surprisingly, by his tenure as director of policy planning in the Eisenhower administration.

In late 1956 and early 1957, as Bowie continued to perform his duties in the Eisenhower administration, he began to seriously consider Harvard's offer and contemplate the possible outlines of the Center. Bundy, for his part, gently nudged Bowie for a positive response in the fall and winter of 1956. It is clear from the tenor of their correspondence that Bundy was especially keen to secure Bowie's services. In November 1956, for example, Bundy wrote to apprise Bowie of developments in the Department of Government. "I do hope that as you consider the choices that you have been debating . . . [and] you are coming to feel the attraction of the job we have discussed. Ed Mason and the rest continue to hope for you." The carrot in this case came in the form of the Government Department's approval of Bowie's appointment as a full professor in the department, should he decide to accept the offer of the Center's directorship. But, as Bundy intimated, the fall of 1956 was a tumultuous time in the very real world of international affairs. The recently reelected Eisenhower administration was still dealing with the consequences of the Soviet repression of the Hungarian rebellion and the Suez Crisis, instigated by the machinations of Great Britain, France, and Israel in October 1956.

Although his timing may have been inopportune, Bundy certainly recognized the harsh realities of Bowie's position. "The world has been whirling," Bundy acknowledged, "and you must have had little time for anything outside the crises." Bundy even accepted the possibility that the circumstances might preclude Bowie from even leaving the government: "it may even be that your sense of timing and choices has been altered." Not to be outdone by the exigencies of American foreign policy, Bundy impressed upon Bowie that this was all the more reason to establish the Center for International Studies at Harvard. "From where we sit here," Bundy entreated, "it seems as if the need for a lively and effective center of study and statement on the realities of our foreign affairs has seldom been greater."[55]

In response, Bowie confirmed that "events since I saw you . . . have left little time for thinking about my own plans," and he was necessarily circumspect in his reply, allowing only that "on the basis of my discussions on the visit to Harvard and with several other people since, I have thought a bit about how such a program should be organized to be effective."[56] Bundy was not prepared to concede defeat to the forces of international crisis, and by February 1957, with his tongue perhaps only slightly pressed against his cheek, he wrote again to Bowie. "In the still more urgent field of American foreign policy, I think we would be in a strong position to mount a more rapid and large-scale attack as soon as we can extract you from the clutches of Harvard men in the Department of State."[57]

Bowie's decision, however, was by no means certain, and he benefited from the counsel and encouragement of friends and colleagues, many of whom were keen to offer both substantive and personal advice. The counsel he received is instructive in terms of how Harvard's effort in international affairs was perceived by those both inside and outside the University. For example, Don Price, then a vice president of the Ford Foundation, alluded to the potential of Bowie's appointment in ascertaining the extent to which academic research could be expected to contribute to the policy-making community: "I have always wondered how much real value there was to the government from research conducted in this field. It seems to me that you are probably in a unique position to test this out from where you now sit."[58] In many ways, Bowie was indeed ideally situated to assess the validity of this proposition; he was also probably the most qualified individual to establish a research center devoted to the fundamental questions of international affairs.

Another correspondent who offered guidance to Bowie was W. Barton Leach, a former colleague of Bowie's at the Harvard Law School and an occasional consultant to the United States Air Force. Leach warned Bowie that the transition from public to academic life might be somewhat deflating. "I rather suspect you would be quite unhappy if you put behind you all these things in which you now play so vital a part and which are all so deadly important to the world." His assessment was not all negative, however, and Leach conceded that Harvard was generally supportive of its faculty engaging in government service, if Bowie chose to retain his government links.[59] Leach was also adamant that Bowie demand the utmost latitude in defining the contours of the Center's research program. The problem, from Leach's perspective—and one he had faced in his own leadership of Harvard's Defense Studies Program—was that "your field of activity is by necessity vague at the boundaries." With this in mind, Leach suggested that Bowie " . . . guarantee never to accuse anyone else of encroaching on your field and you [should] ask the same of your colleagues . . . "[60]

The proposed training component of the Center's program was also a source of consternation for Leach. From his perspective, again probably based on his own experience at the Defense Studies Program, the academic strictures of the traditional Harvard departments might be incongruous with the needs of the Center's potential students. Leach went so far as to suggest that "a different kind of degree" might even be warranted. In any event, if the Center was in fact established with a training component, "the academic diet must be designed for that purpose rather than for some other, and the incentive of an advanced degree must not be denied."[61] Despite his numerous friendly admonitions, Leach was eager to see Bowie accept the offer, and as if to assuage any concern Bowie may have harbored regarding the transition from public service to academia, Leach added, "one's life in a Government Department is often quite substantial when one is of it but not in it."[62]

In May 1957, faced with the choice of returning to his former position at Harvard Law School, joining the foreign service, or accepting Harvard's offer to establish the Center for the International Affairs, Bowie chose the last. On

May 6, 1957, he was formally appointed director of the Center for International Affairs (as it was then officially known) and Professor of International Affairs in the Faculty of Public Administration; both appointments commenced on July 1, 1957.

In addition to recruiting Bowie, Bundy also sought to secure the services of Henry A. Kissinger to serve as the associate director of the Center. Kissinger had earned his B.A. (1950), M.A. (1952), and Ph.D. (1954) from Harvard, and subsequently directed a study on nuclear weapons and foreign policy at the Council on Foreign Relations in New York, from 1955 to 1956, from which his first book *Nuclear Weapons and Foreign Policy* was derived. He was a frequent commentator on issues of foreign policy in the influential journal *Foreign Affairs*, and served as a consultant to a number of government agencies, including the Joint Chiefs of Staff and the Operations Research Office. When the CFIA was created, Kissinger was directing a special studies project at the Rockefeller Brothers Fund. He seemed to be an ideal candidate for the Harvard position, since he was already deeply immersed in thinking about the nature and formulation of American foreign policy and had a great deal of experience at the University. Although Kissinger had already been offered another position at the Council on Foreign Relations, Bundy was keen to secure him in the role of associate director. Kissinger ultimately accepted the offer to become the Center's associate director.

With the two key personnel issues now settled, Bowie wrote to Bundy on May 8, 1957 in order to reiterate and clarify a number of outstanding issues that he deemed essential to the successful establishment of the Center. "We both agree that the Center must enjoy autonomy and be able to operate flexibly in order to achieve the standing and results we both want." This understanding between Bowie and Bundy reflected not only the inchoate nature of the new Center but also the amorphous nature of international affairs as a field of study, at Harvard and beyond. In addition, Bowie made it clear that "it will also be part of the normal pattern for the Director and members of the Center to serve as consultants and undertake specific assignments with public and private agencies in the field of international affairs." Evidently, Bowie had internalized some of the advice he had received, particularly from his former colleague in the Law School, W. Barton Leach, and was clearly eager to retain his links to the public sphere—links that could prove invaluable to both the new center and the conduct of American foreign policy itself. Finally, all that remained was for Bowie to elucidate his desire and expectation to retain the continued support of Dean Bundy as the Center moved forward into uncharted waters.[63]

## Two

# The Program of the
# Center for International Affairs

BOWIE UNDERSTOOD HIS APPOINTMENT TO LEAD THE CFIA AS A MAN-
date to conceive and formulate the Center's role and function: "Bundy agreed
that the first year would be devoted to planning the program, organizing,
staffing, and financing the Center."[1] Bowie was given the 1957–58 academic
year to define and organize the final intellectual and institutional structure of
the Center for International Affairs. In his view "the justification for a center
was to try and get the stimulus of interaction between different perspectives
on these different problems [of international affairs], and that essentially meant
trying to break through some of the departmental tendencies to be parochial,
localized [and] focused."[2] Ultimately, the final manifestation of the new
institution certainly reflected his personal preferences and innovations. For his
part, Kissinger was still occupied with the Rockefeller Brothers Fund and spent
a good deal of time in New York during this period.

### Planning the CFIA

The original planning document composed by Bowie in 1957 is especially
enlightening in terms of understanding how the Center reflected, or indeed
diverged from, earlier faculty proposals. The core of Bowie's final prospectus
was attuned to the international political context of the Center's founding and
focused on the research design that the Center would pursue in the coming years.
An earlier draft of Bowie's program also highlights a number of issues that were

salient during the planning phase, but they were ultimately eliminated from the final plan. Taken together, these two prospectuses enrich our understanding of the direction envisaged for the Center in that formative year.

## Bowie's Program: Enterprising Scholarship, the Fellows, and Long-range Research

The product of Bowie's labors during the 1957–58 academic year is contained in the *Program of the Center for International Affairs*.[3] As Bowie recalls, the publication "was intended as both the founding charter for the Center and as a basis for fundraising."[4] He articulated an expansive, penetrating, and sophisticated conception of what constituted international affairs in the late 1950s. In his view, fledgling nations that were emerging from the archaic and degenerating European empires posed significant challenges to the once unrivalled dominance of these great powers. Communism was only one of many perpetrators that were enervating the old international system: "Under the impact of wars, nationalism, technology and communism," Bowie asserted, "the old order has been shattered."[5] In addition, one of the most ominous catalysts for change in international affairs, in Bowie's estimation, was the development of nuclear weapons: "And over all broods the atom, with its promise and its threat."[6] In his analysis, then, the cold war was but one of the many monumental changes that were fundamentally altering the nature of international affairs.

Bowie stressed the mercurial and opaque nature of the international state system and counseled that traditional means of exercising power were not always the most effective solutions to the problems of international affairs. According to Bowie, "the heavy burden on our physical and financial means tends sometimes to divert attention from the even more critical demands on knowledge, understanding and creative thought."[7] Effective responses to the short-term and strategic needs of foreign policy required the application of this knowledge. Ultimately, the Center was necessary, he urged, because, "nowhere do traditional attitudes fit new realities." Increased interdependence among nations and the consequences of individual countries' foreign policies had never before been so profoundly enmeshed with one another. This political interdependence necessitated the thoughtful and comprehensive formulation of foreign policy. In essence, Bowie contended that Harvard's new research center would be a catalyst for innovative thinking and enterprising scholarship. "*First*" he contended, "is the pressing need for widened knowledge and understanding: for more awareness of the nature and complexity of foreign affairs; for more informed and imaginative thinking." The Center would provide the intellectual and financial resources for the propagation of such thinking, as well as a forum for the preparation and dissemination of these ideas. The Center's second contribution would be to address the "urgent need for wise and skillful people." Creative thinking about foreign policy was not enough; plans for implementing these innovative proposals were also needed: "There must be experts steeped in the study of geographical areas and other specialized knowledge; but also and perhaps even more importantly, individuals able to analyze the deeper causes of events and to pull them together into a whole."[8]

Bowie was convinced that in order to comprehensively study international affairs, however (as others had noted before him), it was necessary to draw on the methodology and insights of a number of related disciplines. In his view, international affairs as a discipline was necessarily a composite of other fields of inquiry, such as politics, economics, and sociology. In this sense, the Center's work had to be interdisciplinary in scope. Nevertheless, simply extracting and synthesizing the accumulated knowledge from these relevant fields was not enough: "Much of the significant data is not accessible to research by conventional means." Such information, Bowie understood, "resides largely in the minds of those who have been responsible for administering programs while technical and social revolutions were daily changing the presuppositions." This singular insight became a cornerstone of the Center for International Affairs in the form of the Fellows Program:

> *Under this program the Center will regularly invite a few qualified people from government, academic, and private life in the United States and from abroad to work at the Center. From the United States, officials invited will include experienced officers from the Department of State, the military services and other agencies engaged in foreign activities. From abroad qualified men will be invited from various regions such as Europe, the Middle and Far East and Latin America. In each case, the aim will be to obtain first-rate men of experience.[9]*

The goal was to integrate the Fellows Program into the academic life of the Center and the University, and in turn the "Fellows" would enrich and enliven scholars' understanding of contemporary international affairs. These practitioners would consequently benefit from access to the Center's academic resources and profit from the time to reflect more deeply on their own professional responsibilities and intellectual development. The Center would provide a forum for such reflections, and facilitate a blend of practical experience and academic expertise:

*In the atmosphere of the Center, the participants should be able to discuss*
*far more freely the problems likely to arise in the future and alternative ways*
*of meeting them. The seminars, research projects and other activities will be*
*directed to presenting, analyzing and prescribing for such potential issues.*
*Free of their normal obligations, the officials could express views as individuals*
*instead of representatives of their countries.*[10]

In addition to Center resources, the Fellows would also have access to the University and would be encouraged to take courses in anything that interested them. As a whole, the interaction of scholars and practitioners focused on studying basic and long-range issues of international affairs was a promising formula.

Although earlier speculative outlines of the CFIA's orientation had considered including practitioners among the cadre of trainees, Bowie's conception of their role as Fellows was much more integral to the research agenda of the Center. Not surprisingly, his own experience in the U.S. government informed his objectives with regard to the Fellows Program. In his view, the unprecedented degree of interdependence in the realm of international affairs—and the attendant potential for instability engendered by the effective collapse of the prewar international system—obliged those responsible for the conduct of foreign policy to possess a richer and more nuanced understanding of other nations' societies and cultures. An increased depth of understanding that went beyond a superficial knowledge of political trends and social customs would, in Bowie's mind, facilitate a more sophisticated and judicious policy. During his time with the Policy Planning Staff, for example, Bowie often invited personnel from the State Department's Bureau of Intelligence and Research to attend meetings, because its staff often had insights about other countries based on either having lived abroad or having developed personal international ties. "I didn't try to get them to be a policy maker," Bowie remembers, "but to be somebody who would help to give us rich context."[11] This experience would inform his notion of what alumni of the Fellows Program ought to be able to contribute to their governments' foreign policies.

Another important rationale for the establishment of the Fellows Program was to counterbalance the insularity of diplomats. According to Bowie, "[diplomats] tend to deal with other [diplomats]." In addition, he was also aware that the nature of this occupation was such that assignments were often short in duration and somewhat capricious in appointment, which meant that foreign service personnel had little time to reflect on their experiences in different circumstances and conditions. While this modus operandi was certainly a necessity in the world of international politics, Bowie felt that "it would be very desirable, for the purposes of trying to create a world in which you had much more cooperation, to have them have some feeling for other societies and their values and priorities." In his view, one of the core functions of the Center's Fellows Program was to engender a deeper, more discerning, and emotive comprehension of the societies in which the Fellows might be posted. In order to facilitate this, Bowie recalls that he "tried to generate that kind of an atmosphere among them, so that they would begin to really interact and educate one another, and end up feeling that they had a better grip on what the world was like." While the Fellows were at the Center, they would have time to reflect on their roles and experiences in an informal and stimulating setting "in which it would be absolutely forbidden that they should represent their government."[12]

## The Research Program

Bowie then turned to the substantive research agenda of the Center and outlined the scope of inquiry that the Center's participants would be expected to undertake. Research associates were to be selected on the basis of their interests rather than specific pre-selected projects. The scholarly enterprise he envisaged was in a far better position than the government to pursue studies of basic issues relating to foreign affairs. While he accepted that research undertaken by government agencies on specific issues of immediate concern was often competent and insightful, the everyday demands of policy often precluded a fundamental assessment of long-term goals and objectives: "policy making must often start with premises which are unexplored for lack of time or staff to analyze them." In Bowie's estimation, outside institutions such as the CFIA were far better equipped to carry out this type of research.[13]

Indeed, Bowie recalls that his own government service was very influential in formulating the Center's program. "I was struck by the fact that in government there is a very strong pressure to concentrate on current issues," Bowie recollects, "and very sparse attention is paid to the longer range perspectives that would help to define our priorities and what your strategy was." The daily task of responding to cable traffic had the potential to undermine policy, because "if decisions are not made within a larger framework they can end up being counterproductive, or contradictory, or just random." From Bowie's perspective, then, long-range strategic analysis languished in government agencies preoccupied with the immediacy of international issues.[14]

That is not to say that Bowie envisaged the Center to be an adjunct of the State Department, responding to the needs and whims of government agencies. In fact, he remains circumspect on that issue, maintaining that "I didn't have it pictured that we were going to be doing things that were commissioned by the government." Indeed, in hindsight Bowie recognizes that "perhaps I didn't think through enough exactly how our work would be infused into the government." Bowie recognized two possible conduits for transmitting scholarship of this type into the policy-making community. On one hand, "my own thinking was that if you had in the general discourse, intellectually, among people who thought about these things, discussion of, and perhaps consensus on certain things…that people in the government…would be influenced by the general intellectual context." In this sense, then, the work of the Center might be expected to percolate into the minds of government officials who were attuned to the intellectual milieu of academia and scholarly debate through the Center's books and articles. The second conduit, of course, was through individuals such as Bowie himself, who constituted a cadre of so-called inners and outers, moving between the academy and the government and therefore functioning as carriers of intellectual capital.[15] With this in mind, Bowie outlined a research agenda for the Center that focused on basic matters of strategic, long-range importance to formulating policy.

Permanent members of the Center faculty—in conjunction with other interested faculty, Fellows, and invited research associates—would direct each area of research at the Center and conduct seminars in their particular field. In all, Bowie outlined five areas of research: European relations; economic and political development; the role of force and arms control; international organization; and the Far East.

First, and perhaps not surprisingly, the Center would concentrate on issues pertaining to "Europe and the Atlantic Community." Although the cold war in Europe would be of special importance, it would represent only one aspect of a much broader enquiry into the nature of international affairs with regard to Europe. European integration—a process already well underway since the inception of the European Coal and Steel Community in 1951—European relations with the United States, which was subsumed under the rubric of the Atlantic community, and Europe-Africa relations were also topics of this particular field.[16]

The second major area of research would focus on economic and political development. In Bowie's judgment, although research was already underway on the economic aspects of development in underdeveloped countries, there were also important social and political aspects that deserved more attention. "Such study," according to Bowie,

> will range far beyond economic aspects. It must seek to discover the changes in traditions, habits and institutions required to make static societies sufficiently dynamic to achieve material and social progress for a growing population. And it must seek to examine and predict the collateral consequences of such change and their effects on stability, interests and attitudes. [17]

The Center's research program would illuminate the possible impediments and pathways to development, and, moreover, the presence of the Fellows among scholars engaged in various aspects of the development process would reciprocally enrich the knowledge of all participants from both the developed and developing worlds.

The cold war was central to the Center's third field of research. The study of "The Role and Control of Force," as the *Program* defined it, would encompass the relationship between developments in modern weaponry and strategic and political doctrine and policy. Obviously, nuclear weapons and their role in international affairs and military planning would be a focal point of this study, as well as a concomitant effort to "analyze these interrelated problems in relation to foreign policy and evolving technological and political developments." [18]

These three fields would prove to be by far the most intellectually lucrative enterprises of the Center in the years to come, led as they were by some of the generation's most able scholars. In addition to these areas, however, Bowie also included two other less well-developed fields of inquiry. "International Order and Conflict," and "Far Eastern Problems" would constitute the final two elements of the Center's research agenda. The former was conceived, somewhat vaguely, as a wide-ranging investigation into the "underlying factors and principles affecting world economic and political relations as well as the maintenance of peace." The latter subject did not become a central facet of the Center's intellectual life until well into the 1970s. This delay was perhaps due to a dearth of existing researchers on the subject rather than a lack of interest by the Center. Moreover, the East Asian Research Center—established in 1955 under the leadership of the Francis Lee Higginson Professor of History John King Fairbank—necessarily inhibited the Center's activities in this area.

Contrary to what one might expect—and indeed contrary to what the progenitors of the idea of such a Center seem to have envisaged—there was no separate research program on the cold war in Bowie's conception of the

Center's agenda. The impact of the Soviet Union and the People's Republic of China did not warrant a separate reference in Bowie's outline of the Center's research program for three reasons. For one thing, Bowie noted that "they will be relevant and often major factors in the analysis of each of the fields listed."[19] Among other things, this was indicative of Bowie's conviction that the Center's research program was to be integrated and interconnected, even at the expense of such a palpably germane focus of study as the Soviet Union and international communism. Second, Bowie clearly was heeding the advice of his friend W. Barton Leach to avoid transgressing too flagrantly on the academic turf of other institutions or academic departments, in this case the Russian Research Center and the East Asian Research Center. Finally, the admonition of the Ford Foundation study's visiting committee also continued to resonate in terms of avoiding the duplication of effort. The imperative of meeting the Soviet challenge is certainly implicit (and occasionally explicit) throughout the document, and Bowie was clearly cognizant of the cold war implications for the study of international affairs. In any event, omitting a dedicated field of enquiry relating to the Soviet Union is noteworthy.

## Teaching and Policy Making at the CFIA

The Soviet Union is not the only "elephant in the room" as far as the *Program of the Center for International Affairs* is concerned. Also missing from the final draft of the Center's program is any reference to teaching and training Harvard students. This had been a constant motif of earlier conceptions of the Center for International Affairs, and its omission from the final program is especially notable, particularly with regard to an earlier draft of the *Program* that devoted a great deal more attention to the teaching mission of the CFIA. This earlier draft promised "certain added benefits at Harvard and elsewhere," and one such benefit was that "the activities of the Center can enrich teaching and training in foreign affairs throughout the University."[20] In particular, the draft program proposed that "the permanent members of the Center faculty will also devote part of their time to graduate training," and it was projected that those faculty members responsible for the Center's principal research areas would conduct seminars and give courses in the appropriate departments and professional schools at Harvard. More tentatively, the draft program also suggested that "selected graduate students with special qualifications might take part in the work of the Center itself."[21]

With regard to undergraduate students, however, even the draft program was more circumscribed. The assumption was that the results and insights of the Center's research would filter into the teaching and research of the broader Harvard faculty. By providing a base for research on international affairs, it was expected that the benefits of participating in the Center's various research programs would infuse the undergraduate teaching of various Harvard faculty: "the instruction and interest of all should be quickened by association with high level officials and other mature associates of the Center working intensively on foreign affairs problems. In this and other ways the influence of the Center is expected to spread to undergraduate teaching."[22] Ultimately, however, all references to the teaching benefits of the Center were dropped from the final program.

There were several factors involved in this decision to remove an explicit teaching component from the Center's program. First, Bowie, Bundy, and Edward Mason forged an agreement, which ultimately received the assent of Don Price, who would be Mason's successor as dean of the Graduate School of Public Administration at the end of the 1957–58 academic year. At a meeting on September 13, 1957, Bowie, Mason, and Bundy approved a division of responsibilities between the GSPA and the Center for International Affairs. Under the terms of this plan, the Center would be responsible for "research and advanced study," while the GSPA would administer "degree training" for those interested in careers in international affairs. This agreement appears to have precluded the Center from offering degrees, as had once been envisaged.[23]

Moreover, Bowie felt strongly that individual departments should control instruction at the University. He recognized that the Center still had an important, indirect, role to play in teaching, but it was essential that the Center avoid competing with the departments in this regard. Through the establishment of half-chairs, Bowie provided core faculty members with joint appointments. In this way, members of the CFIA would enrich their teaching with the research they conducted at the Center.

In the long-term, however, the issues were more complex. As mentioned previously, the position of international affairs as a separate discipline had long been a debated subject at the University, and the question of whether or not to grant degrees— especially the Ph.D.—was an enduring source of contention. One remedy was the International Affairs Program, which was established in the aftermath of World War II under the auspices of the Committee on International and Regional Studies to meet a perceived need for greater emphasis on international studies at the University. It was led at the outset by Rupert Emerson, a professor of political science, and he continued to be a driving force for expanded tuition in the field at Harvard. Indeed, as early as

1946, Emerson had vocalized his opinion that "it would...be an excellent idea to have something at Harvard tagged 'International Affairs.'"[24]

Despite Emerson's patronage, the Program for International Affairs had long struggled to find its appropriate niche at Harvard, especially with regard to its ambiguous role in conferring degrees. Although the program did grant masters-level degrees in the field, at an October 1946 meeting of the Committee on International and Regional Studies there was apparently "some feeling that it would be unwise to offer a Ph.D. in International Affairs, both on the general principle that departments rather than committees should administer these higher degrees and because the same kind of work can be arranged within the present departmental structure."[25] This continued to be an issue throughout the 1940s and 1950s. One of the key disputes centered on the extent to which training in international affairs was practically rather than academically oriented. "The present program is essentially designed to fill the need for a non-academic market" was the consensus of a December 1946 meeting of the Committee on International and Regional Studies.[26] Undeterred, throughout the late 1940s Emerson continued to rally for enlarging the international affairs apparatus at Harvard.[27]

The establishment of the Center for International Affairs provided an occasion to assess this earlier attempt by the University to administer training and advanced academic degrees in international affairs. Emerson had been a member of Bundy's 1956 Faculty Committee, and in November 1956 he publicly called for the creation of a "Center for International Relations" at Harvard. Emerson always believed that such a center should have a prominent teaching capacity, most likely as a way to reinvigorate the ailing International Affairs Program.[28]

Emerson's efforts to raise awareness for the lamentable dearth of substance and clarity in the Harvard curriculum with regard to international affairs received the approval of the *Harvard Crimson* in December 1956. Reflecting an emerging consensus around the University that creating an international affairs center was all but inevitable, the *Crimson* outlined this prevailing conception of the Center's role:

> *The Center would be headed by a director whose main function would be to synthesize a strong degree curriculum from functioning graduate and departmental programs. At the same time, the Center would contribute to meeting an acute need for new courses and personnel at the undergraduate level as well, as more instructors in the area of International Relations would*

*be brought to Cambridge and a tighter study plan could be developed for the undergraduate concentrator.*

According to the report, Harvard undergraduates were "often discouraged from pursuing an education in a sub-area that they view as an intellectual tundra," while graduate students either avoided applying to Harvard or complied with the confines of the Committee on International and Regional Studies.[29] Although the source of the article is not attributed to Emerson, the tenor reflects his repeated calls, both public and private, for the University to place greater emphasis on international affairs.

In a letter to Dean Bundy in November 1957, Emerson sought to clarify the future of the international affairs program: "It would be highly regrettable not to seize the occasion of the establishment of the Center for International Affairs to reconstitute the Program and start it off toward bigger and better things." Although the program was under the aegis of the Government Department, Emerson advocated relocating it either to the Graduate School of Public Administration, which trained persons for public service, or ideally, to the new Center. But apparently Bowie had decided that "the Center should not take responsibility for regular degree and training programs," and so the International Affairs Program continued to languish in the Committee on International and Regional Studies.[30]

In addition to advocating greater responsibility for teaching and training students, the draft program of the CFIA was also more explicit about the role of the Center's faculty in policy making. The draft assertively emphasized the expectation that the core faculty members of the Center would be available for consultation with government agencies on an ad hoc basis. Bowie, of course, had made a point of stressing this in his letter to McGeorge Bundy on May 8, 1957, and reiterated this in the draft program: "By experience and their work at the Center the permanent faculty should be well equipped for such short-term assignments." It was anticipated, therefore, that "the aim would be to staff and organize the Center so that members could be made available for such purposes on relatively short notice as a regular part of its activities." Again, the inclusion of this stipulation bears the imprimatur of W. Barton Leach's correspondence with Bowie prior to his acceptance of the Center Directorship. "Such a plan" according to the draft *Program*, "will help to meet an urgent public need and also serve as a stimulus for members of the Center."[31]

Furthermore, the draft also envisaged establishing a small satellite office in Washington, D.C. that would be available to CFIA affiliates and other pertinent members of Harvard University. These facilities would serve a number of purposes for the CFIA. First, "they would greatly facilitate contact with officials of the United States government and foreign embassies for the purposes of recruiting participants, and obtaining information." In addition, the offices "would be available for use by members of the Center or Fellows in pursuing research requiring material or interviews in Washington." Finally, it was hoped that facilities in the nation's capital would "assist in keeping touch with people interested in the Center or its activities, many of whom would be located in Washington or visitors there from time to time."[32] Ultimately, the proposal was dropped from the final draft of the program and no such office was ever established.

## Assessing the Program of the CFIA

In October 1957, following the completion of the first draft of the *Program*, Bowie distributed copies for the perusal and commentary of relevant faculty members at Harvard University. One respondent was David A. Cavers, an associate dean at the Harvard Law School, who was especially interested in Bowie's idea of establishing a Fellows Program at the Center. "I have begun to think—as you may have all the time—that here might be the priceless ingredient—the element in the program that only Harvard could hope to achieve." The Fellows Program, Cavers mused, "would not render the seminars and the research secondary, but they would add extra meaning to them, and, moreover, if the Fellows of the Center themselves fared well, this might yield portentous results." With this in mind, he encouraged Bowie to "capitalize on what may be a very significant educational innovation," particularly in terms of Bowie's ongoing efforts to attract financial support for the Center. The idea deserved greater consideration, he argued, and ought to be further developed.[33]

Erwin N. Griswold, dean of the Harvard Law School, was also intrigued by the prospective Fellows Program. Although it showed great promise, he was skeptical about "retrainees from Government service." For Griswold, the problem was one of quality control: while "you get some good ones," there was always the danger that "you also get people who are tired, or whose superiors would like to see them out of the way for a while." Griswold also wanted the Center to incorporate teaching into some aspect of the Center's program, however limited, since in his view "the presence of a fair number of real students in the area might help to keep things realistic."[34]

Stanley H. Hoffmann also responded to Bowie's *Program*, and his concerns related primarily to the research agenda of the Center. In his view, the Center ought to more prominently embrace the theory of international relations. He drew a distinction between "philosophical" and "causal or empirical" theories, the latter being the kind of work the Center ought to encourage. "The kind of studies I am suggesting," Hoffmann proposed, "could be a separate 'major field of continuing research,' for it seems to me that the other major fields enumerated in the memorandum would be given depth and perspective if a body of theory were available, so to speak, as a common foundation."[35]

While Hoffmann supported the idea of the Fellows Program, he questioned whether it was wise to place so much emphasis on the extent to which the Center faculty was expected to engage in consulting work for the U.S. government. Since it was difficult to attract scholars and government officials for work on relatively long projects, "the more one stresses the 'training function,' or the more one emphasizes the advantage of having the permanent members of the Center available as consultants or for diplomatic assignments, the more difficult it might be to recruit first-rate people from abroad." This difficulty was only exacerbated "when these men believe that the organization which is asking for their cooperation is in any way connected with a foreign government."[36] It is likely, then, that Hoffmann's advice was heeded in this case, since any explicit reference to the desirability of Center faculty engaging in occasional government service was subsequently removed from the final draft of the *Program*.

Bowie also solicited the advice of some individuals outside Harvard. One such person was an intelligence official, Wallace Lampshire, who was particularly keen to see the Center function as a conclave for the international cooperation and consultation of scholars concerned with the foreign policies of the United States and its allies. His comments reflected the interests of a government bureaucrat; in his formulation the Center would resemble an adjunct of the U.S. government. Lampshire was also much more explicit than Bowie in seeing the Center as an opportunity to consolidate relations among America's cold war allies. In his view, "high-level discussion and study of long-range trends in international affairs might well reveal, far in advance of 'problems,' indications of future allied differences not suspect even to the experienced foreign service officer or intelligence analyst." Lampshire also suggested that the Center should work with the Department of State to improve links with foreign academics and institutions concerned with international affairs.[37] Clearly, there was the potential for a good deal of interest within government circles in the Center's work.

These were not the only individuals to express their views about the direction and substance of the Center's research program. In February 1958,

Kissinger wrote to Bowie in order to express his concerns regarding research at the Center and especially his apprehensions about the prospective Fellows Program: "When the Center started we agreed that there was little point in doing once more what every other research organization and center of international affairs is attempting also," because in his view "the supply of talent is too thin, the subjects to be discussed [are] really relatively so limited, that it is difficult to imagine any distinctive purpose being served by another research organization, even with all the facilities of Harvard at its command." He was also skeptical of the proposed Fellows Program, which would "raise as many issues as it solves."[38]

Kissinger did not necessarily object to the notion that the Center provide the Fellows with the necessary time and environment for reflection and study. The problem, as far as Kissinger was concerned, was that the Fellows would not necessarily offer anything substantive to the Center's research program. Kissinger instead preferred that "the Center became known as a place where outstanding people can find a haven from the pressures of day to day concerns to do truly unusual research. The civil servants can give perspective to the others. They are not likely to do creative work themselves, although they would profit from the training."[39] For him, the Center would prosper only if it contributed seriously and formatively to the discipline of international relations, and as such his concern was that the Fellows would offer little to the realization of that goal.

Kissinger had ruminated upon this in a letter to Bowie in the fall of 1957, and his most pressing concern then had been the need to protect and enhance the embryonic discipline of international relations. He had been concerned that the field could not be expected to mature as an academic endeavor if it were entirely dependent on the fields of political science and economics, and there was a danger that the Center would "become an adjunct of existing departments."[40] Kissinger felt in particular that "[The Center] will face a Political Science Department accustomed to treating International Relations as a subdivision of Government," a prejudice compounded by a widespread propensity around Harvard to "deny the validity of International Relations as a subject."[41] With this in mind, he felt that the Center had to be "ruthless in [its] insistence on independence of conception and execution," and it should jealously guard its sovereignty against all encroachments from the academic departments and contending research centers. "A great tradition can be built only by developing shared concepts, common experiences and common loyalties." Because after all, the issue was not "simply a problem of developing a program; it is also necessary to bring about an attitude and an intellectual discipline. Such a goal is anathema to many trends at Harvard. It is, however, the only real road to achievement."[42]

## Facilities, Faculty, Finances, and Fellows

The research agenda was not Bowie's only responsibility during this period. In addition to formulating the Center's organizational structure and research program, Bowie also had to resolve four other major issues: finding facilities for the Center, recruiting the core faculty, securing sources of funding for the Center's initial operations, and inviting the first class of Fellows.

**Facilities**  In procuring space to house the Center, the goal was to obtain a facility that would foster a collegial and intimate atmosphere and create a sense of identity for the Center. At first, it appeared that the Center might have to be housed in the Littauer building for its first year due to lack of alternatives. For example, one proposal made by Bundy was rejected by Kissinger, no doubt correctly, because it "will be occupied by two other organizations even if we do get space in it, so that we would not gain any particular sense of identity by moving there."[43]

Bundy eventually offered Bowie use of the property located at 6 Divinity Avenue that housed the Harvard Semitic Museum, which was suitably renovated for the purpose of housing the Center. According to the Semitic Museum's *Report to the President of Harvard College* for 1960–61, the decision to house the Center at 6 Divinity Avenue was designed to alleviate the increasing financial difficulties of the museum, not necessarily because it was especially well suited to the needs of the CFIA. The situation was always intended to be temporary, until the Center could be relocated to permanent space either in an existing building or in a purpose-built site devoted to international studies. In the interim, the Semitic Museum's collection had to be moved to first-floor offices or stored in the cellar of 6 Divinity Avenue.[44] The building's second floor was converted into office space for Fellows and visiting research associates and also included a small cafeteria that served as an informal meeting space for the Center's affiliates. The Center library and additional offices were located on the third floor.

Almost immediately, however, Bowie wanted to secure permanent facilities, preferably closer to the Littauer building, where the Departments of Government and Economics were housed. In October 1958, Dean Price of the Graduate School of Public Administration wrote to President Nathan Pusey, expressing his desire to see the Center for International Affairs, along with the other internationally focused research centers, housed closer to both Littauer and each other. "In this process I have kept in touch with Dean Bundy and Mr. Bowie," Price wrote, "since it seems to me, as I said last spring, that a major need is to bring back together in adjacent space the Center and the Littauer School."[45] Bowie felt that this was especially important in order to "encourage intimate contacts with others in the Political Science and Economics faculties having an interest in these [international] activities."[46]

These discussions resulted in a proposal for a purpose-built building that would consolidate the University's efforts in the field of international affairs and facilitate closer cooperation among relevant research centers and programs. In particular, it was felt that bringing the various international research centers adjacent to the Graduate School of Public Administration would "do much to improve the existing poor communication between those engaged in research on related subjects" as well as "greatly emphasize the work being done in the field of international affairs in the University." Ultimately, the convenient location and "the construction of an efficient and attractive facility would do much to encourage and expedite the work of those scholars particularly involved in the study of international and regional affairs and allied fields of study." This would be the beginning of a forty-seven year process culminating in the opening of the Center for Government and International Studies, on a different site, in August 2005.[47]

**Faculty**　Bowie also had to recruit the nucleus of the Center's personnel, all of whom would occupy half-chairs in the Center, and joint appointments within their relevant academic department. To this end, the Ford Foundation endowed two half-chairs—or half the salary of two core faculty members—for a total of $400,000. Bowie was keen to ensure that permanent faculty members would be able to devote half of their time entirely to the Center, free from both teaching and other departmental obligations. At the same time, Bundy and Bowie were eager to retain direct links with the academic departments, and with this in mind faculty members would spend half their time anchored in their departments.

Although there would often be considerable overlap, Bowie sought to match the Center's major areas of research with those of select faculty members, who would then enlist and oversee the efforts of invited research associates and interested Fellows in those areas. Bowie felt it was crucial to begin projects based on people's interests, rather than forcing them into an predetermined agenda. He himself would be primarily responsible for the Center's efforts pertaining to Europe and the Atlantic Community. In the field of development, Bowie turned to a friend and Harvard colleague, Edward Mason. Mason was a longtime professor of economics (and until 1958 dean of the Graduate School of Public Administration), and had been heavily involved in the inception of the Center for International Affairs since the University's application to the Ford Foundation in 1953. Mason was also responsible for the Pakistan and Iran Advisory Groups, funded by the Ford Foundation since 1953, and these two economic development projects would be the genesis for the Development Advisory Service (DAS), discussed at greater length in Chapter Six. Mason was published on issues of economic development, and accrued an extensive resume of government service during World War II, most notably as chief economist of the Office of Strategic Services. In 1945 he was deputy to the assistant secretary of state in charge of economic affairs, and in 1947 he accompanied the American delegation to the Moscow Conference as the chief economic advisor. In many ways, Mason was an ideal candidate to lead the Center's research program in the area of development, not least because of his friendship with Bowie, who considered Mason to be a scholar with a "first class mentality."[48] He was, in Bowie's view, an obvious selection.

The final area of the Center's research would focus on issues of military policy and arms control, and in addition to Henry Kissinger, Bowie would also solicit the energies of a newcomer to the Harvard economics department, Thomas C. Schelling. Schelling came to Harvard from Yale University, and was recruited by Mason—a former professor of Schelling's during his time as a graduate student at Harvard—with a joint appointment in the Economics Department, which meant a reduced teaching load and research support.

Schelling had been deeply involved in the administration of Marshall Plan aid in Copenhagen and Paris, where he worked for Averill Harriman. When Harriman returned to Washington, Schelling went with him, becoming the associate economic advisor to the special assistant to the president in foreign affairs. Schelling's government service culminated in the position of officer in charge of European Program Affairs in the Office of the Director for Mutual Security, a position he held from 1951 to 1953, when he received an offer from Yale University and decided to leave the government. Schelling recalls leaving Washington with the expectation that "I would establish an academic career and then return to government," though despite multiple offers he never returned to full time government service.[49] It was at this time that Schelling and Bowie first crossed paths, when Bowie approached him with

35

an offer to join his Policy Planning Staff at the State Department. Schelling declined the offer on the advice of Bowie's predecessor in the Policy Planning Staff, Paul Nitze, who counseled that Schelling was already in a position to influence policy. His arrival in Cambridge was delayed until the fall of 1959, however, since he had already agreed to spend the previous year at the RAND Corporation, during which time he would cultivate relationships that would benefit the Center for years to come.

These four faculty members formed the initial core of the Center in 1958–59, and they would soon be joined by two more faculty members in 1961–62: Raymond Vernon, who had arrived at Harvard two years before after three years at the helm of the GSPA's New York Metropolitan Region Study, and Alex Inkeles, a member of the Sociology Department. The core faculty would continue to grow at a steady rate over the coming years.

Since Bowie assembled some of the Center's core faculty from outside Harvard—only Ed Mason was a longstanding and continuous member of the Harvard faculty—Bundy was careful to impress that these external recruits did not preclude the involvement of the broader Harvard community. "It must not seem to our colleagues to be a one-man show or an outsider's party," Bundy cautioned, and he was particularly concerned that "...at present [there is] real danger that they may so regard it," especially because the Center's opening operations emphasized activities not involving present members of the faculty in any significant degree. Bundy was aware that the Center would succeed only if it were enthusiastically and effectively supported by the Harvard faculty, and accordingly "its individual members must be brought into its work and feel a share in its operation." Moreover, he also reiterated what had by then become something of a refrain, "we ought to emphasize, and mean it, that the whole enterprise has a Faculty Committee that is not just window dressing." That was not intended to in any way undermine Bowie's leadership, but in the final analysis Bundy was at pains to stress that the Center existed "because it grows out of this Faculty's needs and opportunities."[50]

**Finances**   Throughout the 1957–58 academic year, Bowie pursued with vigor the task of securing finances for both establishing and continuing Center operations. Bundy had already laid the groundwork with some of the major foundations, including the Rockefeller Foundation and the Ford Foundation, two organizations that were among the primary sources of external academic funding in the 1950s and 1960s. Even before Bowie accepted the position of director, Bundy was already sowing the foundation seedbed in an attempt to ascertain the level of interest and possible support that Bowie could expect to encounter.

The first person Bundy called was the president of the Rockefeller Foundation, Dean Rusk, who would later become Bundy's colleague in the Kennedy administration. Although Bundy conveyed that Rusk avoided making a financial commitment, "the kind of enterprise we are trying to mount is one which he can see the reasons for and would be glad to see in flourishing condition."[51] Bundy also approached the Ford Foundation, and reported similarly ambiguous but promising news: "…while I think it is fair to say that the responsible officers there think this is an important thing to do and that you are just the right man to do it, I have not yet had a chance to discuss with them directly the question of possible levels of support."[52] The indicators were positive, however, and all that was needed was Bowie's acceptance of the directorship. "…I must say," Bundy assured, "general experience here in related areas continues to give me the feeling that money enough for effective operations will be easy to get when we have the right leadership."[53] Once Bowie got underway he recalls that "typical of Harvard, I was supposed to go out and find money to support the Center," but there was "fertile soil," especially in regard to international relations. In addition, Bowie was not without contacts in the foundations, and he was able to secure the necessary funding to initiate the Center.[54]

The Center began its life with a range of funding from Harvard University and beyond. By far the largest contributor to the Center's finances was the Ford Foundation, which provided an initial five-year grant of $100,000 that was designated for a range of expenses, including research funding and fellowships, in addition to the two half-chairs it endowed. The Rockefeller Foundation was also instrumental in financing the Center's initial operations by providing a three-year $120,000 grant for general research support. In addition, the Rockefeller Brothers Fund also apportioned $105,000 for three years of "general budgetary support." More support would be forthcoming in the first two years for specific research projects in economic development and defense policy.

The aforementioned foundations were not the only contributors to the Center. Clarence Dillon and C. Douglas Dillon endowed a chair for Bowie, who set the precedent for all future directors of the CFIA by becoming the first Clarence Dillon Professor of International Affairs.[55] The University, of course, was also instrumental in financing the Center's operating costs: $43,300 for the Center's planning phase in 1957–58; approximately $56,000 for the first year; funding half the salary of the other three core faculty members; and providing the building at 6 Divinity Avenue with $100,000 for remodeling. Bowie also secured $25,000 from private corporations, such as Standard Oil of New Jersey and IBM. While the Center had garnered enough funds to support its functions in the short term, the institution lacked endowment for the next forty years, until the Center received a $21 million endowment gift from Albert and Cecilia Weatherhead and the Weatherhead Foundation—and with the gift a new name—in 1998.[56]

**Fellows**    During the first year, Bowie also launched the Center's Fellows Program, and recruited the first group for the following year.[57] For this purpose, he took an extended trip abroad, visiting "the top personnel officials in the key countries that I thought we would want to draw Fellows from." His travels took him to the United Kingdom, France, West Germany, India, Japan, Italy, Netherlands, and Nigeria. Bowie felt that including Fellows from the Soviet bloc would have raised security concerns from the other participants and inhibited the free exchange of views that was at the core of the entire undertaking. The Fellows would come for an academic year and would be limited to about fifteen Fellows in order to maintain the level of informality and intimacy that he sought to foster within the program.[58] He recalls that he got "a very positive reception," for the proposed Fellows Program in each of the countries he visited. Indeed, in India he was even invited to meet with Indian Prime Minister Jawaharlal Nehru, who was "so well impressed that he ordered his cabinet secretary to make sure that the official selected was suitable."[59] The program began with twelve Fellows; six from the United States (armed forces, State Department, and the CIA) and six from abroad. In several years, the cadre reached fifteen, with nine international Fellows. As Bowie recalls of the incipient program:

> *Essential to the success of the program was the caliber of the Fellows. For international Fellows, that was fostered by top-level support, the eagerness of candidates to attend, and the active interest of former Fellows to ensure well-qualified successors. In the United States, the military services had well-established systems for midcareer education, which could include the Fellows Program. This was not yet the case in the State Department. Although the undersecretary, Loy Henderson, strongly supported the program, there was some concern among FSOs that a year away at Harvard might not be helpful to their future careers.*[60]

With finances, facilities, and personnel in place, the Center was ready to begin operations in the fall of 1958. The previous year spent planning and executing a vision that had been gestating since at least 1953 had finally created a research center devoted to the study of international affairs at Harvard University. In his "Report to the President" on the work of the Faculty of Arts and Sciences for the academic year 1957–58, Dean McGeorge Bundy reflected upon the first year of the Center's existence. Although that year was primarily devoted to planning and organization, Bundy nevertheless reported on the need for, and potential of, the new center. Intimating his own personal investment in its establishment and success, Bundy heralded the Center as "a venture for which I have great hope and much personal concern."[61] He explained the need for such a center as the "outgrowth of years of discussion and desire in this and other faculties—all leading to a strong conviction that such a center was badly needed here, both for the strengthening of our own work and for the better discharge of our responsibility as part of a society in terrible danger."[62] Bundy indicated his desire to see the Center become the cynosure of the University's endeavors in the field of international affairs, and a focus for the energies of the various members of the Harvard faculty engaged in research on the topic. Bundy also took the opportunity to advertise one of the Center's potentially most valuable assets: the Fellows Program. According to Bundy, "Mr. Bowie began this program in the strong conviction that the study of great issues of international affairs requires thoughtful exchange between the academy and the marketplace."[63] For Bundy, the early indications emanating from the new center were indeed encouraging.

# Three

# The First Two Years and the Evolving Role of the Fellows Program

## The First Two Years

REFLECTING ON THE FIRST TWO YEARS OF THE CFIA'S EXISTENCE AT the end of the 1959–60 academic year, Bowie avowed with a modicum of satisfaction that "in summary, the Center for International Affairs has taken root." The Center's research agenda and scholarship, while still subject to further growth, "give good grounds for looking forward to a productive future."[1] Although the substance of the Center's intellectual product would invariably be modified upon the basis of experience and the availability of talent, the research agenda remained the same: "Fundamental research on long-range problems of international affairs is the heart of the Center's program."[2] Such research was deemed essential both to the conduct of international relations at the policy-making level and to the maturation of the academic discipline, and with this statement Bowie succinctly encapsulated the essence of the CFIA's raison d'être as he had defined it upon accepting the directorship in 1957.

Though the core premise of the Center's existence remained valid, two years of experience had also enabled Bowie and the other permanent faculty members to hone the methods and contours of the CFIA's activities. The research program was effectively curtailed to three primary fields of inquiry: the process of development, the role and control of force, and the evolving role of Europe. For the time being the analysis of "International Order and Conflict," and "Far Eastern Problems"—at least as they were envisaged in the

Center's original *Program* in 1958—were consigned to the background. Over the coming years, Bowie anticipated that the Center would continue to nurture the three principal research fields, particularly by expanding the Center's focus on "Western Europe, on the political and social aspects of development, and on arms control." While the Center would continue to pursue new avenues of enquiry, these three expansive yet appropriately focused areas of research would form the intellectual core of the CFIA during the first decade and a half of its operation. As Bowie recognized, however, the continued success of this endeavor was ultimately contingent upon the continued availability of both finances and the interests of capable scholars.[3]

Two years of activity had also facilitated the refinement of the Center's modus operandi. The primary mechanism for cultivating research and inter-action among the faculty, Fellows, and research associates was a cluster of research seminars devoted to each of the three core areas of inquiry. "In the early stage, before the research programs had been fully organized, the seminars drew heavily on outside experts." That soon changed, however, because " . . . as the research in progress at the Center has gained momentum and scope, the seminars have more and more assumed their role as specialized research instruments."[4] These seminars helped to provide a shared intellectual and institutional context within which to formulate the Center's research agendas. In addition, the seminars afforded an opportunity to refine the necessary conceptual frameworks that would assure a common ground for discussion and foster the development of the discipline.

## Creating a Community of Scholars

The Center was more than simply a forum for discussion, however, as Bowie professed in the *1960 Annual Report*. He certainly accepted the basic principle that had hitherto guided the research endeavors of Harvard University—"the emphasis is less on organization than on the work of individual scholars"—but he also affirmed that the Center's atmosphere was itself conducive to the research process. "Good research . . . depends primarily on the excellence of individuals engaged in it," he assented, "but the Center can do much to stimulate those individuals and facilitate their research." At the most basic level, "the Center's objective is to provide an exciting place to work." Of course, it was more than that. The Center provided a milieu in which scholars from different national and cultural backgrounds benefited from the "interplay of discussion, analysis, and criticism."[5]

The recollections of the Center's faculty and research associates from that period reveal that this was no hollow boast. Schelling, for example, remembers that "it was a wonderful place; a very exciting place," in large part due to the presence of the Fellows, who he recalls were active and often insatiable participants in the Center's research program, which "made the place exciting."[6] Due to his association with Harvard's Russian Research Center, Alex Inkeles, who joined the permanent faculty of the Center in July 1961, had exceptional insight into this issue. Both centers effectively fostered an extraordinary environment, which broadened the intellectual horizons of their participants and facilitated both fertile and productive atmospheres in which to conduct research. Inkeles argues that although it "did not require the creation of a research center to achieve this salutary effect," such organizations were nevertheless central to the improvement of research on international affairs at Harvard:

> The most important aspect of the Centers was that they brought together individuals from different disciplines and departments who would otherwise not be working together. For many, and for much of the time, it was a very broadening, even transformational, experience. The impact was obvious in the scholarly work of these people, which as a result became less parochial, broader, wider, deeper, less stereotyped and more original and innovative.[7]

Joseph Nye, who began his association with the Center in 1961 as Bowie's research assistant and who would himself become the fourth Center Director, recalls the sense of excitement engendered by the CFIA's interdisciplinary seminars. For a young graduate student, these discussions among the senior faculty members were particularly stimulating: "these were all people who were themselves towering figures, but the fact that they were reaching out across different disciplines and having common discussions, where as a graduate student you could sit in the back row and listen to them argue, made it a very exciting place." For him this was an especially important aspect of what made the Center such a productive and innovative environment, since "university disciplines tend to be things that narrow people or cut them off from each other . . . and that's understandable, but the reason that the Center was important was to get people to get beyond those departments." This not only made the CFIA a particularly vibrant and lively forum for intellectual exchange, but it also facilitated a large degree of original and inventive scholarship.[8] This interdisciplinary model would later have a major impact on his own work, especially his groundbreaking collaboration in 1977 with Robert Keohane, *Power and Interdependence,* on the role of transnational actors in international affairs.

Samuel Huntington, another future Center Director, returned to Harvard as a member of the CFIA's core faculty in 1963 following a brief appointment at Columbia University in New York. One of the most important contributions of the Center was the sense of community that it fostered among the diverse group of scholars broadly concerned with various international issues. From the outset, he notes:

> *People who were involved in the Center thought that it should be a community, and from the very beginning they organized and promoted Center seminars and discussion groups and so forth. I think they took a rather dim view of professors affiliated with the Center simply using their office and the staff assistants, but otherwise not participating in the intellectual life of the Center, which over the years has been of tremendous benefit, certainly to me.*[9]

One surprisingly valuable hub for conversation and debate was the cafeteria on the second floor of 6 Divinity Avenue. As Huntington remembers, "we all ate there . . . [The] cafeteria was arranged so that there were virtually no two-person or even four-person tables; they were all eight or ten-person tables, or twelve." This meant that "you might go down there with a friend and sit down at a table and pretty soon other people would come and sit at the same table and you'd all become involved in one general conversation."[10] This in turn fostered the kind of interdisciplinary intellectual cross-pollination that was one of the most important facets of membership in the CFIA.

Another future Center Director, Jorge I. Domínguez, who arrived at the CFIA in 1969 as a member of the first cadre of graduate student associates, also remembers the vibrant impromptu lunchtime meetings that were generated by the cafeteria's imposed intimacy. In particular he recalls that there was "spectacular group" of junior faculty who met in the cafeteria just about every day. "Sometimes they'd talk about the weather, sometimes they'd talk about chaos at Harvard, but sometimes they had substantive intellectual discussions."[11] These discussions were free of the formality of the Center research seminars, and as such they were often a casual forum for experimental thought and an ideal place for testing new, sometimes unconventional, ideas. Nye also remembers the cafeteria's positive role in fostering discussion with other Center associates. For him, this was also a function of the CFIA's smaller size during its first ten years, in that proximity inevitably engendered a greater degree of dialogue among the Center faculty and Fellows: "it was a lot easier to share ideas at seminars and at lunches for serendipitous reasons, I mean you just have to sit down next to somebody."[12] The cafeteria was integral to the effective functioning of the Center. This outcome was entirely anticipated by Bowie, who intentionally designed the layout of the cafeteria and chose larger tables in order to optimize interaction among Center members. When in later years the increased size of the Center eventually increased the scope of these potential interactions, it also made such informal dialogues more difficult to come by.

In this sense, then, the Center became, in the words of Domínguez, both a "venture capitalist" and a "social capitalist." The Center provided to its members not only financial resources but also a scholarly community, and in this way "one of the values of the Center is to bring people together to talk with each other, often people who would not have assumed that they had anything to talk about." Such interactions, then, often stimulated CFIA associates to broaden their research agendas in ways that they would never have previously considered.[13]

45

## Intellectual Diversity

This is not to suggest that the Center was an idyllic and serene intellectual environment, where unanimity was endemic on the crucial matters of the day. Indeed, it could often be the site of fractious and passionate debates on matters of policy. Despite the claims of those critics who would emerge during the student protests of the late 1960s and early 1970s, the Center personnel were far from unified on matters of substance. There was never anything approximating a "Center point of view." Karl Kaiser, who arrived from Nuffield College, Oxford, in 1963 as a research associate at the invitation of Henry Kissinger, remembers that the Center associates were always attuned to, and often involved in, the broader policy debates of American politics. On the issue of French foreign policy during Charles de Gaulle's presidency of the Fifth Republic, for example, "there were deep divisions in American policy reflected in the seminars; some who had understanding for de Gaulle, others who denounced him as somebody who destroyed the American design of European integration." Such debates only enlivened the intellectual milieu of the Center, and Kaiser notes that these policy disputes were an essential part of what made the CFIA function: "Considering that there were such deep divisions among the scholars at the Center . . . on French foreign policy, on European integration, on nuclear affairs and the [NATO] alliance, the

Center worked very well, and that had something to do with the fact that there was a certain 'live and let live' tolerance for diverging opinions, for which of course the leadership was responsible."[14]

Samuel Huntington concurs with Kaiser's assessment, and notes that the only criterion the Center leadership ever imposed on its associates was ability. Beyond this, Huntington insists that "Center leadership and the director would never try to tell people what to study. If you are a member of the Center you can write on whatever you want. And I think that is a very, very good thing."[15] Indeed, for Huntington it was the multiplicity of backgrounds and viewpoints that made the Center such an invigorating place to work. As he recalls, "the diversity of the people in the Fellows Program, the visiting scholars who have come to the Center, [and] the people who have been hired from elsewhere to participate in Center research programs [ensured that the CFIA had] a very diverse group of people from different backgrounds, different disciplines, and different nationalities."[16]

Domínguez suggests that in many ways this was a function of Bowie's leadership style and intellectual philosophy: "he had a very open and enquiring mind; he didn't have a party line. There were some things he cared about, but what you understood fairly soon is that the things he cared about were not some kind of intellectual dogma, but they were things that he thought were important. So, he thought it was important for the United States not just to act unilaterally but also to manage a relationship in the context of an Atlantic Alliance. That's not a school of thought, that's just an affirmation of salience."[17] There is no doubt that the Center benefited from this climate of intellectual freedom, and the research that was produced under its auspices reflects the creativity this environment engendered.

## The Fellows Program, 1958–72

In writing the Center's first annual report in 1960, it is clear that during the past two years Bowie refined his conception of the Fellows Program, as he reiterated its rationale with a degree of clarity and precision that was perhaps lacking at the outset. The notion that the pressures of the conduct of international affairs precluded the participant from absorbing and integrating new ideas and attitudes had long informed Bowie's conception of the Fellows Program, and he restated this underlying principle in the annual report. The expectation was that "outstanding officials in their forties are, or will soon be, holding key policy-making positions," but as he often stressed, they were not necessarily equipped to engage in that task in the context of a rapidly changing international environment. "It is important" he contended, "for such men to have a chance to re-examine their picture of the world and the new forces at work."[18] According to Bowie, the opportunity to engage in a year of sustained and intensive study and reflection, unencumbered by their professional obligations, would enable the practitioners associated with the Center to return to their occupations replete with a new and more nuanced perspective on crucial contemporary issues.[19]

As he acknowledged, however, the Fellows Program was subject to an adjustment period, as the Fellows and the research staff collaborated to establish the most effective method of collusion and engagement. Nonetheless, by the end of the second year Bowie declared that the parameters of the program were essentially in place. The basic premise was that the Fellows had to be regarded as "colleagues, not as students." In this sense, they were encouraged to compose an academic experience that suited their own personal interests, while at the same time they were given enough freedom to explore anything that might pique their curiosity in conversations with their colleagues and other Center affiliates. Though they were not pursuing an academic degree during their time at Harvard, they were nevertheless encouraged to participate in Harvard seminars and classes that interested them, in addition to the stimulations afforded by the everyday life of the Center. Each Fellow was also expected to write an analytical paper on a topic of interest and present their findings and observations to a seminar composed of their colleagues. Another program highlight was the monthly dinners, at which an array of eminent political leaders informally addressed the Fellows and participated in an off-the-record discussion. Such luminaries as John Foster Dulles, Paul-Henri Spaak, George F. Kennan, and Wilhelm Grewe attended these first unofficial gatherings, no doubt in large part thanks to the connections of the Center Director. One such dinner was even reported to have changed American foreign policy, erroneously, as it turned out.[20]

In addition to six Americans, the first class included a French diplomat, a British diplomat, an Italian civil servant, a Dutch diplomat, a Cypriot bureaucrat, and a Nigerian lawyer. The ratio of Americans to those from abroad would change over the coming years, but this essentially remained the pattern at the outset. On the whole, Bowie steadfastly reported that the program he had so assiduously organized and promoted was fulfilling its role in pervading the research seminars with a level of practical experience and understanding that was otherwise inconceivable. The Fellows themselves concurred, Bowie noted: "The first two groups agreed unanimously that their year at Harvard

47

was a uniquely rich experience." In order to place the Fellows Program on a secure financial foundation, Bowie continued to seek an endowment that would guarantee the program's continued success.[21]

## Faculty and the Fellows

Regardless of the growing pains associated with the Fellows Program, there is almost unanimous agreement among former Center affiliates that the program was a central and successful component of the CFIA during the initial stages of the Center's life. Schelling, for instance, is unequivocal in his assessment of the program's value: "I think that [the Fellows Program] was the heart of the Center. Without that, the Center would have been just a place where people quietly did their own research in their own offices, and this was the activity that involved everybody in the Center."[22] This is a common theme in the recollections of the Center's early faculty members and research associates. Huntington, for example, affirms that "when the Center was founded it didn't consist of much besides the Fellows Program. There was no big academic research program. That gradually developed, but the Fellows Program was the Center in the early years."[23]

Bowie's desire to incorporate the Fellows Program within the broader intellectual work of the Center was a success. "What also contributed to the effectiveness of the Center," Karl Kaiser remembers, "was a close integration of the Fellows Program and the research. There was really no separation; we were all together, and they were good people."[24] Following an invitation from Schelling, Morton Halperin arrived in 1960 as a graduate student from Yale University to become a Center research associate, and he ultimately joined the Government Department as a faculty member. In his view, the Center's research programs for the most part operated independently from one another in the founding years, but "if there was anything that bound the place together it was the Fellows Program."[25]

The Fellows also instrumentally enriched the scholarship of other Center research staff members. Domínguez recalls the impact that Fellows had on his own work, and in particular one paper by Richard Bloomfield (a Fellow from the State Department) that was so interesting it "had a direct impact on work that I would go on to do and have done ever since on U.S. foreign policy toward Latin America." The work of some of the Fellows was so insightful that Domínguez included three Fellows' papers (by Bloomfield, Ricardo Luna, and Arthur Mudge) on his junior seminar syllabus as required reading. Although Fellows often augmented his factual knowledge, these three also contributed to his teaching and "helped to shape how I thought about [things] . . . It was invaluable."[26] Huntington is similarly effusive about the Fellows, who were and remain "an absolutely invaluable resource," and who Huntington continues to invite into his classroom in order to provide personal insights and perspectives on matters of contemporary importance in international affairs.[27]

One problem that persisted during the first two decades of the Center's life, however, was the lack of Fellows from underdeveloped countries, especially from Latin America and Africa. In addition to the difficulty of financing such Fellows, the Center reported in 1963 that "the basic problem here is the understandable desire of governments to husband their limited resources of qualified men." Bowie and his colleagues were constantly aware that the program's success depended heavily on the willingness of the participating government agencies and military services to part with some of their most promising and able diplomats and officers for a year at a time. The burden such a mandate placed on developing countries was seen to be especially onerous. Overall, however, Bowie was confident that the program was proving itself to be valuable not only to the Center but also to the Fellows and their governments. "The fact that governments recognize the desirability of making their best officials available for appointment at the Center," he reported, "is a positive indication of the program's worth in enhancing the effectiveness of these men."[28]

One method by which the Center judged the success of the Fellows Program was the nature of the subsequent assignments that Fellows received following their participation in the program. Bowie always conceived of the program as a preparatory year for especially talented individuals on track to higher office. Indeed, by 1983 the Center had hosted 439 Fellows from fifty-eight countries, many of whom became ambassadors or deputy chiefs of missions. One former Korean Fellow (Il-Kwon Chung, Fellows Program 1960–61) became the ninth prime minister of the Republic of Korea.[29]

The Fellows facilitated the propagation of the Center's research by providing a valuable link with the world of international affairs. It was often through them, Bowie noted, that "the findings of the Center's research program and the objective approach which it exemplifies have a channel to policymakers of many nations."[30] The Fellows also enhanced the overall intellectual life of the Center, and in this regard "their presence helps make the Center a unique forum for testing the hypotheses of scholars against the judgment and experience of senior officials from a variety of countries."[31] Testing hypotheses with Fellows had even more tangible benefits, especially when Center faculty members themselves entered government service. During his tenure with the Carter administration, for example, Joseph Nye spent a great deal of time working on issues of nuclear nonproliferation. He found himself interacting with a former Fellow, Jagat Mehta (Fellows Program, 1969–70), who was the Indian foreign secretary. As Nye remembers, "fortunately the fact that we were friends from the Center made it easier to communicate at a time when India and the United States weren't necessarily seeing things the same way."[32]

The Fellows Program also succeeded in enriching both the University and the broader Cambridge community. Fellows participated in the activities of the undergraduate houses of Harvard College and provided an early, if somewhat informal, link between the Center and Harvard's undergraduate students. Fellows were also encouraged to expand their understanding of the United States through travel and to forge relationships with researchers and faculty members at other universities and institutions around the country. The Center's custom of hosting off-the-record meetings with visiting guests also enlivened both the Fellows Program and the Center as a whole.[33]

## The Turbulent 1960s: Changes on the Horizon

Although the pattern of the Fellows Program remained relatively stable through the first nine years of the Center's operation, in the late 1960s the changes evident in American society as a whole were beginning to influence the tone and substance of the Fellows Program. Indeed, the years from 1967 to 1970 were pivotal ones in the histories of both the Fellows Program and the CFIA as a whole. As the Center reflected in 1970, "there is no doubt that the quality of the typical Fellows' experience at Harvard has subtly changed."[34] The changes were in fact extensive.

With sixteen participants, the Fellows class of 1967–68 was the largest group the Center had ever assembled, and according to that year's annual report it was an unusual time in many respects; the social, political, and cultural turmoil of the late 1960s had permeated the Fellows Program. The composition of the class itself reflected the changing domestic and international context of 1967–68, although for the most part the Fellows continued to be recruited primarily from diplomatic and military services. For example, a female Fellow joined the program for the first time: Begum Gulzar Bano from Pakistan. In addition, the Center also hosted its first Fellow from a socialist country: Ljubivoje Aćimović of Yugoslavia. The program also hosted a French Fellow for the first time since 1961–62, a fact that reflected the rise and fall of Charles de Gaulle and the attendant tensions between the Fifth Republic and the United States. If the class itself was indicative of the shifting political and cultural climate, its activities were equally atypical. The Fellows' educational experience at Harvard that year differed qualitatively from that of many preceding classes: "Their interests often ran beyond their professional concerns. They raised far-reaching and sometimes 'far-out' questions. They focused as much on values and methods as on operational problems. They speculated freely. They seem disposed to play for high intellectual stakes."[35] This was clearly a function of the increasingly tumultuous political and social environment, to which the CFIA was not immune.

This would prove to be no mere anomaly, however, and the next class of Fellows remained attuned to the fractious and contentious context of American society in 1968–69. The Fellows evaluated and reconsidered traditional concepts and norms, and "a resulting feature of the year was the concern that all of them seemed to share for the interplay between domestic and foreign policy, both in the United States and elsewhere."[36] One Fellow reported that over the course of his association with the Center "my views have been subject to more varied challenge than in any other period of my career." Another indicated that the critical reflection and analysis of his own government's role in the world was especially useful.[37]

The Fellows Program continued to evolve, and further change was evident over the course of the 1969–70 academic year. It was apparent that the Fellows were integral to the broader Harvard University community to a greater degree than in previous years, which was a function of both the Fellows' own initiatives and the growing realization among members of the University that the Fellows were a significant reservoir of insight and experience. "More than has been typical of Fellows in earlier years, they made their presence felt."[38] In addition, it was also apparent that faculty and students had become increasingly aware that the Fellows were a valuable resource. In previous years, the Fellows were something of an afterthought for the broader intellectual community at the University, and they tended to find themselves in higher demand in the spring semester than in the fall semester. This changed in 1969, however, when the Fellows were encouraged to participate more fully in planning their own year at the Center. This had the effect of making the Center more relevant to the Fellows, and the Fellows more relevant to both the Center and the University at large:

> Thus the Fellows of 1969–70 got off to a fast start in the fall with the feeling that their presence made a difference at Harvard. They were in the thick of things from the beginning, participating to the fullest extent. Since the word went out that they had something to offer, members of the group were invited to take part in a wide variety of activities in the University and elsewhere. They responded to the challenge and were stimulated by it.[39]

51

That year's group was also particularly adamant that the Center implement a group excursion to Washington, D.C. Previous requests for such a trip were dismissed "for fear of seeming to stress the American viewpoint unduly." But this class was obstinate: "since American policies for better or for worse have worldwide impact, it would be useful to discuss them candidly and in depth at the place where they are made, with the people who make them."[40] The trip was an enormous success, and meetings were arranged with the national security advisor and former Center faculty member, Henry Kissinger, Senator J. William Fulbright, Governor W. Averell Harriman, and a range of other high-ranking government officials, military personnel, and journalists.[41]

The Fellows were also thrust into the ongoing and often violent antagonism between the CFIA and some increasingly radicalized members of the Harvard student body. Discussed in more detail in Chapter Eight, the Fellows found themselves cast "in some obscure sense [as] the instruments of an American imperialist system." As active international affairs practitioners and members of the CFIA community, they were deemed to be complicit in the many crimes for which the Center was held responsible. The Fellows countered such charges, however, and met on campus with various student groups across the political spectrum. One Fellow also confronted the charges leveled against the program on the Letters page of the *Harvard Crimson*. In response to the accusation that the CFIA required the Fellows to take part in a "program which shows the traces of an evil intention," the Fellow wrote: "[this] is simply not true; the Center permits us maximum freedom in the pursuit of our studies and research. Even if it ever wished to impose any limitations in our freedom, I don't think a group of experienced officials, who out of their free will come to the Center, would accept such 'guidance.'"[42] While he accepted that the Fellows were mostly inured against radicalism and did not subscribe to the revolutionary rhetoric of groups such as the Students for a Democratic Society (SDS), it was nonetheless true that "all of us have been exposed to a variety of ideas this year. Upon our return the results will be watched with caution by our employers at home; for them our stay here is also an experiment with unpredictable results. Some of us will have become radicalized in the view of our colleagues." In the final analysis, he averred, "I would see it as a display of defeatism, if the liberal and radical students did not believe that at least some of their ideas found an echo with certain Fellows."[43] Despite calls from some radical students that the program be disbanded, it was this Fellow's judgment that the Center ought to retain the Fellows Program, not only on the basis of its intrinsic merits in broadening the perspectives of practitioners, but because "to those who attribute part of today's evils to bureaucracies and bureaucrats . . . contact with some of the species offers an opportunity to test their thesis."[44]

Despite the turmoil (and occasional abuse), the success of that year, and indeed of the previous two years, indicated that it was important for the Fellows to initiate their own research and embrace the opportunities offered at a University such as Harvard. The Center could only do so much to facilitate their assimilation into the Harvard community, and the fluid and unpredictable environment of the late 1960s seems to have been the ideal catalyst to propel the Fellows out of the CFIA and into the University. The importance of strong interpersonal relationships was also central to the success of the program, and the events of the late 1960s galvanized the Fellows and piqued their curiosity, binding them into a more cohesive and inquisitive group. As the Center reflected on the excitement and challenges of the previous three years, the consequences of these changes were ambiguous, although not altogether unwelcome. From the CFIA's point of view:

> *Is the trend a desirable one? Have Fellows in general begun to spread themselves too thin? A year of freedom in a busy professional career offers a precious opportunity. Can a Fellow gain more of lasting value by focusing sharply on a few issues of paramount concern to him and exploring them to the uttermost?*
>
> *It is useful to raise those questions—not in the expectation of finding a sovereign answer, but as a caution for future Fellows and their associates in the University. A Fellow's year at Harvard can be put to different uses . . . What is important is that each Fellow choose his own mix—and choose knowingly. The Center must help him make the right choice—for himself. It must also protect his right to be different from his colleagues, to be his own man and to go his own way.[45]*

By 1971, however, calm was restored at the University and the Fellows resumed the previous pattern of engaging in intensive study of problems that were particularly salient to their professional and personal interests.

# Four

# The Evolving Role of Europe

THE ROLE OF EUROPE IN THE POST-1945 INTERNATIONAL SYSTEM WAS part of the CFIA's core research agenda and the source of some of its most intellectually productive and valuable research. The research program on Europe was conducted for the most part under Bowie's leadership during the early years, and his professional and academic interest in the subject made him the natural director of these efforts. Bowie conceived of the role of Europe in the same expansive and integrated way in which he perceived the scope of international affairs as a whole. The erosion of Europe's position of primacy in the international state system in the aftermath of World War II, coupled with the resulting cold war schisms, had raised a number of critical and unresolved issues in terms of Europe's continuing role in the world. As Bowie explained in the Center's first annual report in 1960, "though Europe no longer dominates world affairs, the direction in which she moves will continue to have great, perhaps crucial, importance to the world's future."[1]

## In Search of France

With this in mind, CFIA members in conjunction with other scholars undertook one of the most important, influential, and enduring studies produced by the Center. The process began in the fall of 1959 with the inception of the so-called French Seminar, which resulted in the 1963 collection of essays published under the Center's auspices entitled *In Search of France*. The final study assessed the scope, causes, and consequences of the myriad transformations manifest in almost every aspect of contemporary French society, from the origins and implications of social change, to the renovations of the French political and economic system. The authors considered the extent to which these changes were permanent or transitory, contested or tolerated, profound or superficial, and speculated on the possibilities for further change or stasis in French society in the immediate future.[2]

Bowie regarded this seminar as "a good example of how research at the Center benefits from the interchange among scholars of different backgrounds"; one of this investigations most striking elements is that it focused primarily on French domestic issues rather than French foreign policy.[3] As Bowie explained this seeming anomaly in his foreword to the book's first edition, "it was early realized that a penetrating analysis of the interacting changes affecting Europe would require the pooling of the knowledge and insights of experts in domestic politics and foreign relations, economists, social historians, and sociologists."[4] One fruitful approach to the study of Europe was to analyze the experience of individual countries. France was chosen to be the first subject for this kind of collaborative analysis because the necessary talent and volition existed in Cambridge, and it corresponded with the Center's principle goal of undertaking relevant projects on the basis of scholarly interest and desire rather than a particular subject's perceived, abstract importance.

In addition to Bowie, the Center also profited from the presence of a number of scholars whose interests coalesced around this project. Stanley Hoffmann, then an associate professor in the Department of Government, was joined by Charles Kindleberger, a professor of economics at MIT, Laurence Wylie, the C. Douglas Dillon Professor of the Civilization of France, Jesse R. Pitts, a visiting professor from Wayne State University, and Jean-Baptiste Duroselle of the Fondation Nationale des Sciences Politique in Paris, who was at that time a visiting lecturer in the Harvard History Department. The final contributor to the project was François Goguel, secretary-general of the French Senate, who had not participated in the Center seminar.

The process that engendered *In Search of France* in many ways epitomized the founding conception of the CFIA. In fact, of the final authors only Hoffmann had any official association with the Center. The final study, therefore, represented the essence of what the Center was designed to accomplish: facilitating like-minded academics from across Harvard and Cambridge (and indeed from across the Atlantic) in a collaborative, interdisciplinary, scholarly process that probed fundamental questions of long-term significance through seminar discussions,

56

draft essays, and critiques. The French Seminar itself was frequented by visiting scholars and practitioners, including the Center Fellows and visiting statesmen such as Pierre Mendès-France and Valery Giscard d'Estaing, who evaluated the five studies that comprised the final product.[5]

The manuscript production process culminated in July 1961 with a three-day meeting at the Fondation Nationale des Sciences Politique in Paris, where French experts critiqued the final drafts of the book. "Among the benefits of the colloquium, besides a renewed stimulus," Bowie affirmed, "were answers to certain questions, the sharpening of many issues, some changes of opinion, and help in revision of the chapters." In the final analysis, Bowie was assured that "in their search to understand the emerging France, the authors are unanimous in believing that their thinking has greatly benefited from the give and take with one another and with the many others who have cooperated so generously both at the Center and in France."[6]

## In Search of Germany

The success of the French Seminar convinced the Center that embarking on further studies of this nature was efficacious, and it was envisaged that both Germany and Britain would be the subjects of future treatment. Though the British study never occurred, efforts were initiated in April 1964 to formulate a comparable study on the Federal Republic of Germany. The project, led by Henry Kissinger with help from Center research associate Karl Kaiser, would attempt to emulate the successful French Seminar, resulting in a companion volume to *In Search of France*. Like this earlier endeavor, the German Seminar involved an array of scholars on both sides of the Atlantic, including Karl Dietrich Bracher of the University of Bonn and Ralph Dahrendorf of the University of Tübingen, as well as participants from the University of Massachusetts and the University of Michigan. The topics and themes under consideration were similarly influenced by the structure of *In Search of France*, including a focus on the extent of political, social, and economic continuity and transformation in Germany and the nature of German identity in the aftermath of that country's partition.

Although by 1966 the Center's study of contemporary Germany was nearing completion, the CFIA would remain in search of Germany. Instead of a final volume, individual chapters were published as articles or expanded into monographs, including one by Karl Kaiser, who remembers, "the plan was to have a book, but the book never materialized." Kaiser recollects that there was never a formal decision to withhold publication of the final study, but "it may have had something to do with lack of interest in producing a book."[7] Stanley Hoffmann suggests otherwise: the failure to publish a final volume derived from Kissinger's intellectual and political disagreements with some members of the German Seminar. "I think that Kissinger disliked some of the pieces in the manuscript that seemed to him insufficiently 'Atlanticist'; he was close to the German Christian Democrats, and very suspicious of those who wanted above all to overcome the division of Germany, some of whom had written for the volume. As a result he never wrote the leading chapter that HUP expected from him."[8] Whatever the reasons for failing to publish the book, the experience nonetheless validated the founding principles of the Center. Although a final, cohesive publication never materialized, the Center freed the participants to publish their findings elsewhere.

## Eastern Europe

The Center also initially fostered a small research interest in Eastern Europe. Zbigniew Brzezinski, a Center research associate with ties to the Russian Research Center, formed the core of this endeavor and also served as an institutional bridge between the two research centers. His 1960 book *The Soviet Bloc: Unity and Conflict* was one of the first studies to systematically identify and analyze the development of disunity in the Sino-Soviet bloc and had tremendous policy implications. Brzezinski's comprehensively documented treatment of the historical relationship between the People's Republic of China and the Soviet Union ignited a profusion of scholarship on the subject in the political science community.[9]

The Center continued to explore relations within and among communist countries. In 1961, Harvard University Press published F. A. Vali's *Rift and Revolt in Hungary: Nationalism versus Communism*, which analyzed challenges to the communist regime in Hungary. The following year the Center also published a collection of forty-eight annotated Chinese Communist documents in conjunction with the East Asian Research Center. The volume contained translations of major Chinese Communist Party pronouncements and declarations, mostly with an emphasis on domestic policy. The collection was prepared anonymously by a "visiting Fellow of the Center for International Affairs," and as Bowie and John King Fairbank described in their foreword to the anthology, "we can assure those who use this volume that the author has a background and experience which few can match in qualifying him for a work on this subject and period."[10] Despite these promising early forays into the study of the communist world, by 1963 the endeavor had faded entirely from the Center's purview as a separate research focus. It is unclear whether or not this reflected a lack of interested scholars or a fear of duplication, but it is likely that the Center considered work of this kind to be more pertinent to the Russian Research Center.

In 1964, Bowie reflected on the Center's trajectory over the previous six years, and while he was confident that the program was now on a stable and solid foundation, he was eager to continue promoting an original and creative research agenda. As he recognized, "continuity should not, of course, become rigidity." From his perspective it was essential that:

> *The Center must continue to innovate, or its subject matter will elude its grasp. A common framework of study encourages men from a variety of disciplines to focus on critical areas of change . . . Such a framework does not imply repetition; it enables one man to build on the work of another, but it does not exclude new approaches. Thus the Center has tried to gear its program to vital areas of change and to stimulate new ways of perceiving and understanding them.[11]*

59

## The Atlantic Community

If the effort to replicate the success of *In Search of France* had been an exercise in imitation, the Center did renovate its research program on Europe in an effort to yield new results. To that end, the Center inaugurated a fresh approach to the study of Europe with the formalization of a specific research program in Atlantic Studies. Bowie himself had long been concerned with issues pertaining to the Atlantic community, and his 1960 report *The North Atlantic Nations*, discussed in Chapter Seven, was but one reflection of his own research and policy interests in this area. Prior to 1963, the Center's research on European affairs was focused largely on issues specific to individual European countries, as in the case of the French Seminar and the abortive effort relating to Germany. In contrast, in academic year 1963–64 the Center established two distinct yet related tracks, one concentrating on "European Studies," and one with an emphasis on "Atlantic Studies." The distinction, of course, was as much semantic as substantive, but it did reflect a shift from the domestically oriented focus of the French and German Seminars, to more avowed recognition of the importance of U.S.-European relations. This disaggregation of effort reflected in part the critical mass of researchers and faculty whose interests encompassed the relationship between the United States and its Western European allies; In a larger context it was also a consequence of the continuing reorientation of French foreign policy under de Gaulle toward strategic and diplomatic independence from the United States, along with the quickening pace of European integration.

Karl Kaiser, one of the key participants in this aspect of the Center's research program, recalls that Center membership had a distinct advantage when it came to facilitating contacts with governmental actors who had played key roles in the management of transatlantic interactions: "In my own work on transatlantic relations, a few phone calls and I could interview Dean Acheson, or Paul Nitze, and important members of the Senate. It was really wonderful. The Center had such an enormous standing, including the people at the head of it, that it automatically opened doors very high up in Washington."[12] Of course, one didn't need to travel to Washington to meet key actors in the international drama. In addition to the constant infusion of outstanding scholars who passed through the Center on a regular basis, the CFIA also regularly hosted a number of important visitors from Europe in different capacities. In addition to the aforementioned French statesmen Pierre Mendès-France and Valery Giscard d'Estaing, the Center also hosted other prominent Europeans such as Fritz Erler, the parliamentary leader and deputy chair of the German Social Democratic Party, who came to the CFIA in March 1964 to deliver three lectures under the auspices of the Jodidi Fund. The Jodidi Lectures were endowed by the Samuel L. Jodidi and Elizabeth Jodidi Fund in 1955 and were subsequently administered by the Center with the intention of "[fostering] tolerance and understanding among nations."[13] Such associations only helped to enrich the Center's research output and enhance the experience of its visiting research associates.

## Broadening the Program

In a proposal for additional research funds submitted to the Ford Foundation in 1964, Bowie outlined the Center's current approach to the study of Europe, forecasting possible future directions in research. After six years in operation, the CFIA had made significant contributions to the scholarly understanding of how political, economic, and cultural trends in Europe influenced their foreign affairs, but Bowie still felt there was a greater need for multifaceted research that would deepen knowledge of Europe's international relations. "Despite the long-standing interest of American universities in Western Europe, traditional patterns of specialized study centering on separate countries do not meet present day needs." Bowie emphasized the Center's unique capacity to ameliorate this deficiency, stressing that the problems of Europe "demand a more adventurous approach and a pooling of the knowledge and insight of experts in domestic affairs and foreign relations, political scientists, economists, social historians, sociologists, and others."[14] Bowie acknowledged that until the initiation of the French Seminar and the influx of funds from a Ford Foundation grant, "the

Center's activities in the European field were limited by scarcity of resources," both intellectual and financial.[15] In addition to this infusion of money and expertise, the Center also assembled a Faculty Advisory Committee comprising Carl Friedrich, Stanley Hoffmann, Carl Kaysen, Charles Kindleberger, Henry Kissinger, Laurence Wylie, and Robert Bowie, which was designed to steward the Center's efforts in matters pertaining to Europe.[16] Looking forward, the Center proposed to continue investigating three related aspects of European affairs: domestic issues, European integration, and European foreign relations. In all, the Center boasted twelve individual projects underway in 1964 under the rubric of the European research program, ranging across the disciplines of history, political science, and economics.[17]

Indeed, the scope of the Center's activities in issues related to Europe can be ascertained through the remarkable assortment of studies undertaken within the first few years of the CFIA's founding. In 1964–65 alone, for example, the Center hosted eleven visiting scholars from different backgrounds engaged in research on Atlantic and European affairs. In addition to noted academics such as Hoffmann and Kaiser, the Center also hosted a number of journalists and businessmen, further enriching the Center's intellectual capital. One visiting scholar, Ronald H. Grierson, was the executive director of S.G. Warburg and Company, and came from London in order to study issues related to American investment in Europe. Another visiting researcher, Gian Giacomo Migone, was an editorial writer for the Italian publications *L'Avvenira d'Italia* and *L'Italia* who was investigating U.S.-Italian relations. Scholars from other American universities such as Oberlin College and the University of Wisconsin were also well represented at the Center.[18]

## Raymond Vernon and the Harvard Multinational Enterprise Series

Despite the success of the collaborative French Seminar, the Center continued to study Europe either by assisting individual scholars in publishing manuscripts or by fostering small-scale research projects conducted under the direction of Harvard faculty members. The Center was certainly no less prolific for adopting this method, and a number of influential studies emerged under the Center's auspices in the mid-1960s. In 1961–62, for example, Raymond Vernon arrived at the Center to take directorship of the newly established Development Advisory Service. Arguably, however, his work on multinational corporations and their relationship to the international state system—financed by a grant from the Ford Foundation to the Harvard Business School—became his most important intellectual legacy. The Harvard Multinational Enterprise Project, as it was known, provided a bridge between the Center's research programs on development and on Europe, and by involving a number of faculty members from Harvard Business School, Harvard Law School, as well as from other universities, it was a model of what the Center was originally designed to be able to achieve.

The overall study dealt with "not only the management aspects of the growth of multinational enterprises but also the implications of such growth for international trade, international capital movements, and international political relations."[19] The project produced a remarkable research output, and by 1968 it began to yield a number of monographs—coordinated by Vernon and written by faculty members from Harvard and other participating universities—that were published as the Harvard Multinational Enterprise Series. Vernon inaugurated the series with his 1971 volume entitled *Sovereignty at Bay*, a primer on the impact of multinational corporations on the international system. Vernon calculated that in addition to the four book-length studies that comprised the bulk of the project's research, the endeavor also yielded a dozen doctoral theses, forty journal articles, and a 500-page book of tables. This inventory, as he indicated, was "no more than the tip of an iceberg," and Vernon continued to forge new research paths in international political economy over the course of his tenure at the CFIA.[20]

## Germany Revisited

During the academic year 1967–68, the Center also launched a new research program on Germany under the leadership of Kissinger, who had support from his then–research assistant Guido Goldman. The program, which was initiated and administered in conjunction with the Institute of Politics at the John F. Kennedy School of Government, was designed to "[promote] the study of contemporary Germany at Harvard through research fellowships, seminars, occasional conferences of politically-minded [sic] young German intellectuals, and through the creation of a small library." In many ways this was an outgrowth of the previous German Seminar, although unlike that earlier effort the goal of this program was to provide an institutional and academic home for postdoctoral research fellows from Germany who, it was hoped, would produce analytical studies on topics particularly relevant to understanding the distinct problems of contemporary Germany, and its relation to the United States.[21]

The program encompassed a number of facets, including intensive month-long research seminars led by eminent scholars on German politics such as Richard Löwenthal and Ralf Dahrendorf, and a conference in Bad

Godesberg, Germany, on "The Grand Coalition and its Consequences for German Domestic and Foreign Policy." A bimonthly German Politics Lunch Group was also established at the Center, featuring talks by German intellectuals from various academic disciplines. In addition to these meetings and seminars, the Center also assembled a library featuring German periodicals, books, and news clippings from German-language newspapers and magazines. When Kissinger left the Center in 1969 to join the Nixon administration, the program continued to prosper under the leadership of Guido Goldman and remained an active and productive part of the Center's overall research program on European issues, until it was transferred to the newly created Committee on West European Studies.

## The Committee on West European Studies

The Committee on West European Studies was established in 1969–70 to foster teaching and research on "West European" problems.[22] "The founders of the committee wanted to promote teaching about Western Europe," Hoffmann remembers, "and were interested not only in foreign policy and strategic issues but in internal ones (including European integration). The emphasis of the CFIA was both more global (development, transnational relations) and more America (and policy) centered." Although he admits that "relations with the CFIA were a bit tense for a while," CFIA executive committee members Bowie and Vernon both served on the Committee on Western European Studies, along with two other Center faculty members, Karl Deutsch and Hoffmann himself, who became the committee's chair.[23] The committee retained significant links with the CFIA in the early 1970s, co-sponsoring a seminar on U.S.-European relations and jointly benefiting from a Ford Foundation grant designated for research in Western European affairs. In 1973, however, the Committee on West European Studies was formally transformed into the Center for European Studies (CES), which effectively ended the CFIA's European research program, and by 1974 the Center no longer hosted any explicitly European activities, deferring such issues instead to the newly created CES. The Center did maintain, however, a continued interest in the role of Europe as it pertained to U.S. foreign policy.

After sixteen years in operation, the Center had hosted a wide range of scholars working on various aspects of European politics and economics. In many ways, while not a direct institutional product of the CFIA, the emergence of the CES was a natural outgrowth of the CFIA's efforts in the field of European and Atlantic affairs. While the foundation of the CES owed much to the decision to enhance Harvard's teaching curriculum, as well as to the energies of faculty associate Stanley Hoffmann, it also represented the culmination of the CFIA's European program. From the beginning, the Center had focused on both the domestic and international dimensions of Europe's political, economic, social, and cultural development, but by 1973 it was clear that the CES provided a more coherent and cohesive institutional home for those research efforts.

The migration of the European research program to CES was an important watershed in the development and maturation of the CFIA. Indeed, the Center was the progenitor of several autonomous research centers and programs at Harvard University, such as the Harvard Institute for International Development (HIID) and the Center for Science and International Affairs (CSIA). In many ways these migrations represented a loss for the Center, both in financial and intellectual terms. In the long run, however, such institutional offshoots demonstrated the abiding relevance of the Center, its founding principles and research agenda, and its role as intellectual incubator.

# Five

# The Role and Control of Force

THE CENTER'S RESEARCH PROGRAM IN MILITARY POLICY AND ARMS control constituted an intellectual cornerstone of the CFIA in its first decade. The jewel in the crown of the Center's efforts in this regard was a body of arms control theory that would resonate far beyond 6 Divinity Avenue. The resulting critical mass of scholarship generated some of the most significant theory and analysis ever produced on nuclear arms control and military strategy. Two principal factors converged in contributing to this remarkable outpouring of literature. In the first place, the astounding array of talented and concerned scholars concentrated within the Cambridge area stimulated the formation of a core academic community that was intellectually and politically motivated to both define and disseminate arms control theory. Concomitantly, the need to come to terms with the function and potential application of nuclear weapons amidst an intensifying nuclear arms race that showed no signs of abating provided an urgent political context for formulating and promulgating a rationalized—and indeed rational—corpus of arms control theory.

The field of military policy, broadly conceived, had been identified early by the CFIA as a core concern. As Bowie remarked in his summary of the Center's first five years, "military-political strategy has been a major subject of study at the Center from the beginning." He highlighted the fact that this interest derived from the unprecedented developments in weapons technology that had occurred since the end of World War II—developments that were intensified by the conflict between the two superpowers: "The starting point for this concern," Bowie mused, "was the evident fact that revolutions in weapons and politics and the postwar dominance of the U.S. and the U.S.S.R. had undermined traditional concepts of strategy and the role of force in international relations." In light of this unique international context, he contended that national defense problems "had to be stated and analyzed in new terms and weighed against new criteria."[1]

In many ways, problems of this nature constituted the primary justification for the CFIA's foundation. Bowie had envisaged from the outset that a research center of this kind was uniquely equipped to engage in long-range study and research, whereas governments were unable to respond in this way because they were hamstrung by immediate crises and short-term international developments. In the context of rapidly changing conventional and nuclear weapons systems, governments were often forced to make far-reaching diplomatic, military, and strategic decisions promptly, and sometimes all too hastily. In addition, the Center's core research staff understood that military and strategic decisions were not formulated in a political vacuum. As Bowie recognized, "the postwar world has been struggling to develop concepts and analytical methods applicable to the radically transformed political and military environment." The Center's focus on the political implications of military decisions engendered a far more comprehensive approach to the problems of nuclear and conventional weapons than previously, both in the academy and the government. The Center was certainly not alone in attempting to address these issues, and the work was far from over, but as Bowie reflected with justified optimism in 1963, "the beginnings that have been made are potentially of great importance."[2]

### The Role of Force: Beyond Arms Control

Although several faculty were frequent and important participants in various Center activities on political-military affairs—Bowie on military strategy and Morton Halperin on arms control—the Center's efforts on political-military issues were led at the outset by Kissinger and Schelling. Kissinger had already established a reputation in the field through his 1957 book *Nuclear Weapons and Foreign Policy*, which was based on the proceedings of a Council on Foreign Relations study on the subject. The book was a national bestseller and prizewinner, and for the most part it had received enthusiastic reviews from his peers.[3] Kissinger argued that U.S. military doctrine had been distorted by the then-obsolete insistence on the maximum application of force targeted toward completely destroying the enemy. This dogma derived in particular from the experience of World War II, but in the nuclear age such a doctrine was infeasible for two reasons. On the one hand, it effectively rendered the application of U.S. military force impotent, since rarely would the stakes be high enough to warrant a full-scale nuclear strike against the Soviet Union. Moreover, it precluded the United States from achieving limited objectives vis-à-vis the Soviet Union, and this in turn enabled the Russians to incrementally undermine American containment. According to Kissinger, "all-out war has therefore ceased to be a meaningful instrument of policy."[4] Limited war, including the potential employment of tactical nuclear weapons on a localized battlefield, would provide an intermediate and graduated strategic alternative that would enable the United States to achieve limited objectives and to respond more effectively to any gradual aggrandizement by the Soviet Union. Though written before he arrived at the CFIA, the scope of Kissinger's study on political-military strategy reflects the extent to which the Center and its associates were cognizant of the broad political, economic, social, and even cultural context that informed strategic and military thinking.

67

Although the Center's efforts in military policy were primarily devoted to arms control, it was by no means the exclusive focus of the political-military component of the CFIA's research agenda. At the outset, the Ford Foundation provided the Center with a $220,000 five-year grant to explore national defense policy and host a number of scholars who were concerned with significant political-military issues. The first such scholar was Henry S. Rowen, who came from the RAND Corporation in the summer of 1960 at Schelling's invitation to develop a manuscript on nuclear proliferation. Halperin recalls that Schelling was instrumental in identifying potential research associates for the Center's program on military policy. Indeed, a steady supply of RAND associates populated the Center as a result of the contacts Schelling made during his prior association with the RAND Corporation.[5] At various times RAND associates such as Albert Wohlstetter and Herman Kahn—two of the most significant, influential, and controversial early theorists of nuclear strategy—attended the Center's political-military seminar. A wide range of other scholars and practitioners also attended the Center's seminars and meetings, including Robert Komer from Bundy's National Security Agency staff, and General Adolf Heusinger, then commander of NATO ground forces.[6]

From the beginning, Schelling's work at the Center propelled the theoretical and analytical boundaries of political-military scholarship, starting with his 1960 collection of essays *The Strategy of Conflict*. That same year, the Center received a grant from the National Science Foundation to fund Schelling's early inquiries into the potential applications of game theory to instances of conflict and cooperation in international affairs. In cooperation with Bernhardt Lieberman of the Boston University Psychology Department, Schelling started to develop a game designed to "simulate some of the situations and choices in such conflicts."[7] Thus began a forty-five-year fascination with game theory's implications and applications, which culminated in a Nobel Prize in Economics for Schelling in 2005.

### Defense and Nuclear Weapons in Asia

In conjunction with the East Asian Research Center, the CFIA also undertook two studies on behalf of the U.S. Arms Control and Disarmament Agency (ACDA), led by Halperin (CFIA) and Dwight Perkins (East Asian Research Center). In July 1964, prior to China's first atomic detonation, the two centers brought together twenty-five specialists on China and arms control to assess the impact of China's possible procurement of nuclear weapons, especially with regard to its implications for arms control measures. The resulting study, composed by Halperin and Perkins, was published under the title *Communist China and Arms Control* in 1965. After China's first successful nuclear test in October 1964, a second conference was held during the following summer, again under the auspices of the two centers and on behalf of ACDA. Indeed, during this period Halperin became a prolific scholar on the implications of Chinese nuclear power, publishing widely and incisively on the subject.

The Center's research on the Chinese nuclear question not only facilitated greater cooperation with the East Asian Research Center but also stimulated the CFIA's growing interest in political-military issues pertaining to Asia in general. In addition to Halperin's work on China and nuclear weapons, the Center also began to consider the role of Japan in the international state system. In April 1966, for example, Harvard and the Carnegie Endowment for International Peace sponsored the visit of a number of American scholars to Japan, including Bowie, Schelling, and Halperin. The group met informally with a range of Japanese academics, media professionals, and government officials to discuss issues of regional and international concern.[8] Although the CFIA had already benefited from the presence of a number of Fellows from East and South Asia—including India, Pakistan, Japan, and Korea—the Center's research agenda had focused primarily on development issues in these regions. It was not until after China's nuclear test that the Center began to fully consider the region's importance in international affairs.

This increasing interest in East Asia quickly broadened into a flourishing but diffuse array of studies focusing on security and defense issues in the Pacific in general. The impetus continued to be China's nuclear program, and the strategic implications of that nation's growing power and influence. It is noteworthy that this issue was a far more pressing concern than the war in Vietnam to many of the Center's research associates engaged in research on military issues in Asia and the Pacific in the mid to late 1960s, and the situation in Southeast Asia was always much more germane to the CFIA's initiatives on development and modernization.

## New Directions

By 1970, the Center's research program on political-military strategy and arms control began to capitalize on an evolution in thinking that had been apparent at the CFIA for at least two years. Since its inception, the primary focus of the program had been on the "use of force in relation to problems of national defense and on the direct control of arms through tacit or overt negotiations." Ten years of intensive and productive activity in this area had yielded enormous insight into the myriad processes by which force could be applied and countered in the international system. It had become manifest by this time, however, that "underlying theoretical understanding of these threats and of how to deal with them has been greatly advanced, especially with respect to weapons capable of producing mass destruction."[9] Recent negotiations between the United States and the Soviet Union validated both this contention and the insights of the Center's arms control seminar, which is discussed in more depth below. Diplomatic discussions over the deployment of antiballistic missile systems and the initiation of the Strategic Arms Limitation Talks (SALT) demonstrated the efficacy of the research conducted by the Center during the previous decade: "No one had to go back to the beginning in order to think usefully about these problems."[10] The challenge, however, was to expand the Center's research program in order to consider the entire spectrum of influences that informed national security and defense policy, including "domestic political processes and decisions about weapons research, development, and acquisition," and "the relationship of the sending and reception of messages and signals."[11]

Schelling's imprint here is clear, but several new directions were now evident in the Center's research, stimulated in large part by some of the generation's most intellectually influential theorists, including Robert Jervis, Kenneth Waltz, and Gene Sharp. For example, Jervis, then a professor in the Department of Government, was engaged in his groundbreaking study

69

of perception and misperception in international relations that culminated in two significant books: *The Logic of Images* and *Perception and Misperception in International Politics*. Waltz, who propounded one of the first systematic studies of international relations theory in his 1959 book *Man, the State, and War*, was an intermittent research associate of the Center and worked on his 1967 book *Foreign Policy and Democratic Politics* while at the Center. During his periodic stays at the CFIA, Waltz also continued to refine his theoretical understanding of international relations, investigating the various facets that constituted the structure of the international system. In addition, the Center hosted Dr. Gene E. Sharp for an extended period beginning in 1965, during which time he developed many pioneering and enduring theories of nonviolent action, which would ultimately find expression in his three-volume opus, published in 1973, *The Politics of Nonviolent Action*.

## The Control of Force: Forging an Arms Control Community in Cambridge

For all the Center's contributions in the general field of political-military policy, it was the CFIA's formative role in developing arms control theory that yielded some of the most remarkable research and analysis in the Center's history. The fact that by 1960 there was such a remarkable profusion of literature on arms control requires further exploration. Undoubtedly, the intensifying nuclear arms race impelled the growing interest of intellectuals in the subject. Ever since the Soviet Union broke the U.S. atomic monopoly in 1949, the logic of nuclear arms had compelled both numerical and technological escalation in the minds of American and Soviet policy makers. In 1950, NSC-68's projections of Soviet atomic capability occasioned a quantitative and qualitative acceleration of America's nuclear weapons program, including the recommendation to develop a thermonuclear hydrogen weapon. The outbreak of the Korean War that same year seemed only to validate the dire predictions of Soviet aggression as outlined in NSC-68. The Soviets deployed a new generation of long-range bombers in 1955 and two years later launched an Intercontinental Ballistic Missile (ICBM), facilitating a quantum leap in Soviet delivery capabilities that finally rendered the United States potentially vulnerable to a nuclear strike; the United States responded with a reciprocal missile development program.

In addition to this patently perilous international context, participants in the Cambridge arms control community during that period identified several additional factors that impelled the vigorous and urgent study of such topics. From Schelling's perspective, two factors played an important role in the proliferation of arms control theory in the early 1960s. One important catalyst was the fact that the myriad complex issues surrounding nuclear weaponry and its employment were so new that "the military acknowledged that it didn't have the experience to deal with these things. They needed new thinking and new people, and therefore . . . the military was thirsting for help in dealing with the kinds of issues that they'd never had to deal with before." This in turn provided an opening for the research and analysis in which Schelling and his colleagues at the CFIA and beyond were actively engaged. Secondly, Schelling notes that "I think people discovered that you could apply reasoning to military problems the way you could apply them to almost any other kind of problems, and that attracted a lot of economists," such as himself.[12] Carl Kaysen, on the other hand, recalls in particular the contributions of the Harvard and MIT scientific communities, especially those individuals who had actively participated in the genesis of the atomic era: "they felt the impulse which so many of the scientists at the Manhattan Project felt, [that] we've created this terrible thing and we ought to do something about it." This feeling was exacerbated by the sense that by 1960 the world faced "a very dangerous, unstable situation."[13] One former Manhattan Project participant, Paul M. Doty, remembers that the change in administration in January 1960 also played a major role in encouraging some natural and social scientists to devote more energy to this issue: "I think it was probably the expectation of friendly relations with Kennedy himself. That was certainly what set me into spending more time on it."[14]

## Two Catalysts

It was in this context that the CFIA, in conjunction with the Center for International Studies (CIS) at MIT, commenced one of its most important and durable contributions to international relations in the fall of 1960: the Harvard-MIT Joint Arms Control Seminar. The seminar originated from two unrelated studies conducted under the aegis of the American Academy of Arts and Sciences (AAAS) in the summer of 1960, and both were attended by CFIA faculty and other Harvard and MIT scholars who were interested in the technical, political, and military implications of nuclear weapons and their management. These two studies culminated in a number of seminal works on arms control that would shape the field at a critical time in its development. One meeting took place at the AAAS in May 1960 and resulted in a special edition of the Academy's journal, *Daedalus*, which was later expanded into book form. The second study was organized by Bernard T. Feld, an MIT nuclear physicist and Manhattan Project alumnus. Feld's "Summer Study on Arms Control" brought together participants from Cambridge and farther afield over the course of the summer and provided the stimulus for Schelling and Halperin's highly influential *Strategy and Arms Control*. Without hyperbole, Jennifer Sims argues, "these publications recorded a revolution in the conception and practice of national security and nuclear strategy. Within months, the revolution and the debate that it swept forward was known worldwide. Decades later 1960 was seen as a turning point; 'The Golden Age' of nuclear arms control had begun."[15]

In the spring of 1960, the editor in chief of *Daedalus* commissioned over twenty leading authorities on nuclear weapons and arms control to produce a special volume for publication the following fall. The AAAS convened a guest editorial board to conceive and organize the effort, which became a seminal volume on nuclear arms control. The editor in chief, Gerald Holton, recruited his editorial board almost entirely from Harvard and MIT, and it included Bowie and Kissinger along with technical experts such as Donald G. Brennan of the Lincoln Laboratory and Manhattan Project veterans such as Bernard Feld, both of whom were instrumental in establishing the foundations for the technical implications of arms control. As Holton stated in his prefatory note to the final volume, "as recently as a year ago a coordinated group of papers of this range and quality could not have been assembled." By the end of 1959, however, Holton felt compelled to devote an entire issue of *Daedalus* to the subject, since in his estimation there had been a "change both in atmosphere and in substantive work [that] made it possible to assemble what may be regarded as a handbook on the problems of arms control and national policy."[16] Approximately sixty participants met at the House of the Academy on May 20 and May 21 to discuss the papers that had been submitted for the publication; the final papers were published in a special edition of *Daedalus* that fall. In addition to Bowie, Kissinger, and Schelling, the *Daedalus* volume contained articles by a plethora of esteemed political scientists, natural scientists, philosophers, psychologists, and legal scholars. Edward Teller, the so-called father of thermonuclear weaponry, Senator Hubert Humphrey, and the prominent psychologist Erich Fromm all contributed articles on issues ranging from the need for supranational organizations and openness, to the desire for complete unilateral disarmament. It would prove to be an enormously important and influential endeavor. For one thing, Kaysen suggests that the *Daedalus* volume played a major role in establishing arms control as a legitimate field of study among scholars: "I think it is fair to say that the *Daedalus* issue crystallized the discussion and made it a sort of academically respectable subject."[17]

The scope of the articles submitted by Bowie, Kissinger, and Schelling demonstrate the breadth and variety of thinking on the issue at the CFIA in the early 1960s. Bowie was concerned with the broader international context of arms control agreements, and he focused on the conditions necessary for effective agreements between the United States and the Soviet Union: "No arms-control plan will remain effective and dependable unless it continues to serve the national interests of each of the parties, as its leaders conceive those interests." With this in mind, instituting an arms control system that provided enough flexibility to allow either side to withdraw from the agreement might be necessary. Such a system would provide sufficient latitude for stabilizing nuclear deterrents, deemed essential by most arms control theorists, in order to both prevent a possible preemptive nuclear war and enable progressive steps toward arms limitation and, ultimately, arms reduction. A realistic inspection and verification system would also be essential to an effective arms control regime, since "by cooperation through such means," Bowie suggested, "the major opponents might be able to work out ways of maintaining the strategic deterrent at lower levels of resources and expenditures."[18]

Kissinger provided an essay derived from a future publication, *The Necessity for Choice: Prospects of American Foreign Policy*, which would be published in 1960. Kissinger was concerned primarily with the politico-military implications of nuclear weapons, especially with regard to military doctrine and strategy. In this essay, he continued to analyze the efficacy of limited nuclear war that he had begun three years earlier in *Nuclear Weapons and Foreign Policy*. In that previous study, Kissinger had advocated integrating limited, tactical nuclear capabilities into military and political planning in order to achieve limited objectives without resorting to a full-scale nuclear exchange. In this 1960 essay, however, Kissinger revisited his earlier emphasis on tactical nuclear weapons, arguing that it had become infeasible to rely too much on such weaponry. Instead, Kissinger recognized that "a substantial build-up of conventional forces and a greater reliance on conventional strategy is essential," though not necessarily decisive.[19] In this regard, Kissinger argued that the implications for arms control rested upon "the paradox that the best road to nuclear-arms [*sic*] control may be conventional rearmament," since a credible conventional deterrent was just as important as a credible nuclear deterrent.[20]

Schelling's article reflected his enduring interest in the implications and consequences of advancements in nuclear technology. It was not enough to simply remain enmeshed "in the traditional confinement of 'disarmament,'" he argued, for beyond that lay "the entire area of military collaboration with potential enemies to reduce the likelihood of war or to reduce its scope and violence."[21] The problem, as Schelling understood it, was that "we and the Russians are trapped by our military technology." This predicament had one potential solution, which was to foster reciprocal agreements that would negate—or at least mitigate—the propensity of new technology to accelerate the nuclear arms race. This would require a systematic "strategic analysis" of every aspect of the nuclear program, including weapons systems, verification techniques, and deployment patterns, in order to ascertain which element of the nuclear equation was most liable to produce either stability or volatility. Such diplomatic agreements between the Soviet Union and the United States would not necessarily be explicit, but could be achieved through implicit or even unilateral gestures, something Schelling called "mutual arms accommodation."[22] Though Schelling identified many problems inherent in this form of informal arms control, his argument is important because it demonstrates his ability to think beyond the conventional parameters of formal, diplomatic, arms control systems.

The second major study undertaken in that remarkable summer was Feld's "Summer Study on Arms Control," which began in June and ended in September 1960. The seminar was financed by the Twentieth Century Fund and convened at MIT's Endicott House, drawing approximately fifty scholars, mostly from MIT and Harvard, but also from around the country. The seminar's general objectives "were to advance some aspects of the intellectual state of the art in arms control," wrote the director of the Twentieth Century Fund in the foreword to Schelling and Halperin's *Strategy and Arms Control*, "and to provide some concrete data on a few technical and strategic problems of potential importance."[23] In a memorandum to Feld written prior to the summer study, Schelling outlined both his reflections about the inchoate field and his feelings about what they might achieve in the coming summer. This document provides a unique insight into the early thinking of one of the most influential arms control theorists. Indeed, Schelling was far from optimistic about the possibilities in early 1960. For one thing, he professed himself to be "impressed with how ill-equipped we are, as a group, within the time available, to solve any appreciable number of technical problems relating to arms control, or to give technical evaluations of concrete schemes." The technical difficulties were not the only problem: it was likewise difficult "to reach a group consensus on a concrete arms proposal, or even a set of alternative proposals, that we might jointly dignify with a decision to spend the rest of the summer on."[24] For Schelling, achieving concordance was more profound in its dimensions at this early stage, perhaps even epistemological, since it was deeply rooted in the imprecise and immature nature of the field. He recognized that the subject of arms control was at present too nebulous and too divorced from more traditional thinking on military and strategic issues to be immediately constructive. In this analysis, Schelling felt that one of the summer study's primary goals should be to determine the scope, context, and substance of both theoretical and practical arms control topics. The following quotation, taken from Schelling's letter to Feld, is especially instructive and in many ways represents one of the embryos that would spawn modern arms control theory:

> I am impressed, as I have been for a year or two, with how far we are, and everybody
> else is, from having a reasonably mature and sophisticated conception of what arms
> control is all about, what genus of activity it belongs to, how to characterize it,
> what it depends on, what it aims to do, and how it relates to more general areas
> of policy like diplomacy and military affairs. My personal hunch is that as the
> subject is explored further, the definition will be further broadened, until perhaps
> we no longer think of it as a distinct, novel, unique, and well-delineated area of
> activity, but instead think of it as an area of military and diplomatic activity
> that has simply received little emphasis and even less recognition for what it is,
> in the past, than more traditional lines of activity. I think some of our discussions
> . . . reflect not only a need to explore the domain of arms control to find out what
> it contains, but perhaps also an initial preconception, maybe a misconception, that
> arms control is something very new and different, in concept as well as in policy. I
> think we are still just discovering what it is all about, and may yet have a number
> of revolutions in our thinking ahead.[25]

In the aftermath of the summer seminar, Schelling remained unconvinced that a consensus had emerged. Although he found Feld's proposed summary of the proceedings to be "very well written, sober, well balanced, [and] intelligent," he nonetheless strongly disagreed with some of its findings. Schelling's reticence did not reflect any derision of Feld's summary; on the contrary, he acknowledged that he himself could not produce a better summation. The problem, Schelling conceded, was endemic to the scholarly process in which they were engaged: "I am inclined to think that the statement we can all agree on is likely to be a pretty weak statement."

What is clear from this correspondence is that Schelling remained as equivocal about the early efforts of the arms controllers in the aftermath of the summer study seminar as before it began. While one reason was the inherent, and perhaps not entirely negative, difficulty in achieving consensus among a wide range of arms control theorists, another was the intrinsic complexity of the subject itself. "I rather think that arms control is about as complicated as military policy, and that many of the glaring gaps in our knowledge would never be filled, and some might require large amounts of money."[26] Nonetheless, over the next twelve years Schelling and his colleagues in the Harvard-MIT Joint Arms Control Seminar would grapple with these problems, and propel "revolutions in thinking" both within the academic community and the policy-making community.

## Emerging Principles

Despite Schelling's pessimism, it is clear that a number of basic premises emerged from that summer study. Morton Halperin, for example, remembers the novelty and innovation that would impel the arms control community to some of its most enduring and insightful research. He recollects that there *was* a consensus, in the broadest sense, on the basic premise of arms control:

> *The approach of everybody in that room was that properly designed arms control agreements could actually contribute to the security of two states who were adversaries by avoiding inadvertent conflicts that neither wanted while leaving them both free to pursue the use of threats of force as part of their foreign policy. Well, that was a totally new idea . . . I had just been through graduate school and had been taught what all graduate students were taught . . . that arms control is nonsense; that the real cause of war was tensions and hostility between states and that states are forced to talk about arms control because publics want it.*

The whole endeavor, then, in his estimation pivoted around the "profoundly important but very simple idea that . . . given the nature of nuclear weapons there could be military agreements among hostile nations that would actually increase the security of the nations." Prior to this, Halperin attests, the assumption was that "the arms race was simply a manifestation of the political conflict among nations, and would end or dissipate when either there was a war or political conflict ended by a political treaty of some kind."[27]

In addition, and despite the wide range of approaches to the subject, recognizing that nuclear arms control did not necessarily demand abolishing nuclear weapons outright was another thread that unified almost all of the participants in the greater arms control community. In his foreword to the *Daedelus* volume, Jerome B. Wiesner, director of the Research Laboratory of

Electronics at MIT and member of President Eisenhower's Science Advisory Committee, hoped that the special issue would "provide some of the basic information and understanding needed for an intelligent public discussion of the disarmament problem."[28] The "disarmament problem," however, was as much a problem of definition as it was a problem of impending nuclear annihilation. Arms control did not necessarily connote advocating the complete elimination of nuclear weapons, nor did it preclude such an outcome. As Donald Brennan suggested in his contribution, "the approach should be thought of as oriented toward improving the national security of each of the nations involved by adjusting at least some armament capabilities and uses to those 'actually' desirable in the light of the intentions, actions, and adjusted capabilities of the other nations." Depending on the circumstances, therefore, in the interests of arms control and maintaining deterrence it might even be necessary to increase the number of nuclear weapons available to either side.[29]

77

As Schelling remembers, this often meant that those who demanded general and complete nuclear disarmament derided those who advocated some form of arms control: "what you might call the culture of disarmament was such that all of us—almost anybody who used the term arms control—were despised by the disarmament community. We were considered captives of the military industrial establishment." Among those who criticized Schelling and his colleagues, he insists, "disarmament and arms control in 1960 were considered incompatible, competing notions."[30]

For those engaged in defining arms control theory, however, this was always an erroneous distinction. In 1961, the *Daedalus* volume was published in book form and edited by Brennan, who noted in his preface that among the authors concerned with the subject "there are differences over ways and means, and in sophistication; but *there are no basic differences in the morality of the authors* [italics in the original]." As Brennan emphasized, conceptions of arms control were arrayed across a spectrum of possible responses and outcomes, including the potential for general and complete disarmament. Some writers, he argued, preferred a limited definition of the concept. In his book *Arms Control, Disarmament, and National Security*, Brennan addressed such writers, who proposed that arms control " . . . is a distinctly wicked doctrine, and those who advocate it (as opposed to 'disarmament') are made to appear as immoral proponents of the continuation of the arms race."[31]

The underlying premise of arms control, then, was ultimately a pragmatic one. As Schelling reflects, it derived from an understanding that "we have to live with nuclear weapons. We can't trust the Soviets, they can't trust us. We've got to try and design weapons systems that are minimally susceptible to false alarm, or miscalculation, or accidental launch, or something of the sort." However unpalatable accepting nuclear weapons might be in the abstract, there was no way to undo the discoveries of the atomic age. As such, it was essential to come to terms with their existence and find ways to manage and mitigate their potentially catastrophic consequences. Arms control was envisaged as an attempt to do just that, and nuclear weapons continued to be relevant to the two superpowers. For Schelling, it was essential to recognize that this often meant supporting efforts "to design weapons in such a way that they make war less likely."[32] The tension between the arms control community and the disarmament community would soon be rendered moot by the inauguration of the Kennedy administration, which was broadly sympathetic to the principles of arms control.[33]

### The Control of Force: The Harvard-MIT Joint Arms Control Seminar

Following the success of the two AAAS studies, CFIA and CIS members decided to pool their considerable intellectual resources in the fall of 1960 and establish the Harvard-MIT Joint Arms Control Seminar. This measure was intended to institutionalize an informal series of meetings that the CFIA had conducted since 1959 and to capitalize on the achievements of the AAAS gatherings that summer.

The decision to institute the seminar followed a meeting between Schelling and Halperin from the CFIA and Max Millikan and Ithiel de Sola Pool from CIS, in which it was agreed that the two centers should cooperate in this growing field. The initial underlying basis of the seminar was to consider the fundamental question: "How should American military policy be adapted to take in arms control considerations and to prepare for possible arms control agreements?" The group would meet once every two or three weeks to discuss pre-circulated papers prepared by one or more of the participants.[34] The two centers received a jointly administered $50,000 grant from the Rockefeller Foundation to fund the seminar's activities. As stated in the proposal to the foundation from September 1960:

> The seminar hopes to serve as a catalyst to encourage people to do research on arms control. It will also function as a clearing house where people in the area doing work on arms control can exchange drafts, discuss their work, and discuss policy implications of arms control research. The relatively large number of people in the area currently doing research in the field of arms control suggest that the [proposed] program will be very useful.[35]

The seminar was designed to exploit the fact that "numerous individuals, working from equally numerous disciplines, were engaged in research and writing and in academic and governmental work relevant to this field of wide ramifications and increasing national urgency."[36] Despite this ongoing uncoordinated endeavor, however, there was a need for a broader and more intensive collective effort. Substantively:

> The Seminar program was designed to improve communication by clarifying terminology, exchanging manuscripts, and exploring the policy implications of currently proposed or contemplated arms control measures. In addition, the Seminar was intended to spur original creative effort among its members by establishing a forum for argument and diverse comment, by inviting individuals from outside the community for special presentations, and by limited sponsorship of new research and writing.[37]

In addition to engendering greater interaction and cooperation among like-minded scholars in the field, it would also "offer a catalyst for broadening and deepening the understanding of its members and for encouraging so far as possible the availability of their competence to universities, the government, and the public."[38] In this regard, then, the seminar reflected the essence of the CFIA's broader mandate: to provide a forum for discussion and to stimulate a wide range of scholarly research from a variety of perspectives and disciplines.

## The "Cambridge Approach" to Arms Control

In her book *Icarus Restrained*, Jennifer Sims outlines the central premises of the resultant "Cambridge Approach" to arms control, although she correctly recognizes that "not all the contributors to this body of thought subscribed to the entire approach . . . Although most accepted the majority of its features and recognized the remainder to be at least plausible."[39] Indeed, some would subsequently renounce certain aspects of the approach or disavow the endeavor entirely. But at the outset unanimity was most apparent on the notion that nuclear weapons were quantitatively different than other weapons, and therefore their employment and management necessitated a completely new mind-set. These exceptional weapons had engendered a unique international environment, and as such their use required a unique approach. At the same time, however, the basic underlying structure of the international system remained rooted in the Westphalian system of independent, often competing, sovereign states, dominated by the competing blocs of the East and the West. In that regard, it was reasonable to assume that the governments of the nuclear powers and their allies "can recognize the above truths and reduce the likelihood of war by acting on their common interest in controlling or avoiding technical instabilities while observing the constraints of the system." Finally, Sims identifies a broad recognition among the Cambridge arms controllers for the need to maintain the "weapons-stability nexus." This she describes as a belief in the seemingly paradoxical notion that nuclear weapons themselves provide security against their use, especially in the context of a constantly shifting balance of relative nuclear capabilities.[40]

The "Cambridge Approach" had three common objectives with regard to nuclear arms control. First, most participants considered it essential to "establish and maintain the threshold between conventional and nuclear weapons." By invoking a clear boundary between what might precipitate a nuclear strike and what actions warranted only a conventional response, both sides were aware of the limits and therefore could judge the potential consequences of their actions. Second, in order to maintain this threshold it was deemed necessary to preserve the notion that any "first use of nuclear weapons could potentially lead to general use."[41] This also meant that in the interest of arms control and maintaining the threshold, it was necessary to oppose any weapons system or tactical deployment that might blur the boundary between nuclear and conventional weapons. This included the doctrine of limited nuclear war, or developing low-yield, tactical nuclear weapons, whose relatively reduced destructive capacity might tempt their limited employment.[42] Third, the arms race had to be stabilized, and for many that meant promoting robust and secure second-strike capabilities for both sides that would ensure "mutually assured destruction" and therefore significantly reduce the likelihood of a first strike. In order to promote this stability, it was also essential to implement formal and informal measures of "crisis stability," such as direct lines of communication between the Kremlin and the White House, and reciprocal verification and inspection regimes. In the short-term these measures were expected to reduce the possibility of an accidental or ill-conceived first strike; in the long-term the "Cambridge Approach" sought to reduce the friction between the United States and the Soviet Union so that a concerted effort to ameliorate, if not eradicate, the nuclear arms race could prosper.[43]

The first meeting of the Harvard-MIT Joint Arms Control Seminar convened on October 4, 1960 at the Harvard Faculty Club and set the tone for a lively and constructive future. Participants from Harvard included Bowie, Kissinger, Schelling, Bundy, and Doty, as well as Millikan, Pool, Lincoln Bloomfield, and Walt Rostow from MIT, in addition to thirteen others from the area. Three papers were circulated in advance, including Schelling's and Pool's contributions to the *Daedalus* volume. The discussion began with an analysis of possible arms control methods, derived in large part from Schelling's conception of more subtle, tacit, and implicit agreements. The discussants debated the relative importance of the politico-military context in which arms control agreements were expected to be reached, and the meeting ended with the consideration of U.S. policies toward arms control and its ultimate purpose.[44]

Future meetings followed a similar pattern and were interspersed with discussions about relevant international events. These meetings also benefited from the various governmental and nongovernmental assignments of its members. For example, at the December 13, 1960 meeting, several members reported on their recent attendance at the Moscow Conference on disarmament—one in a series of the so-called Pugwash Conferences—at which scientists from the Soviet bloc met with scientists from the West in order to discuss issues pertaining to nuclear weapons. Doty, Schelling, Louis Sohn, and Jerome Wiesner had all attended the conference, shared their often divergent impressions from their meetings with Soviet scientists, and fielded questions from the other seminar participants.[45]

In addition, the seminar almost immediately attracted attention from the policy-making community. As early as the second meeting on October 24, 1960, Lincoln Bloomfield announced that one Defense Department official had asked to attend a session. Bloomfield also suggested including an interested State Department official at a later meeting.[46] The Center also attracted guests from the U.S. military, including two participants from the Joint Chiefs of Staff.

There was a certain degree of dissension within the group during the first year, however, on the extent to which the seminar ought to be orienting itself toward explicitly policy-relevant questions. At the final meeting of the 1960–61 academic year, for example, Schelling introduced the topic of President Kennedy's recent defense budget, noting that "the thinking reflected in arms control circles had taken some root in military circles and was reflected in the Kennedy Defense Budget." In response to the following discussion, Milton Katz questioned in what direction the seminar should move. In his view, "in the last three years an effort has been made to think seminally and fundamentally," and he felt that this was still a pressing and urgent problem for those engaged in thinking about arms control rather than trying to influence policy. David Cavers of the Harvard Law School concurred with his colleague, stressing that "it was important to be ahead of the thinking in Washington, and not to be responding to it." Henry Rowen, a former CFIA research associate who had since joined the Defense Department as deputy assistant secretary of defense for policy planning, was in a unique position to assess the role of the scholar in this field: "academics should deal with the long-range political implications of arms control proposals and not with the short-range political problems."[47]

In the end-of-year questionnaire provided to the participants, there was certainly no resolution to this disagreement. When asked if the seminar should be explicitly "policy-oriented," the responses were mixed; for some respondents, the seminar maintained "greater influence by being detached," while others insisted that "there have been enough abstract studies; what we need are results." A more circumspect respondent suggested that the participants ought to simply "play it by ear, and consider our primary objective the maintenance of an alert and vigorous Cambridge intellectual position."[48] Nevertheless, after one year of meetings the seminar had a wide-ranging influence, not only through the scope and volume of its resulting publications but also through the participants' activities within the U.S. government, the international scientific community, and in the classroom. According to the seminar's annual report:

> Seminar members carried out an increasing regime of consultation with government bodies and public speeches and appearances at panels and forums. Several members of the Seminar were active in the unofficial Pugwash Conference in Moscow in December 1960, and have kept up their contacts and correspondence with foreign counterparts. Concepts and approaches developed in Seminar work have in addition been applied and presented in courses offered in the curricula of the two sponsoring institutions.[49]

One of the most significant publications to emerge from these discussions and the earlier "Summer Study on Arms Control" was Schelling's and Halperin's *Strategy and Arms Control*. The book was conceived as "an effort to fit arms control into our foreign and military policy, and to demonstrate how naturally it fits rather than how novel it is." In common with the majority of the Cambridge arms control advocates, Schelling and Halperin stressed the strategic value and flexibility of arms control measures, whether in explicit bilateral diplomatic agreements or unilateral and implicit posture modifications. Disarmament was but one possibility on a spectrum of potential actions and reactions.

In Schelling's and Halperin's assessment, arms control "rests essentially on the recognition that our military relation with potential enemies is not one of pure conflict and opposition, but involves strong elements of mutual interest in the avoidance of a war that neither side wants, in minimizing the costs and risks of the arms competition, and in curtailing the scope and violence of war in the event it occurs."[50] In the previous fifteen years, in which the arms race seemed to be escalating without impediment, this insight alone was tremendously valuable. The study ranged broadly across a multitude of issues, from the dangers of an accidental nuclear war to an exposition on the logic of premeditated, preemptive nuclear strikes. They speculated about the various scenarios that might result in a nuclear exchange, and prescribed a number of potential arms control remedies that could be expected to eradicate, or at least mitigate, the potential for nuclear war. Though they accepted that many of the measures they suggested had inherent risks and flaws, Schelling and Halperin nonetheless provided a framework for thinking about various arms control strategies that had real policy significance. Just how significant would become clear as soon as the Kennedy administration got underway.[51]

The book was in many ways an outgrowth of Schelling's contribution to the earlier *Daedalus* volume, refined and renewed by the summer's discussions and the collaboration of Halperin and the members of the Harvard-MIT Joint Seminar. Schelling remembers that the seminar essentially provided "a captive audience" for developing their ideas during the fall of 1960: "We simply fed them chapters of our book. And for the whole fall term they became our sounding board, for chapter after chapter after chapter. And it was good for them because it gave them something pretty tangible to chew on. They became a perfect audience for Mort and me to indoctrinate." The seminar had the added advantage of providing an audience of future Kennedy administration officials, such as McGeorge Bundy, Walt Rostow, Henry Rowen, Carl Kaysen, and Abram Chayes, men who would soon be in a position to formulate policy. This meant that, as Halperin affirms, "the rest of us had an outlet of people that we knew to talk to about these issues and it became politically relevant."[52]

Besides the Schelling and Halperin volume, the seminar's discussions over the following twelve years were tremendously expansive and equally impressive. From the relative merits of expanding the arms race into space, to the politics of alliance management, the seminar extended broadly and incisively across the whole spectrum of the political, military, economic, technological, and social sources and implications of arms control. One discussion, for example, focused on the possible consequences of engaging in a concerted effort of civil defense preparation. Harvard professor Arthur Smithies introduced the topic by outlining some questions that might arise from a large-scale shelter program: Would shelters increase the likelihood of a preemptive Soviet strike,

83

since shelters would remove populations from their position as hostages? What effect would such a program have on relationships with America's allies, for whom diverting the enormous resources required to implement an effective shelter system was fiscally infeasible? Might such an initiative detract from U.S. military spending?[53]

In another notable meeting, the seminar convened on October 22, 1962, in the midst of the most dangerous nuclear crisis of the entire cold war; the scheduled discussion for that evening was laid aside in favor of considering the events surrounding the ongoing Cuban missile crisis. The participants discussed the potential motivation of the Soviet leadership in deploying missiles to Cuba, the options available to the United States in resolving the crisis, and the conceivable outcomes. Schelling, for instance, suggested that the crisis "will teach us something about the [Soviet] value system. This kind of information will be valuable to us in other crises elsewhere and will affect the position of the U.S. government." The fact that Schelling anticipated further crises indicates that he did not think this Soviet deployment would result in a nuclear exchange, but even in the shadow of a very real nuclear crisis—and in the glow of the television procured to watch President Kennedy's historic address to the nation that evening—the participants in the seminar remained transfixed on what could be learned from the experience, and how it might enrich their understanding of arms control and nuclear weapons policy.[54]

Such discussions, viewed from a distance, may appear macabre, and perhaps they reflect a certain emotional distance from the stark realities of nuclear annihilation. One historian, for example, derisively insists "in Schelling's hands, nuclear war becomes an extraordinarily bloodless and cerebral affair, an enterprise suitable for tweedy professors smoking pipes."[55] Such characterizations, however, detract from the measured and seminal research in which the seminar members engaged, and the real policy value of such discussions and the publications they facilitated. While they might sometimes appear hyperrational, the stakes were such that lucidity was a vital, and sometimes altogether too rare, commodity. Schelling, in particular, remains characteristically perspicacious on the issue: "I don't mind being called a cold warrior, but I would insist that I wanted deterrence to work, in both directions, so that there could be no war, and I never felt I had to apologize for that."[56]

At the end of the 1962–63 academic year the seminar met to consider the question, whither arms control? Some members had become less sanguine about the seminar's constructiveness, impact, and insights; indeed, Schelling himself began the discussion with the rather pessimistic announcement, "the sense of momentum in arms controls has declined." The feeling of novelty and innovation that had characterized the founding moments of the arms control movement had, in his view, dissipated. He felt that the seminar concentrated largely on strategy and foreign policy and as such had only generated one major insight since 1960—"the view that disarmament need not be based on equality; there may be an interest in negotiating asymmetrical agreements." Otherwise, there was little in the realms of either theory or practice to suggest that arms control had made any significant headway in the previous three years. In fact, Schelling proposed that the "most tangible development is the enmity between disarmers and arms controllers."[57]

Taking the contrary position—there had been significant results in both policy and theory—Louis Sohn was more optimistic that "the research can take effect only in the long run." Joining the regular participants on this occasion was the acting director of the U.S. Arms Control and Disarmament Agency, Adrian S. Fisher, who contended that the seminar remained crucially important since "the task of intellectual leaders is to educate the public, especially Congress, and the Russians." From his perspective as an ACDA official, "it is very difficult to keep ideas alive against inertia and opposition." Roger Fisher of the Harvard Law School was also circumspect. He accepted that new ideas were lacking, but he was confident that "the old ones have been sold to the government, and possibly the Soviets." He did express concern, however, that "the Seminar is failing in that it is not leading, not thinking through new ideas." Halperin concurred that the seminar's insights had inculcated U.S. government thinking on arms control, and welcomed the fact that "arms control has become part of strategy: questions like war termination conditions or negotiation during war are taken seriously by the government."[58]

Despite these criticisms and reflections, the seminar continued with renewed vigor in the 1963–64 academic year, although Schelling's complaint that the seminar tended to focus more on strategy and foreign policy retained its salience. Nonetheless, the Center continued to draw upon government officials' expertise, including former seminar members who had left academia for government service. At the first meeting of that academic year, for example, John McNaughton returned as a guest from his new post as general counsel of the Department of Defense to discuss the recent Test Ban Treaty negotiations alongside former Center associate Carl Kaysen. Although the seminar continued to host policy makers and influential strategists, the seminar would never again recapture its early zeal for formulating arms control theory.[59] Partly, as some participants had already noted, this derived from the fact that the need was no longer so acute, since the groundwork that was laid in those early meetings had provided a solid foundation for exploring more general, yet no less important, issues related to arms control. In addition, the seminar's growing focus on strategy and foreign policy to some degree reflected the CFIA's core belief in contextualizing and connecting the various facets of international affairs.

As the years progressed, however, seminar meetings occasionally ignored the problem of arms control entirely. At the beginning of the 1964–65 academic year, for example, the participants discussed devoting part of that year to civil conflict or domestic violence questions. Roger Fisher outlined a possible rubric for such analysis, suggesting that the group consider "wars of liberation, coups d'etat, general strikes, and boycotts." In a departure from his earlier criticisms, Schelling himself was also in favor of such enquiry, "analogies abound between great power conflict and domestic violence." Arms control remained the prominent factor in their meetings, but guerilla warfare and urban insurgency were also discussed, and in later years the conversations were increasingly concerned with the situation in Vietnam. Ultimately, observed Schelling, "any form of strife is worth considering, even if no analogy to international conflict is immediately apparent."[60]

Despite periodically reinvigorating the seminar, as the 1960s drew to a close its direction had become progressively less clear. One factor ensuring continued discussion of arms control issues was the Chinese attainment of atomic capability in 1964. As discussed earlier, Morton Halperin was instrumental in developing this subject, along with his sometime collaborator Dwight Perkins. As the arms race developed in the 1960s, the seminar also devoted attention to the development of antiballistic missile systems, the Strategic Arms Limitation Talks, and the Nuclear Non-Proliferation Treaty.

An advisory committee was assembled in late 1970, chaired by Alex Inkeles, in part to prepare a report on the long-term direction and priorities of arms control research at the Center. Several Center faculty members were on the committee, as were other faculty from Harvard and outside. Although the report is lost, it apparently registered some "general disenchantment" with the field of arms control and military-political issues. In March 1971, the Center's visiting committee met to discuss the recommendations of the Inkeles Report. Despite some visiting committee members' protestations that "arms control still cries for organizing intelligence in the light of the experience of the last decade," the seminar met for the last time during the spring semester of 1972.[61] In the Center's annual report for that year, it was announced that "because of the difficulty in finding a focus that could take advantage of research on arms control being done in the Cambridge area, it was decided that the seminar should be recessed." Despite this decision, it was reportedly widely accepted by the participants that arms control remained a crucial issue, and as such the topic was revisited the following year to ascertain "what kind of seminar, if any, would provide the best forum for work being done by the Cambridge Community and would best serve its intellectual needs."[62]

The seminar did in fact reemerge under the broader mandate of a new CFIA Program for Science and International Affairs, established with the support of the Ford Foundation on July 1, 1973. This new endeavor—which would eventually become the Belfer Center for Science and International Affairs housed at the John F. Kennedy School of Government—was designed to promote, among other things, "a variety of research and educational programs aimed at examining the role of arms control in international relations and the interaction between arms control measures and their political, economic, and strategic consequences." Additionally, there was to be a renewed "effort . . . to pool the technological with the other components of these problems and to seek out approaches that will diminish the risks of war."[63] This mandate was certainly congruent with the original scope of the Arms Control Seminar, and with this in mind, the Harvard-MIT Joint Arms Control Seminar was resuscitated in 1973. Under its new design, the seminar continued to be a forum for discussing issues relating to the implications and applications of arms control measures, although now it featured guest speakers from various governmental and nongovernmental agencies as well as academia.[64]

## The Legacy of the Harvard-MIT Joint Arms Control Seminar

Reflecting on the CFIA's role in the field of arms control for the Center's twenty-fifth anniversary in 1983, Paul Doty observed "in its early years, the Center contributed substantially to the maturing of strategic analysis and arms control conceptions that have structured the way we think about the radically new dilemmas of the nuclear age."[65] The Center's contribution can be measured in a number of ways. Quantitatively, for over twelve years the seminar was the catalyst for a profusion of literature on arms control topics that was nothing short of prolific. At the same time, the seminar and the research it facilitated significantly raised the CFIA's national and international profile. During the first two years alone, the participants produced 130 papers, lectures, editorials, journal articles, and books on various facets of the arms control problem. In addition, the seminar's success significantly extended the influence of the CFIA with the policy-making community through the authority of its research and

87

the mobility of its participants. As Ernest May has argued, direct pathways of influence are extremely difficult to trace, since "no one can measure objectively the indirect or direct influence of any given book or article."[66] Nevertheless, May further suggests that although intellectuals in general might not often have had a direct effect on "declaratory policy," it is clear that they could and sometimes did "exercise important influence in fixing the terms of strategic debate" and in this way "they may perhaps have contributed to a basic trend toward stability rather than volatility in the relationship between the United States and the major Communist powers."[67] There seems to be little doubt that the research produced by the arms control seminar participants had a significant effect on American policy. The seminal, and in many ways unprecedented, research that was produced under the seminar's auspices helped to create the basic premises that would guide thoughtful arms control negotiations for the next fifteen years.

As May also notes, however, intellectuals often achieve their greatest influence if they were willing to "either work for an operating client . . . [or] get into the muck themselves."[68] In this regard the seminar's influence comes into even sharper relief. In 1985, for example, Schelling reflected on the achievements of arms control both in theory and in practice over the previous thirty years in an article for *Foreign Affairs*. He noted that disseminating arms control theory by producing scholarly publications was only one way in which the insights of the Harvard-MIT Joint Arms Control Seminar were promulgated to a broader audience.

> *[A] number of participants in the Harvard-MIT seminar took positions in the Kennedy White House, Department of State and Department of Defense; others from RAND and elsewhere, who had been part of this intellectual movement, moved into the government as well. So it is not completely surprising that those ideas became the basis for U.S. policy and were ultimately implemented in the ABM treaty. I consider that culmination of 15 years of progress not merely the high point but the end point of successful arms control.*[69]

Schelling's own career provides a case in point. Although he eschewed formal government appointments, he nevertheless continued to contribute to policy and strategy formulation in a consulting capacity. In 1961, for example, Schelling was appointed chair of a consultative committee on War by Accident, Miscalculation and Surprise, and the following year he chaired a committee of military officials who conducted a study on the various strategic issues that the

United States might be expected to face in the next decade. He also conducted war games and assessments for various military and government agencies throughout his tenure at the CFIA. Schelling (along with other members of the Center faculty) enjoyed access to key government officials, many of whom were former Center associates or occasional participants in the arms control seminar. As he recalls, "in the Kennedy administration, and through the Johnson administration, so many academic friends of mine were appointed to high positions that I was always in close touch with people in the Defense and State Departments or the White House."[70]

Indeed, the concepts generated under the auspices of the Harvard-MIT Joint Arms Control Seminar contributed to the Kennedy administration's amendment of the Eisenhower-Dulles policy of Massive Retaliation. Robert Levine, a Rand economist who had spent a year at the CFIA during the intellectual zenith of the Arms Control Seminar, notes "coming into office in 1961, [Robert McNamara] was appalled by the indiscriminate nature of Massive Retaliation and its inappropriateness for most conflict situations. The needed changes had been made clear by studies from the Harvard-MIT and RAND centers, from an elite commission headed by Ford Foundation president H. Rowen Gaither, and from within the Defense Department itself."[71] In its place the Kennedy administration instituted a strategy of Flexible Response, which inculcated many key concepts of the arms controllers in Cambridge, especially the notions of stability, deterrence, mutually assured destruction, and a general acceptance that arms control measures might be introduced unilaterally. Levine further argues that "the never-never abstract and theological nature of nuclear strategy combined with the Kennedy administration's suspicions of the uniformed military establishment meant that more of the raw unrefined product than usual seeped through and entered national strategy."[72]

There can also be little doubt that the 1963 Limited Test Ban Treaty and the installation of a so-called hotline between the United States and the Soviet Union both bear the imprint of Cambridge arms control advocates, and these measures are rightly regarded as two of the first halting steps toward ameliorating the nuclear arms race between the United States and the former Soviet Union. The 1972 Anti-Ballistic Missile Treaty also bears the hallmarks of the arms control theory that emerged from the Center in those early years. In addition, one of the most compelling and observable links between the Harvard-MIT Joint Arms Control Seminar and a significant arms control agreement can be found in the initiation of the Strategic Arms Limitation Talks (SALT) in 1969. In his 1973 account of the SALT

89

negotiations, John Newhouse argues that "in 1968, [Morton] Halperin . . . became the crucial figure in SALT. Rarely has a single individual played so large a role in maneuvering a sensitive, highly controversial initiative through the bureaucracy."[73] According to Newhouse, Halperin and his small team almost single-handedly "filled the bureaucratic void and somehow managed to nudge a SALT proposal all the way up to the desk of Lyndon Johnson."[74] Without question, then, the influence of the Center's work on arms control was far-reaching and profoundly significant.

Despite the successes of the 1960s, by 1972 the Center's original program on political-military strategy had begun to dissipate. Kissinger's appointment to the Nixon administration in 1969 and the effective loss of Schelling to the Public Policy Program at the John F. Kennedy School of Government in 1972 removed the Center's original personnel in this area. Halperin had already left Harvard and the CFIA in 1966 to take up a position as a deputy assistant secretary of defense with responsibility for political-military planning and arms control. These personnel departures, coupled with the temporary waning of the Harvard-MIT Joint Arms Control Seminar, forced the Center to pursue new directions during the second decade. The departure of Halperin, Kissinger, and Schelling also ensured, however, that the insights gleaned over the previous fourteen years would continue to pollinate government efforts toward meaningful arms control agreements with the former Soviet Union.

# Six

# Development and Modernization

WITHOUT QUESTION, THE CENTER'S MULTIFACETED RESEARCH program on development and modernization was one of the most prolific, far-reaching, and intellectually influential aspects of the CFIA's activities during its early history. In contrast to the rest of the Center's research agenda, the development component was much more explicitly anchored in both theory and practice. The Center's work on political-military issues and arms control certainly exerted a great deal of influence in the realm of policy, and its primary focus was the formulation of a theoretical and practical basis for arms control agreements. Members of the Center's research staff unquestionably helped to promulgate these insights throughout various U.S. government agencies and beyond, but they did so often in an informal and unofficial capacity. The structure of the development and modernization program was equally concerned with the theoretical foundations of economic and political development, but the establishment of the Development Advisory Service (DAS) in 1962 propelled the Center into the arena of international government consultancy on an unprecedented scale, with unparalleled scope and access, and ultimately mixed results.

The Center's Development and Modernization Program was originally led by Edward S. Mason, who joined the CFIA as one of its original faculty members in 1958. Of this initial core, Mason was the only one who was already a member of the Harvard faculty, having joined the Department of

Economics as an instructor in 1923, and he was well respected throughout the University for both his scholarship and his administrative skills. At the outset the Center pursued three theoretical facets of the development process. First, CFIA associates pursued a wide-ranging study of the economic dimensions of the development and modernization process. Second, the Center leadership recognized that economic development, whether intentionally or unintentionally, wrought social and cultural changes that would also require attention and analysis. Third, the return of Samuel Huntington to Harvard in 1963 afforded the opportunity to delve more deeply into processes of political development. These three often interrelated issues were touchstones for investigation throughout the first decade, and all three proved to be dynamic and productive components of the Center's research agenda.

## Economic Development and the Development Research Group

In 1959 the Center secured $300,000 in funds from the Ford Foundation to begin a comprehensive research project on "The Role of Private Business and of Government in Generating Economic Development." The project was undertaken in order to ascertain what blend of government and private economic activity could be expected to stimulate growth in a number of different countries, and what specific circumstances could be expected to enhance or inhibit growth. Initially this encompassed five different case studies—Brazil, Mexico, Southern Rhodesia, Pakistan, and Iran. Under the auspices of these five studies the Center was able to incorporate faculty members from the Graduate School of Business Administration (Lincoln Gordon and Raymond Vernon), as well as Gustav Papanek from the Graduate School of Public Administration and two outside scholars.[1]

The project soon blossomed into an intellectually lucrative constellation of studies that spanned five continents and joined the efforts of scholars from all over the world, including Brazil, Pakistan, and Lebanon. The resultant monographs, articles, and working papers considered such diverse subjects as the transition from subsistence agriculture in Southern Rhodesia and the role of entrepreneurs in Lebanon. The project culminated in an interpretive volume produced by Mason entitled *Foreign Aid and Foreign Policy*, which was based on his series of Elihu Root lectures at the Council on Foreign Relations.[2] By 1965, it had facilitated the research and publication of seven books.

The Center's research program on economic development also benefited enormously from the existence of the Development Advisory Service at the CFIA. The DAS provided an outlet for theoretical and analytical studies conducted by its advisors working in the field, and for members of other international aid agencies and financial organizations eager to produce their own manuscripts. In this sense the theoretical and practical aspects of the Center's development program were reciprocal and mutually beneficial. Gustav Papanek, for example, then deputy director of the DAS, applied his practical experience in Pakistan to a manuscript on the roles of Pakistani government and business, as well as an edited volume on the subject. A testament to the DAS's commitment to field research, in 1965 Papanek's two volumes on development in Pakistan were reported to have been delayed so that Papanek could incorporate the recent findings that Pakistan's rapidly changing economic situation demanded.[3] Similarly, Wolfgang Stolper, a former senior economic advisor to the Nigerian Planning Division and Center research associate, was afforded the opportunity to prepare a monograph based on his experiences in Nigeria.[4]

93

Despite the conclusion of Mason's program on business and government, the Center retained an energetic interest in economic development. Hollis B. Chenery, a Harvard economics professor and former assistant administrator of the U.S. Agency for International Development (USAID), joined the Center faculty in 1965 and initiated a quantitative research project on the subject. More than any other work conducted under the auspices of the economic development program, Chenery's project benefited from close association with the DAS, which in turn profited by this new quantitative research. Chenery's project also brought to the Center a number of young assistant professors from the Economics Department.[5] The project received a grant of over $500,000 from the Agency for International Development, and focused on "using techniques of quantitative analysis to study the economic problems of underdeveloped countries and to provide a basis for development policies."[6] The Center calculated that in the course of five years, the project had produced over one hundred articles and twelve books.

Based on the success of the project and its collaboration with the DAS, in 1970 the Center combined aspects of both programs into a "Development Research Group" (DRG). An executive committee with members from both organizations would give the group focus, review research applications, and dispense funds. As the Center reported that year, "it is expected that such an arrangement will provide a better framework for conducting comparative studies and for drawing systematically on DAS field projects." By integrating the DAS into the broader research program of the CFIA, the Development Research Group would play a pivotal role in the continued relevance of the DAS to the University at large.[7]

The DRG marked a watershed for the CFIA's study of economic development. As Bowie noted in the 1970 annual report, before that year the Center's efforts had been primarily concerned with policy-related research, applying quantitative and qualitative methods to analyze actual problems faced by governments of developing countries and proposing solutions to those problems.[8] Thanks to its diverse group of research associates, as well as its advisory presence in numerous countries, the Center's work had been largely comparative. Although it would remain policy-oriented and comparative after 1970 "in substance as well as in organization," Bowie reported at the time, ". . . there will be important changes." He envisioned the DRG intensifying the process of integration between the applied work of associates in the field and the more theoretical studies conducted at the Center.[9]

Gustav Papanek remembers that the DAS provided an important service to both the CFIA and the entire University. The quantitative data and qualitative analysis of DAS advisors overseas represented an important resource for many across the Harvard community and beyond. "There were a lot of PhD dissertations being written. . . . The [DAS] projects had access to information, to new ideas. . . . it brought interesting students to Harvard, it gave some faculty members insights into problems in the world that they normally wouldn't have had, and [DAS members] had begun publishing books and articles based on the experience."[10] The significance of the DAS as an academic resource cannot be overstated in any assessment of its activities.

The DRG was also designed to refine the Center's economic development research agenda, and with this in mind, the group proposed to concentrate its efforts on fewer topics. Bowie identified four prospective research studies to build on earlier successes at the Center and to propel them into the next decade. A major new initiative on comparative development was planned to consider various strategies in twenty-five different countries and to identify the social and economic impact of these countries' sources of growth. Earlier work on the role of government in the development process was also revived, with a new emphasis on the political and social ramifications of government involvement. The improvement of economic planning models would also receive attention, along with a fresh investigation of the unequal income distribution that so often accompanied rapid economic growth.[11]

The DRG proved to be a successful enterprise, thanks in large part to its ability to absorb and assimilate both the practical and theoretical aspects of the Center's economic development program. Indeed, over half of those working under the auspices of the DRG in 1971 were DAS members, who found an outlet for their field research at university presses, scholarly journals, and in the Center's series of Economic Development Reports. As Vernon reported in 1973, "in no small part the work of the DRG benefited substantially from the field involvement and overseas work of the DAS and from the ability of the DRG to draw upon the experience that various staff members have gained while working overseas. As a consequence, the DRG continues to be relevant to the actual needs of the developing countries."[12] The undertaking also attracted considerable financial support from USAID, the Ford Foundation, the National Science Foundation, the Department of Health, Education and Welfare, and the Twentieth Century Fund.[13]

By 1974, however, the Center's research on economic development abruptly ended, due to the dissolution of the DAS and the creation of the Harvard Institute for International Development (HIID), which created a University-wide structure accountable directly to the Office of the President. The precipitous conclusion of the CFIA's once vigorous contribution to the field of economic development—ranging across a wide variety of subjects from the role of technology to the dynamics of private investment—reflected the significance of the DAS's contribution to the Center. In addition, the Center had lost one of the chief architects of the DRG in 1970 when Hollis Chenery left Harvard—first temporarily, then permanently—to join the World Bank.

## The Social and Cultural Implications of Development and Modernization

Bowie had argued from the beginning that "the 'modernization' of societies, even economic growth as such, is far from being solely an economic process," so it was unsurprising that in 1960 the Center initiated a seminar on the social and cultural aspects of modernization.[14] This effort was led by professor of sociology, Alex Inkeles, who became a member of the Center in the summer of 1961. His appointment to the core faculty represented an important addition to the research staff, which until that point had been dominated by economists and political scientists. Having already spent a number of years at Harvard's Russian Research Center, Inkeles valued the opportunities provided by the University's research institutions through which "one could obtain the resources most departments were not able to provide in adequate degree, if at all, from their teaching budget," such as physical space, research assistance, partial relief from teaching, and a forum for the publication of research findings. He remembers his move to the CFIA as a natural progression. Inkeles was "interested in finding a new base from which I could explore socio-cultural issues of national development without the geographical constraints set by Russian and Soviet studies," and the new Center provided him with the opportunity to pursue those interests.[15]

From the outset the CFIA convened a seminar in conjunction with the Social Relations Department that assembled an interdisciplinary cluster of faculty to discuss these issues at the Center. This effort brought together sociologists, anthropologists, psychologists, political scientists, economists, and legal scholars in an attempt to holistically consider the broader implications of economic development. Inkeles and his colleagues sought to analyze the processes by which individuals in developing countries coped with, and adapted to, the transition from "traditional" to "modern" society. Their work provided a lens through which to assess the impact of modernization and development upon ordinary citizens rather than on those elites who often directed and catalyzed the process of economic development. This involved an extensive survey of issues, including:

> orientations to time, to technical competence, to education, and to non-traditional authority; attitudes toward cooperation, competition, and rational organization; dispositions to consume, to save, to enjoy leisure or to postpone gratification; aspirations for advancement for self, children, community and nation; conceptions of rights, justice, and orderly government procedure; and readiness for change and mobility.[16]

In order to ascertain how these aspects of life were changing among citizens in the developing world, Inkeles worked with scholars in Pakistan, Chile, and Nigeria to construct a questionnaire that they administered to a representative sample of the population in each of those countries. Despite the many logistical difficulties associated with a qualitative survey of this kind, by 1964 Inkeles and his colleagues in Chile had carried out over five hundred interviews, and Center research associate Howard Schuman working in East Pakistan had accumulated almost one thousand responses. The project also embarked on data collection in Argentina and in India, though riots in the mineral-rich industrial city of Jamshedpur hampered the interview process there.[17] Among a host of other issues, the questionnaire probed the respondents' attitudes toward education, political engagement, aspirations for inter- and intragenerational social mobility, and toward industrial work practices.[18]

Codification and analysis of the data began in 1965, employing IBM punch cards, computer tapes, and the skills of a number of computer programmers, but it would be almost ten years before this enormous feat of programming and analysis was completed and finally published as *Becoming Modern: Individual Change in Six Developing Countries* in 1974. This remarkable study reached a number of conclusions regarding which social processes or institutions were the most significant in modernizing members of developing societies. Not surprisingly, mass media and education were found to be crucial. In addition, Inkeles and Smith found that the factory itself was an important catalyst for the modernization of individual workers. Not only did industrial work compel workers toward cities, "factory work, through its inherent properties, provided training in new ways of orienting oneself toward man, nature, and the social order."[19] This process was a function of the fact that the factory constitutes "a particular form of social organization, characterized by rational planning, ready acceptance of new technology, authority based on technical competence, coordination of the efforts of large numbers of individuals, and treatment according to impartial rules."[20] Inkeles and Smith further concluded that such results could be achieved under the right circumstances even in agricultural workplaces, as long as the organizational setting provided a similar degree of stimuli. This study remains one of the most important monographs to emerge from the Center in its fifty-year history, and the process that led to its publication became a model of what a research institution like the CFIA could achieve.

## Political Development

Prior to the inception of a designated research program on the political dimensions of development and modernization, the Center, somewhat seren-dipitously, provided the locus for a number of studies relating to Africa. Professor of Government Rupert Emerson did much to direct the CFIA's efforts in this field. The research on Africa focused on two fundamentally important questions relating to the independence of African states following decolonization. First, how are the new African governments dealing with problems of internal economic and political integration? Second, what role will African states play in the international state system? In order to answer these questions, the Center invited a number of African, European, and American scholars to the CFIA and supported their research on topics as varied as the Ghanaian legal system and the political implications of externally imposed borders on the viability of newly independent African states. This work provided a vehicle for the study of African political, economic, and social issues at the University. As Bowie reported, the Center's contribution "emerged as a significant regional interest involving a variety of disciplines and [is] serving as a focus for the stimulation and enrichment of research and teaching on Africa in many parts of the University." The CFIA had not set out to assemble such a rich and diverse group of academics devoted to the study of Africa, but it took advantage of a critical mass of scholars to forge a wholly new facet of the CFIA's research agenda.[21]

It proved to be a transient moment in Center history, however, as by 1964 the CFIA enveloped its nascent African studies research program into a newly formed nucleus of studies broadly conceived under the rubric of political development. This new endeavor was intended to broaden the Center's focus to include Asia and Latin America. When Samuel Huntington returned to Harvard from Columbia in 1963, the Center's efforts were infused with a new vigor and direction. As well as probing the role of political parties, the new research agenda emphasized "the processes of building political institutions: their stability; their principal forms; and their relation to social reform and economic progress." The political development component of the Center's research intersected with ongoing work on development and modernization being conducted at the CFIA.

The most immediate and significant result of this new program came in the form of another collaborative venture with MIT in 1964. The Harvard-MIT Joint Seminar on Political Development, or JOSPOD, as it was known, reflected the success of the ongoing Harvard-MIT Joint Seminar on Arms Control, and was conceived with a similar rationale in mind: to take advantage of the growing number of scholars in the Boston area who were studying political development, and to provide an intellectual focal point to discuss ideas and research. As Huntington remembers with reference to the field of political development, "there had been very little serious academic work done on that subject and it seemed to me it would be useful to create an arena, or seminar, where scholars around the Cambridge area from different universities could come together once a month or so." JOSPOD provided an opportunity to define a relatively new discipline, much like that of arms control four years before.[22] It was hoped that "efforts [would] be made to identify and to define general concepts and propositions useful in the analysis of political change and to test existing theories of political development against the experiences of a variety of countries and political systems." In addition, an analysis of the historical examples of the developed world would illuminate possible paths to development in the underdeveloped world, work in which Huntington was already engaged.[23]

Besides ongoing work on political development in Africa, one visiting scholar, Ergun Özbudun, was researching the role of the military regimes in developing countries, with an emphasis on Turkey. Candido Mendes de Almeida, a research associate from Brazil, embarked on a study of that country's transition from colonial rule to independence and the implications of that evolution for Brazil's development prospects.[24]

With the receipt of a $250,000 grant from the Carnegie Corporation in 1966, the program began to gather momentum. This grant funded research, led by Huntington, into the relationship between political stability and social reform. From the beginning the agenda was broad, and researchers investigated an array of factors including land reform, tax reform, corruption, racial and communal conflict, the role of political parties, and the relationship between power and social change. In addition to the ongoing research on Africa (which continued to be directed by Emerson) the Center also instituted a project on student politics and modernization, led by professor of government and social relations, Seymour Martin Lipset, discussed in more detail in Chapter Nine.[25]

The program, and indeed the subject of political development itself, reached a new level of maturity during the 1966–67 academic year. A plethora of conferences and seminars were organized that took advantage of the Center's growing expertise in the field and began to connect its work to that of the broader academic community. An international conference was convened in Brazil, for example, that brought together academics from the United States, Brazil, Switzerland, Italy, Israel, Argentina, and Chile. Scholars from around the world also attended a five-day conference in Nairobi, entitled "East Africa and the Orient: Problems of Pre-Colonial History," organized by Center associate Robert I. Rotberg. In addition to JOSPOD, a seminar on relations between the United States and the Dominican Republic was established that attracted scholars from around the country.[26]

By 1968 the Center confidently reported that "in terms of the volume of data being assembled and analyzed, and in terms of the variety of issues under investigation, research in this crucial area may well be nearing its peak."[27] That year Huntington also published his landmark study *Political Order in Changing Societies*. His opening contention that "the most important political distinction among countries concerns not their form of government but their degree of government" swept aside long-held assumptions about the presumed chasm between totalitarian communist states and liberal-democratic states. Instead, Huntington highlighted the extent to which the United States, Great Britain, and the Soviet Union shared a common emphasis on governance and political order, reinforced by mature political institutions, all of which embodied "consensus, community, legitimacy, organization, effectiveness, [and] stability."

The greater distinction, he observed, was between these states and "many, if not most, of the modernizing countries of Asia, Africa, and Latin America," whose polities were characterized by "a shortage of political community and of effective, authoritative, legitimate government."[28]

In this context, Huntington sought to explain why there appeared to be such a remarkable increase in violent incidents and instability in the developing world during the two decades after World War II. He concluded that "it was in large part the product of rapid social change and the rapid mobilization of new groups into politics coupled with the slow development of political institutions. . . . The primary problem of politics is the lag in the development of political institutions behind social and economic change."[29] Political institutions mediate competing claims and foster communities of interest among the various social forces that constitute a given society, Huntington argued, and are therefore essential to the stable and ordered functioning of complex societies. The modernization process places increasing pressures upon societies; it often erodes traditional patterns of community, creates new layers of authority, and increases levels of participation, all of which requires the stabilizing influence of effective political institutions.[30]

> By mobilizing new people into new roles modernization leads to a larger and more diversified society which lacks the "natural" community of the extended family, the village, the clan, or the tribe. Because it is a larger society . . . the modernizing society is often a "plural" society encompassing many religious, racial, ethnic, and linguistic groupings . . . As the scope of social mobilization in such communal groups extends downward, however, the antagonisms between them intensify . . . Modernization also brings into existence and into political consciousness and activity social and economic groups which either did not exist in the traditional society or were outside the scope of politics in traditional society. Either these groups are assimilated into the political system or they become a source of antagonism to and of revolution against the political system. The achievement of political community in a modernizing society thus involves both the "horizontal" integration of communal groups and the "vertical" assimilation of social and economic classes.[31]

According to Huntington, the most important factor in mitigating the potential antagonisms engendered by the modernization process is the existence of political parties, which function to assimilate potentially revolutionary groups.[32]

His seminal work is a cornerstone in the political development literature and remains required reading in colleges across the country.

As the Center entered its twelfth year in the fall of 1969, two new facets were added to the political development program. A research project entitled "Participation Patterns in Modernizing Societies" was established under a contract from USAID. It was a joint Harvard-MIT initiative, directed by Huntington and MIT professor, Joan M. Nelson. "The principal purpose of this research is to explore the relationships among different forms of economic, social and political participation in societies in transition from tradition to modernity."[33] Among other things, this project used computer programming to generate models for understanding the political processes that characterized developing countries. A second new project dealt with the "External Dimensions of Political Development," which built on elements of numerous studies conducted at the Center in the past.[34] Just as these two new endeavors emerged, the founding project on political institutionalization and social change reached the end of its tenure at the Center. In all, twenty-eight scholars had been involved in the project over the previous five years, producing twenty-eight monographs, including Huntington's classic work, and over forty articles.[35] By 1973, the project on "Participation Patterns in Modernizing Societies" had also concluded, yielding another ten book-length manuscripts in four years.[36]

Despite the termination of these two highly productive research projects, the program continued with renewed energy. The recently instituted program on the external dimensions of political development was recast as a study called "International Relations of Political Development," which benefited from another new research venture, the program on international order, discussed in Chapter Nine. In addition, Jorge I. Domínguez joined the effort, augmenting the program with a new emphasis on problems of political development and international relations in Cuba and Latin America.[37] As the Center reported in 1973, "in the absence of an institute for Latin American studies at Harvard, the Center for International Affairs has attempted to play a positive role in encouraging research on the problems of this continent." At the outset, responsibility for filling this lacuna in Harvard's research and teaching fell almost entirely to Domínguez.[38]

In 1972, the CFIA reported that "studies of development and modernization again made up the largest component of the Center's research effort, whether measured in terms of people involved or money spent."[39] Just two years later, however, this once prodigious component of the Center's research agenda became significantly circumscribed. One reason for the abrupt attenuation of this program was the simple fact that designated, project-specific research funds had been spent—like many Center initiatives it had a deliberately limited tenure. In the context of a general reduction in funds for international research, subsequent financial support became harder to secure. As the Center's priorities changed, some projects were consolidated under new headings, such as that of the Program on Transnational Processes and Institutions. The retirement of Edward Mason in 1969 and the dissolution of the DAS in 1974 also contributed to the demise of the program on development and modernization, which is not to say that the Center entirely abdicated its once formidable role in the field of development and modernization. Issues of economic and political development continued to receive considerable attention under various guises throughout its second decade. JOSPOD continued unabated and remained a prominent part of the Center's research program into the twenty-first century. It ran successfully for thirty-five consecutive years, first under the leadership of Huntington and then under Domínguez, making it by far the longest-running seminar in the Center's history. Indeed, the theme of political and economic development continued to weave through much of the Center's activities throughout that period, and like the programs on Europe and the role of force, its significance and influence continued to resonate through much of the CFIA's research.

## The Development Advisory Service

Prior to the establishment of the CFIA, Edward Mason, in his capacity as the dean of the Graduate School of Public Administration, initiated a small-scale economic consultancy program in Pakistan and Iran, beginning in 1954 and 1958, respectively.[40] Mason had been approached by the Ford Foundation, which convinced him to help dispatch a small group of advisors to Pakistan to consult with a newly established economic planning board. As Mason later wrote, "the contract, involving Harvard, the Government of Pakistan, and the Ford Foundation, was to run for 18 months beginning March 1, 1954." In fact, the relationship would continue until 1970. The arrangement with Iran was short-lived, however, ending four years after its inception in 1962.[41]

These two advisory groups formed the basis for what would become, in May 1962, the Development Advisory Service. Mason recalls that the creation of the DAS was due in large part to the success of the Harvard projects in Pakistan and Iran. The Ford Foundation continued to receive applications for planning assistance, and by 1962 it was prepared to offer the University $750,000 to assist in establishing a designated institution under the auspices of the CFIA.[42]

For his part, Bowie outlined the Center's interest in the formal creation of the DAS in a letter to F.F. Hill of the Ford Foundation in March 1962:

> Our proposal is to create in the Center for International Affairs at Harvard a career advisory service to assist the developing nations in planning, research and training for development. Our purpose would be to develop and maintain such services on a more permanent basis so that a cadre of qualified men could carry on such work as a career for an extended period. These career men would serve as leaders of advisory groups, which would be filled out with other experts serving on a more temporary basis.[43]

He recognized that the DAS would constitute a dramatic departure not least for the CFIA, but for the University as well. Nonetheless, it would represent a valuable addition to Harvard's international efforts, allowing the University "to participate more adequately in overseas work and to discharge its obligations in this field on a basis compatible with the integrity of its primary responsibility for training and research." The proposed advisory service also promised to augment the Center's own research agenda in the field of development and modernization. Looking beyond its impact on the CFIA, Bowie foresaw a reciprocal relationship between the DAS and the University as a whole, since the experiences garnered by DAS field advisors would enhance Harvard's teaching mission by transmitting real-world, even real-time, data and observations on international economic development into the classroom.[44] Even putting all its objectives aside, the founders of the DAS were creating something new, a kind of laboratory for "[learning] about the problems and value of maintaining and operating such a program by a university."[45]

The endeavor got underway in the spring of 1962 under the directorship of Raymond Vernon, with support from then–deputy director Gustav Papanek, who had already gained extensive experience in this field through his leadership of the advisory group in Pakistan. Mason remained involved in an advisory capacity. Within a year, in addition to its ongoing activities in Pakistan, the DAS had instituted four new projects, in Indonesia, Colombia, and two in Argentina. DAS advisors worked directly with government planning agencies in their host countries, such as the Planning Commission in Pakistan or the Ministry of Finance in Colombia. The goal was to provide economic advice to the often inchoate agencies charged with implementing development and modernization projects in their respective countries. In some cases the DAS worked closely with private research organizations such as the DiTella Institute in Argentina. Here DAS advisors assisted in training local personnel in economic development and planning. In both cases, "the aim of these groups [would] be to 'work themselves out of a job' as soon as possible, by helping countries to set up their own planning agencies, economic staffs and research and training institutes."[46]

It is impossible within the confines of this study to detail all DAS activities during its twelve-year residence at the CFIA.[47] A number of issues, however, deserve closer analysis, since they highlight some of the successes and failures of the operation and illuminate its sometimes complicated relationship to the CFIA, the University, U.S. foreign policy, and those governments that played host to DAS advisors.

## The DAS, the CFIA, and the University

One of the most complex issues that faced DAS members was the Janus-faced and sometimes ambiguous position they held in both the academy and in the service of foreign governments. Functioning as advisors to foreign governments while sustaining academic careers in which they translated their practical experience into scholarly insight required balance. Ever cognizant of this issue, the DAS considered the question in its 1966 annual report: "The Development Advisory Service, whose charter would have it work both in the academic world and in the world of government policy, is constantly tempted to stress one at the expense of the other. While the service takes as its guiding premise the dependence of productive academic output on direct involvement with governments abroad, it is prey to the lure of each extreme." This was a constant dilemma for DAS staff members, who often faced competing pressures from the two constituencies that relied upon their services.

*One the one hand, there is the seductive opportunity of participating in the shaping of policies that determine the growth of economies, of being close to power. On the other hand, advising on policy can be frustrating and with few tangible results in the short run; how seductive, therefore, to concentrate on more theoretical academic activities which gain kudos from the international professional fraternity and are less affected by inadequate data, multiplicity of factors, confusing relationships, and uncertain results.*

Ultimately, it was clear that the right combination of politics and theory was essential if the DAS was to fulfill its responsibilities to both Harvard and their government clients.[48]

This raised further questions about recruiting and retaining DAS advisors. Willingness to serve abroad for extended periods was essential, but this often meant deferring an academic career. To staff and support these advisory missions, the University established two new categories of employment: long-term development advisors, who generally returned from their field assignments to spend every third year in Cambridge; and short-term, fixed-contract advisors, who spent the majority of their time abroad. Development advisors were given tenure appointments on an indefinite contract, but should the University terminate their employment, they were entitled to an eighteen-month grace period to research or teach at Harvard.[49] Gustav Papanek remembers that this system of "industrial tenure," as it was known, was essential to the success of the DAS. "When you work overseas, everybody forgets that you exist. You are not publishing much, because you are spending your time advising the government on day to day problems." By establishing a reserve fund that would finance advisors for eighteen months to two years once their overseas assignments ended, the DAS was able to assure "that when you came back you had a period of time to reestablish yourself; to publish, to give seminars so your colleagues could become reacquainted with you." Essentially, Papanek observes, "it was an incentive for first-rate people to go abroad."[50]

This was vital not only to the success of the DAS overseas, but also to the production of quality scholarship. As Papanek suggests, however, talented individuals often found themselves in an ambiguous position within the University, and especially within the academic departments with which they were affiliated. In his history of the DAS and HIID, Mason contends "despite contributions to teaching and research by DAS staff, its members continued to be regarded, by themselves and others, as not quite full-fledged members of the University."[51] As it turned out, difficulty arose simply in filling the ten designated appointments available for permanent career-development advisors.[52]

Another challenge that faced the DAS as an institution was the complexity of managing and administering the service. Foreign governments often asked to deal with the person in charge, thus the director had to wear a number of hats: "ideally [he was a] superlative administrator, a committed teacher, and first-rate economist capable of maintaining an academic career at Harvard all while managing an organization that spanned the globe." To satisfy Harvard's stringent criteria for scholarship and teaching and to provide at the same time a public face for the DAS at home and abroad, was a task for which, Papanek notes, "nobody has the level of energy necessary." Papanek personally visited the major projects twice a year while director of the DAS from 1965 to 1970, but acknowledges "most of us fell short in one dimension or the other."[53]

In 1968 a University committee was formed to examine the relationship between the DAS and Harvard. In response to the committee's findings, the DAS conducted a self-analysis of its contributions to research and teaching, concluding that "most field advisors find they do not have much time to do professional writing while in an advisory capacity." Even though DAS employees were granted time in Cambridge, the arrangement proved unsatisfactory, since most of the permanent staff found themselves spending it concerned with "professional catching-up." Inadequate funding also limited the amount of research they produced. The DAS did conclude, however, that the establishment of the DRG at the CFIA facilitated more cohesion by integrating DAS advisors in the field with their Cambridge counterparts.[54]

It was evident that dealing with questions of policy augmented both research and teaching, and helped to focus attention "on crucial issues of development, rather than on those that are merely interesting or fashionable at the moment." The DAS acknowledged, however, that their current research was of interest primarily to economists, and they had yet to find an effective way to engage with political or social scientists. Even so, any attempt to integrate advisors from other disciplines would require caution and due regard for the needs and expectations of the host governments, who, the report noted, were often suspicious of disciplines such as anthropology and sociology.[55] This proved to be an intractable problem, and was one of the major reasons for the creation of the Harvard Institute for International Development in 1974.

With regard to teaching, the DAS clearly felt that the University was not making sufficient use of its available talent and experience, especially in areas in which Harvard had limited course offerings or lacked qualified teaching personnel.[56] Even as the CFIA reaped the benefits of the DAS, there remained a long-standing gulf between the unique opportunities presented by the experiences of its staff members and the University's willingness to invite them into the classroom.

## The DAS and American Foreign Policy

Although this subject is considered in greater detail in Chapter Eight, it bears at least cursory examination here. A crucial component of the DAS mandate was that, as Mason notes, "no direct financing could be accepted from the U.S. Agency for International Development or any other bilateral program." It was understood from the beginning that DAS advisors, if they were to succeed, could not appear to be agents of American foreign policy, or for that matter, of any other government's foreign policy.[57] The concern was that any suspicion would undermine the legitimacy and independence of their advice, especially given the ongoing cold war context.

On the Harvard campus in the late 1960s, amidst mounting student anger toward the Vietnam War and U.S. foreign policy in general, the DAS was forced to address this issue. In late 1969 it would write in its own defense:

> the DAS has adopted a number of practices which are specifically designed to assure its independence of the American Government and of any particular ideology. It refuses to accept funds from the U.S. Government to finance its overseas activities . . . . The contractual arrangements which the DAS enters are directly with the governments it helps; no intermediaries or third parties are allowed to intrude into this direct relationship.[58]

At the heart of this effort to maintain independence was the stipulation that DAS project teams should be multinational. Mason noted that in 1963–64, for example, of thirty-eight advisors and consultants employed in the field, only eighteen were American. The balance comprised staff from Great Britain, Norway, Australia, Netherlands, France, Sweden, Belgium, Burma, and Brazil.[59] One benefit of this arrangement, as far as the DAS was concerned, was that many non-American advisors, especially those from Northern Europe, were socialists. Indeed, the DAS would later claim to have "attempted on various occasions to recruit economists from eastern European countries" and that "prior to the Russian invasion of Czechoslovakia . . . .it seemed that arrangements could be made with several Czech economists."[60] Certainly, this was stressed for domestic consumption, intended in part to appease the rancor directed toward the DAS during the student protests. But, more importantly, it served to establish the group's credentials with foreign governments, to show itself free from partisanship or conflict of interests.

Dwight Perkins, a former advisory group member and future director of the successor organization to the DAS—the Harvard Institute for International Development—further emphasizes the importance of international recruitment. Recruiting internationally "was virtually a necessity" in order to find enough people willing to work abroad for long periods of time. It was not simply a function of seeking to avoid unwelcome criticism. In the final analysis, however, "the whole spirit of DAS and HIID was that our job was to work for the country; to help it help itself. Our loyalties were really to that activity, to that country, as long as we were working on that problem . . . .our job was not to carry out American policy." Though Perkins recognizes that it was not always easy to convince the host government that this was the case—and though myriad pressures were evident from international organizations, foreign governments, and philanthropic foundations—the DAS succeeded, Perkins believes, when it established itself as an independent entity concerned with the welfare of the countries in which it worked.[61]

### The DAS and Host Governments: The Case of Pakistan

At the same time, DAS members were aware that their potentially intimate relationships with host countries could threaten their intellectual autonomy, and could even taint their research findings. To a certain extent, this was mitigated by the fact that "an obvious advantage to working with a government is greater access to the decision-making process and to statistical and other information which often remains unpublished." In this respect, then, DAS advisors were privy to more information and data than they would otherwise have access to as independent academic researchers, but as with much in the history of the DAS, these associations were not without complications.

From the host governments' point of view, however, one unqualified benefit of these relationships was that it ensured that the advice provided was germane to their needs, "rather than work which makes an interesting theoretical or methodological contribution alone or is preoccupied with obstacles and reasons why solutions are difficult." Implicit in this statement is the assumption that scholarly interchange involves purely academic analysis, that the questions asked and the answers given tend to reflect the interests of the scholars rather than the very real needs of the developing countries. The work of the DAS contradicted such an idea: because of its unprecedented access to decision makers—ultimately one of its most remarkable features—it could reasonably argue that "transmitting knowledge to those in a position to act is undoubtedly more effective when it comes from the inside rather than the outside."[62]

The project in Pakistan was the longest in the history of the DAS, and according to Mason, the most successful.[63] A draft report on the project following its termination in 1970, written by its longtime director, Richard Gilbert, addresses many issues that affected relations between the DAS and the Pakistani government. It provides a particularly interesting case study, illustrating some of the broader questions raised by DAS involvement in economic planning commissions across the developing world.

According to Gilbert, the Pakistan advisory project had all the hallmarks of an exemplary DAS model: "The Harvard Project in Pakistan is unique in the history of technical assistance. No other project has continued for so long, included so large a group of economists and achieved so intimate a relation at the very centers of government." Papanek recalls that one of the minor reasons the DAS was able to float ideas within the government in Pakistan was the fact that Gilbert's wife established a friendship with the president's mistress.

> The key, though, were two factors: first, the advisors were resident and an integral part of the government machinery. Their work did not appear as that of outsiders, second-guessing and upstaging the Pakistani staff; their work appeared as the product of government agencies which redounded to their credit. Second, the advisors were an unusually able group of economists . . . . Initially there was only one Pakistani agricultural economist working in the government. As Pakistani economists returned with a Ph.D., they formed a close bond with the foreign advisors. Then in the 1960s Richard Gilbert became team leader and developed a close relationship with the minister of finance as well as the leadership of the Planning Commission, thanks largely to his unusual skills as a policy economist. He came up with a number of brilliant ideas that helped Pakistan achieve an unusually high growth rate and political credibility.[64]

Therefore, DAS advisors, through their close ties to the Planning Commission, were able to exert influence on their Pakistani counterparts. As Gilbert relates, "The Harvard Group thought of itself as working for the Government of Pakistan and was accepted into its counsels, if not on the level of civil servants, at only a step removed. The intimacy of relationship which developed over the years was without precedent."[65]

Central to the success of the project in Pakistan was the fact that "the Group was from the beginning international in character, free of national bias, unlike bilateral technical aid programs." The maintenance of objectivity and independence from the machinations of foreign governments was considered crucial in gaining their host governments' trust. Gilbert also stresses the extent to which "over the years it included many eminent economists, with a wide range of viewpoints and experience in socialist as well as capitalist governments." Though he acknowledged that the advisory group "did not itself include any representatives from communist countries," he was keen to stress that it did work with economists from socialist countries who were engaged with UN technical assistance programs.[66] This facet of the program ensured at least some kind of neutrality for the DAS group during a cold war steadily radiating outward from its European epicenter.

Gilbert also emphasizes the importance of the "the Harvard connection" in providing an institutional and intellectual base for DAS advisors. Harvard "provided the opportunity for extended periods at the University for study and evaluation of experience," and its rigorous recruitment policy "sustained the level of competence and kept the Group abreast of current economic thinking and skills."[67] Papanek observes that the Harvard connection provided another important asset to the governments that sought assistance: requesting the help of Harvard University did not necessarily reflect badly upon the competence of their own nation's often inchoate planning commissions.[68]

Nevertheless, Gilbert is realistic about the DAS advisory group, allowing that its role was, ultimately, "advisory," and that "its powers were essentially the powers of persuasion." While he acknowledges that the advisors played an important role in exerting influence on international aid organizations, "it was the policies themselves which elicited the support of the donors, not some magic in the Harvard name . . . .While the Group played a role in formulating objectives, targets, and policies, the recommendations were made by the Pakistanis in the planning organizations and the decisions made by the Government of Pakistan." The DAS group, in Gilbert's analysis, was not responsible for the success of economic development in Pakistan, but neither was it responsible for the failures.[69] Given the scope of DAS involvement in the Planning Commission in Pakistan, this seems an unlikely proposition on both counts, and underrates its influence.

Gilbert does, however, highlight some of the problems raised by the close association of the advisory group with the inner circles of government. His observations apply to Pakistan, but they hold true for DAS operations throughout the developing world. He notes that the Planning Commission with which the DAS worked generated a certain degree of bureaucratic animosity within the government, since it tended to be the repository of the country's most talented and influential economists. In addition, he contends, this situation engendered "a degree of arrogance and abuse of power by the planning institutions." Gilbert largely blames the resultant enmity on the other agencies concerned with economic development in Pakistan, but he does concede that "while the Harvard Group is not responsible for the failure to build up the strength of the other organizations, its presence in the planning institutions, nonetheless, helped produce the imbalance." In a broader sense, the DAS advisory group "was inevitably held responsible, at least in part, by those who felt themselves aggrieved by government policies." One of the most damaging results of this was that it made "the people with whom the Group worked vulnerable to the charge that they were puppets of foreigners, and the policies they recommended the result of foreign influence."[70]

He also questions the long-term effectiveness of the DAS advisory group. If Bowie had earlier envisioned that the DAS would eventually "work themselves out of a job," Gilbert suggests that in fact the opposite was true in the case of Pakistan. "The project acted as a crutch. The Government of Pakistan did not have to move more quickly and firmly to develop the necessary level of competence in its own staff, since the Group was available to help carry part of the burden." In this respect, then, the presence of the advisory group could be counterproductive.[71]

Perhaps most importantly, however, Gilbert suggests that the DAS advisory group "must share some responsibility for the priority given to growth at the expense of equity." Gilbert also reported that "others . . . charge that our presence lent respectability on the international scene to a government following crudely inequitable and corrupt practices, and our advocacy of reform, to the degree that it was successful merely postponed the necessity of more fundamental changes." Indeed, these were the very charges being leveled against the DAS back home in Cambridge by an increasingly radicalized student population. Gilbert, for his part, accepted that "these charges contain some elements of truth."[72] This criticism suggests that some DAS advisors were not always sufficiently attentive to the social and political ramifications of the development process, which in the case of Pakistan had encouraged a disparity of wealth among the regions and population.

Perkins and Papanek both comment on another side of the DAS's involvement with foreign governments. Advisors and consultants had to be politically astute, cognizant of the more than simply economic reach of their advice. Perkins recalls that "the politics of it was very important. You had to understand the politics at least to some degree in order to be able to function effectively. Certainly you had to understand bureaucratic politics. If you went in there just as a pure technician you weren't going to be terribly effective." At the same time, "you had to disguise that. You couldn't be overtly political."[73] Papanek affirms that for this reason advisors were meant to remain in their host country for as long as possible. "It was essential not only for economic reasons, but you [also] needed to know the political issues."[74] Any economic guidance DAS advisors provided needed to be sensitive to the political context.

Finally, Papanek raises the issue of cultural insensitivity, which on occasion impeded DAS members in Pakistan. For example, he was informed during a routine visit that a member of the DAS, taking advantage of the abundant wild marijuana that grew on the outskirts of Islamabad, was hosting "pot brownie" parties for junior members of the Planning Commission. Another advisor had to be fired because of inappropriate recommendations to the government of Pakistan—he recommended that increasing pork production would be the best way to increase the protein intake of the population, despite the fact that Islam forbids eating pork. This, coupled with his suggestion that women ought to be brought into the workplace, and his observation that the annual fast of Ramadan made the workforce inefficient, ensured that his advice was no longer suitable material for the DAS in Pakistan.[75]

Political conditions could also change rapidly within the countries served by the DAS. The DAS advisory group in Pakistan reported in 1969 that it was increasingly the target of anti-Semitic and anti-Western antagonism in Islamabad, as the presidency of Ayub Khan began to unravel amidst seething social, political, ethnic, and economic ferment. Indeed, this was one of the primary factors in the decision to terminate the project the following year.[76] Similarly, a coup d'état in Greece in April 1967 abruptly ended the DAS advisory presence there. Papanek wrote the following to the vice president of the Ford Foundation (and former DAS member) David Bell: "Since we remain convinced that our responsibility must be to the government we work with, the government needs to be one we can, in good conscience, be responsible to. . . . In this case, from what we know about the attitudes of the present leaders, and what they have done, we do not see how it would be possible to continue there."[77]

## The DAS in Perspective

Over the course of its twelve-year existence the DAS was responsible for seventeen projects in thirteen different countries. The most significant of these included ten projects in which DAS advisors worked directly with government planning commissions: Pakistan, Iran, Indonesia, Malaysia, Ghana, Liberia, Ethiopia, Greece, Argentina, and Colombia. In addition, DAS advisory groups in Tanzania, South Korea, Nicaragua, Indonesia, and Argentina provided assistance to newly formed institutes dedicated to research in economic development. Not every project was a success, and some were ultimately failures, but there is no question that the effort was unique. It is therefore all the more puzzling that the DAS has, for all intents and purposes, escaped the attention of historians interested in the genesis and implications of development and modernization theory. A number of excellent monographs have recently explored the role of development theory in the cold war, but the DAS receives almost no attention. Historians have instead tended to focus on the role of the Center for International Studies at MIT, whose efforts in this regard were much more closely tied to the ideological struggle of the cold war.[78]

113

One of the most difficult challenges that faced the DAS over the course of its fourteen years, as Mason affirms, derived from the balancing act it was required to perform in satisfying the myriad and sometimes competing interests of its benefactors and employers:

> *The fact of the matter is that the DAS undertook to serve a number of clients not all of whose interests were identical. The University was primarily interested in contributions to teaching and research. The financing agencies—certainly the Ford Foundation—were primarily interested in training and institution building. The host governments were primarily interested in advisory services and, to a lesser extent, in training and institution building. Balancing these diverse interests was not always an easy task.*[79]

In large part because of the inability of the DAS to reconcile these interests, in 1974 the Development Advisory Service was dissolved and HIID was created in its place. There had been intimations that such a decision was pending since 1968. Successive investigative committees—one initiated by the University (the Dorfman Committee) and one initiated by the Ford Foundation—had largely praised the DAS in its overseas efforts, but lamented its sometimes underdeveloped links to the University at large. Though efforts were underway within the CFIA under the auspices of the DRG to rectify this deficiency, it was becoming clear that a new organizational structure was required. Indeed, the HIID was a University-wide endeavor that reported directly to the Office of the President, and as such its scope and function was considerably broadened and its relevance to the University augmented.[80]

Perkins recalls, "quite frankly, in the last years [the DAS] didn't belong to the CFIA anyway. The tail was bigger than the dog by a rather considerable margin, and the CFIA was not set up to manage it." Though the Center had already begun to shift away from its earlier emphasis on economic development and modernization, the departure of the DAS represented a significant financial and intellectual loss to the CFIA. Still, Huntington concurs that the DAS "had developed [its] own identity, and had grown quite large, and it was physically impossible to house [it] in the Center. So I certainly thought it was very appropriate for them to go off on their own."[81] The excision of the DAS from the CFIA was, therefore, from a certain angle, inevitable. The creation of HIID, however, would not necessarily solve the many other issues encountered during the tenure of the DAS.

114

# Seven

# The Center's Relation to Policy

THE CENTER'S ROLE IN POLICY FORMULATION DURING ITS FIRST TEN years deserves further consideration, since at the outset the CFIA's relationship to the policy sphere was a great deal closer than it is today. Indeed, during the first decade of the Center's existence many of its faculty and research associates engaged in formal government consultation and informal dialogue, and in some cases Center affiliates would enter government employment on either a temporary or permanent basis. As Bowie recalls, it was never his intention to institutionalize or formalize any specific form of government interaction: "My conviction was that if we produced convincing analysis in books, articles, journals, and other places, that it would affect how people thought about foreign policy, and broaden perspectives."[1] Samuel Huntington, the Center's third Center Director, concurs: "I don't think [Bowie] conceived of the Center as a foreign policy think tank, and certainly that has not been the way in which the directors of the Center and people at the Center have thought about it. We've thought about it as a scholarly research institution."[2] In particular, Huntington stresses that the CFIA was never designed to be analogous to the avowedly policy-oriented institutions that proliferated in the United States during the 1960s.

Nevertheless, as has already been demonstrated, the CFIA's scholarship on issues concerning each aspect of the initial research program—European affairs, development, and arms control—would inform various aspects of American foreign policy, and in turn the Center's research output would benefit from this connection to numerous government agencies. In the case of the CFIA's contribution to the study of development, the influence of the Center could be felt even further afield, as DAS advisors worked with high-level officials in countries around the world.

In his first annual report, Robert Bowie considered the extent to which the Center was discharging its responsibilities in the two arenas that the CFIA was expected to inform the broader intellectual discourse: policy formulation and general academic dialogue. In so doing, Bowie identified a number of conduits through which the Center's intellectual product and influence could be disseminated. First, in addition to books and articles by Center associates, Bowie reasoned that "Fellows and Research Associates who are exposed to the studies at the Center" would continue to propagate the Center's findings when they "return to other surroundings." In this way the Center's research would pollinate the broader intellectual milieu in which its practitioners and scholars moved. Second, and just as importantly, the Center's faculty and other associates were also deeply involved in both scholarly and policy-oriented discourse outside the confines of the CFIA, and in this regard the Center's intellectual product was mobile, far-reaching, and ultimately influential. Through government consultation, outside lectures, participation in international conferences, and national and international advising roles, the Center's research staff promulgated their ideas and insights in a wide range of venues and to a broad array of constituencies. For example, Center faculty member Edward Mason was a member of an International Bank for Reconstruction and Development mission to Uganda in late 1960, and the advisor to the Fellows Program, Jo W. Saxe, continued his ongoing association with the United Nations. Bowie himself, as "a consultant to the Department of State on future tasks of the North Atlantic nations," was preparing a report that will be discussed at greater length below.[3]

## Ideology and Foreign Affairs

Two examples warrant closer examination at this juncture. In 1959, the Center received a government commission, in this case from the Senate Committee on Foreign Relations. The study originated in a decision by the committee to embark on a systematic and comprehensive assessment of U.S. foreign policy. According to the committee chair, Senator J. W. Fulbright, "it was felt that such a study of this nature might serve to develop fresh ideas and approaches to the foreign policy of the Nation and lead to a better national understanding of international problems and to more efficient and effective administration of our international operations."[4] This Senate initiative evolved from conversations among a small Senate executive committee and "a group of distinguished, private citizens" that included Bowie, Henry Luce, Dean Rusk, William Bullitt, and William Diebold. Proposals were solicited from universities and other institutions concerned with the conduct of American foreign policy, and ultimately fifteen papers were commissioned by the committee.[5] The Senate's directive to the Center was to produce "a study of the role played by ideology in international relations and of the implications of ideology for United States foreign policy." This study culminated in a report entitled *Ideology and Foreign Affairs*, which was published by the Senate Committee on Foreign Relations in January 1960.

Bowie submitted the Center's final report on November 23, 1959, although he was keen to highlight an important caveat that reflected his attitude toward studying international affairs as embodied by the Center for International Affairs. In his letter to Fulbright, Bowie was adamant that "concentrating on any single factor in foreign affairs entails the serious risk of conveying a distorted conception of the relative role of that factor. The reader should bear in mind that this report is one of a series of studies which cover other important aspects of international affairs and is expected to be read in that light."[6]

The report was very much a collaborative effort, drawing on the expertise of Center affiliates as well as other Harvard faculty who were not directly associated with the Center. In this regard it exemplified the ways in which the Center might be expected to engage with the wider Harvard faculty and also provided a model for future interdisciplinary and cooperative studies. Zbigniew Brzezinski coordinated and compiled the final report, and he has the distinction of being responsible for the first two publications produced under Center auspices. Brzezinski was one of the first research associates to join the Center in 1958, and he would remain at the CFIA until June 1960 following the publication of his monograph *The Soviet Bloc: Unity and Conflict*.[7]

The report itself focused on the relationship among the "three political ideologies commanding the greatest allegiance in contemporary times: constitutional democracy, nationalism, and communism," with the bulk of the study devoted to the interplay between communism, nationalism, and the developing world as a source of ideological conflict in the cold war.[8] The implications of these ideological interactions for American foreign policy were also given consideration in the report. In many ways, the study reflects the Center's primary concerns as outlined by Bowie in his 1958 program report, although it is important to note that this report in no way represented a single, cohesive,

"CFIA mind." Schelling, for example, arrived from his year at the RAND Corporation too late to participate in the study, and he did not agree with the tenor of the final report.[9]

From the authors' perspectives it was essential to consider the role of ideology as "not merely abstract theory but as a social and political force."[10] This was especially important due to the growing interdependence of the international system and the increasing importance of postcolonial nations in Africa and Asia. It was within this context that communism, nationalism, and democracy were interacting, and in some cases these three ideologies were struggling for supremacy. Communism in particular was not immune to nationalism, according to the report, and the relationship between these two forces within both the communist bloc and the nonaligned developing world was the subject of much of the report's analysis. As for the implications for U.S. foreign policy, although the study was limited by its mandate to discuss broad trends, it did conclude: "Democracy will not survive merely by reacting to the threats of tyranny. Our foreign policy, therefore, must have wider perspectives than those stimulated by the continuous clash with the U.S.S.R."[11]

When the paper came before the Senate Foreign Relations Committee in February 1961, Brzezinski had left Harvard to take a position at Columbia University. Bowie nevertheless recommended that Brzezinski testify before the Senate committee as the principal author of the study, although Brzezinski was quick to point out that "I do not speak for the center in any official sense."[12] The paper was endorsed by the committee chair, Senator Fulbright, who remarked before Brzezinski began his testimony:

> Before you begin, I want to say on my own behalf that I consider this perhaps the most significant study of all those undertaken by the committee, and I think the material in this is the most significant for the future of our country and certainly for the formulation of our foreign policy. I hope that the committee can help spread the ideas and the thoughts that you have developed so well in this study . . . if there is any possible way we can inspire the interest of the press to help us educate our people and our own Government on the contents of this report, I will certainly do anything I can.[13]

In fact it was not only the American press that noticed the Center's report. Both the Soviet and Chinese presses also took an active interest in the study—Soviet theorists even published a number of rebuttals in communist periodicals in response to the paper's claims of disintegration in the Sino-

Soviet alliance—while the Chinese press accused the Center of engaging in "outspoken slanders."[14]

## The North Atlantic Nations: Tasks for the 1960s

The Senate Committee on Foreign Relations was not the only government body interested in soliciting the expertise of the CFIA research staff. In early 1960, Bowie was called back to government service as a consultant to the State Department. In early 1960 Christian Herter, Eisenhower's secretary of state following the death of John Foster Dulles in May 1959, invited Bowie to compile a report on "The North Atlantic Nations: Tasks for the 1960s," which would ultimately become known as the "Bowie Report." He was assisted in this endeavor by an expert staff, selected by him from foreign affairs agencies and think tanks, and the Center and its associates were not directly involved. The genesis for this report originated in a meeting of the NATO Council of Ministers the previous December, during which the Council had issued a call for a comprehensive plan of NATO objectives for the coming decade.[15] As Bowie recalls in his foreword to a published edition of the final report:

119

> The Report . . . sought to outline an overall strategy for the foreign and security policy of the U.S. (and its allies) for the coming decade. Its basic concept was that this entailed two broad tasks: one was the positive effort to build and manage a cooperative order for the prosperity and security of the noncommunist nations; the second was to safeguard this order from Soviet disruption, while fostering Soviet evolution toward a less hostile relationship. Within this context, the Report undertook to identify the major political, military, and economic issues which the Atlantic nations would confront during the 1960s in their relations with each other, with the Soviet Union, and with the developing world, and to recommend approaches for dealing with them, through NATO or other means.[16]

The report did not simply propose a nuclear solution to the problems that might face the Atlantic community in the 1960s. Bowie also devoted a great deal of attention to the Atlantic community's relations with the developing world: "To achieve an orderly international community, the less developed countries must be able to participate in it as independent, effective, and responsible nations."[17] With this in mind, Bowie recommended that the Atlantic nations aid developing countries in their efforts at modernization, not only economically through aid programs, trade, and assistance with communications, but also politically, culturally, and militarily.[18]

"Relations with the Communist Bloc" were also considered, and Bowie highlighted the necessity to "reconcile the requirements of simultaneously *competing with* and *dealing with* [italics in original] the Bloc," which required both " (a) an unremitting awareness of Bloc hostility . . . and (b) a continuing desire for useful relations with the Bloc, even when tensions are at their peak." This required a concerted and coordinated effort to continue restrictions on trade, while also increasing points of exchange in conjunction with increased efforts toward arms control.[19] Bowie also encouraged the Atlantic community to mobilize more of its resources and intensify its efforts toward some form of political unity.

120

Most famously, however, Bowie's report contained a proposal for establishing a multilateral nuclear force (MLF), which was designed to accomplish a number of goals in the context of U.S.-European and NATO relations. The concept of a multinational nuclear force had grown in popularity as the Soviet Union began to approach nuclear parity with the United States. In Bowie's formulation, the United States would establish a seaborne nuclear force under the control of NATO and the Supreme Allied Commander in Europe (SACEUR), General Lauris Norstad. American Polaris submarines would form the basis of this force, which would be "jointly financed, owned, and controlled and manned by mixed crews (i.e., non-national)." That this MLF should be sea based and operated by a combination of participants drawn from NATO members was an essential aspect of the plan, since it would "ensure joint control, prevent national withdrawal of components, reduce vulnerability, and avoid other problems of a mobile landbased [sic] system."[20]

The MLF proposal, as Bowie rendered it, was designed to achieve several objectives in this increasingly perilous international nuclear environment. First, joint control of a NATO nuclear force would assuage the fears of America's European allies that the United States might not be willing to "trade New York for West Berlin," as a popular maxim of the period depicted the United States' strategic dilemma. In addition, the proposal would mitigate the propensity for America's European allies to develop their own independent nuclear forces, as the UK had done since 1952, and as France had begun to do with its first atomic test in Algeria in February 1960. Third, the MLF would also resolve General Norstad's request to deploy Medium-Range Ballistic Missiles (MRBMs) in Europe, thus providing Europe with a medium-range nuclear shield that was not vulnerable to the numerous political and strategic disadvantages associated with a land-based deployment. Finally, Bowie also conceived the MLF as a potential catalyst for European integration, since it might form the basis of a European military force. Bowie met with President Eisenhower in August 1960 to discuss his report, which received Eisenhower's support, and by December 1960 the proposal was presented to the NATO Council of Ministers by Secretary of State Herter.[21] The MLF proposal would continue to draw Bowie into discussions in Washington throughout the Kennedy and Johnson administrations.[22]

Taken together, these two studies established two possible precedents for the Center's role in formulating American foreign policy, in addition to filtering knowledge through publications and discourse originally envisaged by Bowie. One study—commissioned directly by the U.S. government to enhance foreign affairs—represented the collective wisdom of some Center associates (in conjunction with other Harvard faculty members) and seemed to begin a close direct institutional relationship with the government. The Center could therefore be expected to meet the intellectual needs of the government directly through collaborative, interdisciplinary research conducted under the overall auspices of the CFIA. The second paper represented an alternative method, in which Center research staff—in this case Bowie, acting independently of the Center—could inform and influence policy. Conceivably, however, those engaged in such activity would have inculcated the Center's intellectual output, which would in turn inform their assessments and proposals. It was in fact the latter method that would become the dominant conduit through which the Center's research would permeate the reservoir of intellectual capital available to the policy-making community. The former method—directly commissioned studies by the federal government—would become somewhat anomalous in the Center's history.

## Scholarship and Foreign Policy: Problems and Opportunities

All of this took place during the increasingly complex cold war, which significantly complicated American foreign policy and frequently required input from academic experts and area specialists. The academic community potentially formed an intellectual reserve for the federal government, and their knowledge often proved enormously valuable to both the intelligence and foreign-policy-making communities.

This was by no means a simple relationship. In the absence of an institutionalized link between the academy and the U.S. government, the scholar's role and influence in American foreign policy has been extremely varied and ambiguous. The traditionally sacrosanct independence of intellectual inquiry often precluded effectively utilizing academic research and analysis, which in turn prohibited the researcher from engaging the policy maker, and vice versa. Nevertheless, there have always been those in power who, for reasons of expediency, efficacy, or choice, have solicited the perspectives of the academic specialist, just as there have been those scholars who have requested hearings in the corridors of power.

This embrace of academics and their research was not simply a function of a ubiquitous government, intent upon co-opting the nation's intellectual resources to prosecute the cold war, as some critics contended during the Vietnam War.[23] Many scholars benefited from, and indeed sought, closer ties to the government, and their reasons varied. Some were motivated by a desire to enter public service. John Kenneth Galbraith, recalling the early days of the Kennedy administration noted, "there were a lot of people, as in my case, that had more information than they could contain, stronger opinions than they could conceal, and therefore were available for advice and action."[24] Many sought financial resources for their research projects or institutions. Still others sought to apply their theoretical models to practical situations, which could often only be achieved with the resources of the federal government.

In this context, the Kennedy administration is often cited as the apotheosis of the scholar-statesman relationship during the cold war. As Galbraith recalls:

> Kennedy always had a detached view of Harvard and the professoriate, and at the same time relied very strongly, there should be no doubt about that, on the academic community [at Harvard] and elsewhere. Dominantly Harvard, but also, there were people from Yale, Princeton, Chicago . . .You could have a scholarly discussion every night in Washington . . . there was a dominant role for a wide range of university professoriate.[25]

Indeed, the Kennedy administration would attempt to employ the talents of the academic community, to the extent that it could manage and administer the creative process, which in many cases it did not. In February 1963, for example, the State Department's Bureau of Intelligence and Research (INR) hosted a meeting at Camp David with members of the academic community in order to discuss a common approach to producing pertinent research. The meeting focused on attempts to formulate a shared theoretical conception of "political systems analysis," yet throughout the proceedings the conversation turned to how external scholarship might serve the Kennedy administration's foreign policy. It was widely accepted that "new ideas and insights from varied sources are needed to guide government action," and that, "in this area, contributions by outside scholars can be of great assistance."[26] Some participants, however, reflecting a broader societal debate, voiced their concern about whether it was appropriate or indeed useful to apply nongovernmental research to policy formulation:

> *There are those who think it is possible for the academic world to provide policy papers by joining the scholars' theoretical knowledge with his awareness of policy problems. Others look upon this kind of analysis as impossible . . . Also, there was a feeling that such a marriage between the Government and the academic communities would cause the scholars to lose their purity of outlook.[27]*

123

This latter notion derives from the central tenet of academic professionalism—intellectual autonomy—that for many academics has engendered a sincere belief in the necessity for a separation of academy and state. Indeed, as William Polk has argued, "tension between the academic community and the government is a corollary of the American concept of politics."[28] One Harvard faculty member, for example, had already concluded that it was inappropriate for scholars to aid and abet the policy makers in their work. In his 1959 presidential address before the Association for Asian Studies, John King Fairbank declared:

> *We who specialize in Asian studies should not be expected to deal with American foreign policy. Our task is to concentrate on scholarship. . . . [Otherwise] the Asia specialist may wind up as an Asia expert busily serving to the American public those answers which are already in the common mind in a process of public give and take which is touted as democratic discussion, or even as policy formulation, but which may be no more than collective autointoxication.[29]*

Indeed, as Eytan Gilboa has argued in one of the few systematic studies of the association between the scholar and foreign policy, "the relationship between knowledge and power, theory and action, intellectuals and politicians, scholars and policy-makers, and universities and governments has always been tense."[30] Many scholars are averse to a closer relationship with policy makers, which is attributable to numerous ethical, institutional, and practical concerns. Gilboa argues that many scholars felt that bureaucrats either failed to clarify the research requirements or sought evidence only ex post facto to support the government's position. Moreover, policy makers frequently imposed deadlines on their academic collaborators that often precluded exhaustive and rigorous analysis. Some policy problems, simply put, were considered beyond the scope of scholars confined to university libraries and labyrinthine archival repositories.[31]

## The Limits of Long-Term Scholarship for Foreign Policy Making

The scholars were not alone in their distrust and reticence toward closer cooperation between the policy-making community and the academy. James N. Rosenau conducted a survey among State Department officers in 1969 and elicited a similar inventory of doubts about engaging both scholars and their scholarship. He found, for instance, that many bureaucrats considered external research to be out of date, or couched in technical language that precluded easy digestion, particularly in such a time-sensitive arena as international diplomacy. Furthermore, some policy makers considered scholarly research—which was often produced in a political vacuum—to be irrelevant.[32]

Former assistant secretary of state for far eastern affairs, Roger Hilsman, was especially cognizant of the interrelationship between scholarship and policy, having entered government service from academia in 1961 to head INR at the State Department. Speaking before a plenary session of the 1964 meeting of the Association for Asian Studies on the relationship between the scholar and the foreign policy maker, Hilsman was equivocal about the relevance of external research in the policy-making process. Initially pessimistic about the efficacy of scholarly input in policy decisions, Hilsman demurred, "much of what is done in scholarship is really of relative little utility to the policy maker" because "the twists and turns of foreign policy . . . are, I think, beyond the reach of effective writing by scholars."[33] Although he conceded that scholarship was useful in areas of fluidity and uncertainty, challenges remained: "The problem is not just one of focusing scholarship on these problems in areas where they can be most productive but rather one of a cultural lag between work that is done and the making of policy."[34]

Throughout his tenure, Hilsman made efforts to improve access to academic research for use in INR intelligence assessments. In preparation for a Senate Appropriations Committee hearing, for example, he drafted a paper supporting continued funding for the INR's Policy Research Studies Program, which according to him had been established in 1961 to "develop an institutionalized bridge" between government and academia.[35] Hilsman argued that previous initiatives under this program had demonstrated the value of policy-oriented studies conducted by outside scholars. Crucially, however, such studies did not result from the common scholarly process of politically disinterested academic inquiry. Rather, they were solicited by the State Department and the White House to ensure their relevance and applicability to the administration's foreign policy imperatives. Moreover, Hilsman assured Congress that, "as further insurance that a study when finished will be as relevant as possible, the Bureau of Intelligence and Research advises and assists the outside scholar."[36] Notably, the method advocated by Hilsman was the very method that many affiliates of the CFIA had eschewed in favor of direct employment as consultants.

Walt Rostow, another Kennedy administration academic who made his way from Cambridge to Washington in 1961, offered this assessment of scholarship's impact on the policy-making process: "I can attest that there is an enormous gap between the best level of University thought, and even between the best level of thought in the working levels of our bureaucracies— and the thought ultimately brought to bear on high policy decisions."[37] In many ways, this gap reflected the perception that the government was disinterested in engendering closer ties to the academic community, whereas the scholar was reluctant or unable to proffer an explicit response to specific foreign policy problems.

One of the most compelling insights into the gap between scholarship and policy making is evident in the recollections of one CFIA research associate turned policy maker, Zbigniew Brzezinski. Brzezinski, who had published extensively on the emergent Sino-Soviet split in the early 1960s, recalls "I was called down to Washington a number of times, by various people connected with the NSC and the CIA, for discussions regarding the Sino-Soviet schism. There was a great deal of interest in the issue. Since I was writing on the subject, I was being consulted, but I cannot assess the impact of my views."[38] Based upon his subsequent experience as President Carter's national security advisor, however, Brzezinski concludes, "the biggest barrier is the lack of understanding by scholars of the pressures and conflicting dilemmas that policy makers confront when shaping policy. As a result, a great deal of their work tends to be 'academic' and hence of predominantly . . . academic interest."[39]

The Department of State was especially ambivalent about employing scholars and utilizing their research in formulating foreign policy, despite the best efforts of Hilsman and the INR. The State Department's reluctance to engage academic research was due to its official view, which considered external research of "limited applicability to the ordinary work of a political officer,"[40] according to Eytan Gilboa. Writing in 1969, Robert Nisbet concurred, suggesting that there exists "between the State Department policy sections and the American academic community . . . distrust founded upon the State Department's lack of confidence in the concrete results of social science research."[41]

## The Kennedy Administration Strikes

Despite this mutual apprehension about the appropriate relationship between scholarship and policy, the value of the Center's affiliates to the policy-making community almost undermined the CFIA before it could even consolidate its existence. The remarkable talent assembled by Bowie and his fellow core faculty members were subject to the intellectual equivalent of a hostile takeover bid by the newly inaugurated Kennedy administration in 1961. This aggrandizement did not merely reflect the insatiability of the Kennedy administration. Of course, the Center's research staff included many men who had served the federal government or the United States military in various capacities during World War II and the subsequent political and economic reconstruction of Europe, as in the cases of Bowie, Schelling, and Mason. In this regard, many of these individuals were consummate "inners and outers," who were comfortable and capable public servants with myriad connections throughout the multifarious government bureaucracies.[42]

In large part, the close ties between the Center and the new government in Washington were facilitated by the links between the Kennedy administration and the CFIA through the personage of McGeorge Bundy, who left Harvard to become national security advisor at the commencement of the Kennedy presidency in 1961. As dean of the Faculty of Arts and Sciences, Bundy had of course been instrumental in creating the CFIA; he would likewise prove to be instrumental in the near disintegration of the Center only three years into its tenure.

Most notably, in July 1961 Bundy attempted to recruit Bowie from the CFIA to become an undersecretary of state in the new administration. Bundy solicited counsel from foreign policy luminaries such as John J. McCloy and Hamilton Fish Armstrong, who gave Bowie a glowing endorsement. In a memorandum to President Kennedy dated July 13, 1961, Bundy reported: "Armstrong can think of no one better for the chief job in intelligence or the Under Secretary's job in the State Department."[43] As Bowie acknowledges, the offer was tempting, but could not be accepted. "I had to tell them no. I felt that I had taken on a certain obligation to the Center . . . and I had just got it going, and I didn't really feel I could legitimately leave."[44]

Schelling was also offered a position in the Kennedy administration as Paul Nitze's deputy for arms control, a position he ultimately turned down. From his perspective, "I had, I think, more fun and more influence being an available consultant rather than going on the payroll." For one thing, Schelling remembers that Bundy's presence in the White House provided an expeditious conduit between Cambridge and Washington that enabled a great degree of reciprocal influence between CFIA members and the Kennedy administration. "Whenever I had an idea I felt free to go down to Washington and talk to Bundy" recalls Schelling, "he was accessible if you wanted to reach him."[45] Indeed, Bundy himself might have agreed with Schelling's assessment. In a 1961 letter to another academic, Robert Osgood, Bundy speculated " . . . I have the impression that location is not the decisive point here. People from Harvard and Rand are in fact closer to the processes of government than many others who are right here [in Washington]."[46]

Despite his reluctance to accept a permanent position, Schelling certainly exerted his influence on many occasions as a consultant to various administrations, particularly on issues relating to nuclear weapons and strategic doctrine. In 1967 he was again asked to come to Washington as a full-time consultant to the State Department in order to "develop a 'systems analysis' approach to foreign policy," designed to rationalize the U.S. government's disbursal of foreign aid.[47] By May 1967, however, he had decided to forgo the offer having "gradually realized that the Department's organization was too complex to develop a system for programming in one year."[48]

## Henry Kissinger and the Kennedy Administration

A third member of the Center's core faculty did, however, find himself in the employ of the Kennedy administration. Eight days after the presidential inauguration, Bundy wrote Henry Kissinger to broach the subject of him becoming a consultant to the White House on national security issues. "As I said in our shorthand telephone conversation," Bundy wrote, "the President has asked me to talk with you at your early convenience about the possibility of your joining up down here." Bundy was apparently not alone in seeking Kissinger's assistance, however, as other government agencies were interested in his services, including the Department of State. Dean Rusk, Kennedy's new secretary of state, was especially keen to have Kissinger join his staff, and Bundy had to interject directly with the president to ensure that Kissinger was not compelled to join Rusk.[49] According to Bundy, "[The President] does not want

127

to seem to interfere with any particular department's needs, but he does want you to know that if you should be interested, he himself would like to explore the notion of your joining the small group which Walt Rostow and I will be putting together for his direct use."[50]

Kissinger had evidently already given some thought to the role of the intellectual in the context of the cold war. In his book *The Necessity for Choice*, published in 1960 under the auspices of the CFIA, Kissinger reflected on the appropriate relationship between the intellectual and the policy maker. He lamented the lack of clarity and efficiency that plagued this association, despite the government's often impulsive propensity to call upon intellectuals in response to myriad problems and questions. In fact, in his view one of the biggest problems derived from this often injudicious proclivity to gorge upon intellect. This often meant that "intellectuals with a reputation soon find themselves so burdened that their pace of life hardly differs from that of the executives whom they counsel." As a result, "They cannot supply perspective because they are as harassed as the policy makers."[51]

The tendency of government bureaucracies to selectively call upon those intellectuals whose views tended to support the status quo was another consequence Kissinger felt inhibited the productive employment of the scholars' talents. Alternatively, the process of finding common ground among an assembly of specialists with widely different competencies and opinions often enervated their individual contributions to such an extent that "the result is more often a common denominator than a well-rounded point of view." Moreover, since the intellectual is often not directly involved in the decision-making process, "all too often, what the policymaker wants from the intellectual is not ideas but endorsement."[52] Ultimately, then, such an assessment had ramifications for institutions such as the CFIA itself:

> *Thus, though the intellectual participates in policymaking to an almost unprecedented degree, the result has not necessarily been salutary for him or of full benefit to the officials calling on him . . . Nor has the present manner of utilizing outside experts and research institutes done more than reduce somewhat the dilemma of the policymakers. The production of so much research often simply adds another burden to already overworked officials . . . Few if any of the recent crises of U.S. foreign policy have been caused by the unavailability of data. Our policymakers do not lack advice; they are in many respects overwhelmed by it. They do lack criteria on which to base judgments.*[53]

*Robert R. Bowie in April 1958, soon after he was named as the founding Center Director.*

*Members of the Center for International Affairs in 1959–60.*

*From left to right—Bunroku Yoshino of Japan, Counselor for General Affairs in the Economic Affairs Bureau of the Japanese Ministry of Foreign Affairs; Soemarman of Indonesia, Secretary General of the Ministry of Home Affairs; Il-Kwon Chung of the Republic of Korea, Ambassador to the United States, General in the Korean Army, and former Chair of the Joint Chiefs of Staff; and A.D. Pandit of India, Joint Secretary in the Ministry of Works, Housing and Supply in the Government of India—were Fellows of the Center in 1960–61.*

*Thomas C. Schelling was associated with the Center for International Affairs for ten years, beginning in 1959, before moving to the newly established John F. Kennedy School of Government. He was awarded the 2005 Nobel Prize in Economics.*

Edward S. Mason was associated with the Center from its founding in 1958, when he left the deanship of Harvard's Graduate School of Public Administration, to 1969, when he became acting dean of the Faculty of Arts and Sciences. He was also instrumental in the Development Advisory Service.

Henry Kissinger holds his last seminar at the CFIA on December 16, 1968, before leaving for Washington to become national security advisor in the Nixon administration.

*Lee Kuan Yew, then prime minister of Singapore, visited Harvard in the spring of 1975.*
*He spoke with Raymond Vernon, who was Center Director from 1973 to 1978.*

*Director of the Center for International Affairs from 1978 to 1989, Samuel P. Huntington continued his active association with the Center through the 2007–08 academic year.*

CFIA advisor to the Fellows, Benjamin Brown, nurses a bloody ear following a September 25, 1969 attack on the Center by the Weathermen faction of the Students for a Democratic Society (SDS).

Damage to the CFIA library following the detonation of a bomb planted by unidentified assailants in the early hours of October 14, 1970.

The Center was attacked for the third time in April 1972. A small fire was set in one office, and other offices were ransacked by an estimated two hundred demonstrators. Here, Jorge I. Domínguez (Center Director, 1996–2006), then a graduate student at the Center, and CFIA Executive Secretary Lawrence Finkelstein view the damage.

Delivering the Jodidi Lecture on February 19, 1980, Zbigniew Brzezinski spoke to an overflow audience of eight hundred people on "Equity and Security: The Challenges to American Foreign Policy." Brzezinski wrote the first two publications produced under Center auspices, and was one of the first research associates to join the Center in 1958; he would remain at the CFIA until June 1960 following the publication of his monograph The Soviet Bloc: Unity and Conflict.

Benjamin Brown (right) directed the Fellows Program from 1960 to 1983. Center Director Samuel Huntington and the rest of the Center community gathered to celebrate Ben's generous presence upon his retirement.

Center for International Affairs directors Robert D. Putnam, Samuel P. Huntington, Raymond Vernon, Robert R. Bowie, Joseph S. Nye, and Jorge I. Domínguez gathered to inaugurate the newly named Weatherhead Center for International Affairs in April 1998.

*Center group photo 2006–07.*

Despite these reservations, by March 1961 Kissinger was officially appointed as a consultant to the National Security Council, and Bundy expressed his belief that "I think you are one of the very few people whose advice will be really helpful on this relatively informal basis." Bundy envisaged that Kissinger would be available for consultation "particularly in the general area of weapons and policy and in the special field of thinking about all aspects of the problem of Germany." Although Bundy could not judge the extent of the workload for which Kissinger would be responsible, "the best model which has occurred to me since our conversation is that of the President's Science Advisory Committee, the members of which are on call for advice on special problems in a fashion which is determined by the problems and not by any a priori plan."[54]

129

Kissinger's role with the National Security Council meant that he would be receiving classified documents at the Center, which required that his office be secured. The CIA arranged for such safeguards, including Kissinger's receipt and storage of sensitive information. Secret material was sent by registered mail, and top-secret material was delivered by CIA couriers. A safe was installed in Kissinger's 6 Divinity Avenue office, in which sensitive material was stored and monitored by an alarm system.[55] Both Kissinger and his CFIA secretary were granted top-secret security clearance.[56] Prior to installing this safe, Kissinger received confidential materials through the Center for International Studies at MIT—which also handled classified documents—requiring Kissinger to travel to and from MIT three times a day.[57]

By May 1961, Kissinger was ready to begin his assignment, and he proposed to Bundy several areas on which he would be interested in consulting. "It seems to me very important that an analysis be made of our existing war plans, from the point of view of their political impact." Furthermore, Kissinger expressed an interest in "almost any subject in the NATO area," as well as arms control, although he added the caveat " . . . before the White House can be effective, a better position must be produced by the Disarmament Administration."[58] During the following eighteen months Kissinger's responsibilities ranged widely across these various subjects, issues that were central to the CFIA's research program during these early years. He was at liberty to impart his thoughts to Bundy and on occasion directly to President Kennedy himself, on subjects such as the Soviet violation of the moratorium on testing nuclear weapons, American negotiating positions in disarmament discussions with the Soviet Union, and issues pertaining to Germany and the status of Berlin.[59]

There was always a degree of ambiguity that created a somewhat difficult relationship, however, which derived in part from Kissinger's stature as a Harvard professor and prominent commentator on national security issues in the nation's press and scholarly periodicals. In this regard, his experience demonstrated the potential disadvantages of attempting to combine the roles of public academic and government consultant. In June 1961, Kissinger wrote to Bundy to declare his intention to remain an "*ad hoc* [italics in original] consultant" to the Kennedy administration rather than to accept a full-time (but temporary) position over the summer. In his letter Kissinger outlined the "two ways in which an outsider can contribute to the policy making process." While the first method is to deliver new ideas, the second method " . . . is to help in developing a sense of proportion and direction. Of these, the latter seems to me by far the more important, even though the former is the most frequently demanded." In order for Kissinger to have compelling input, "I must be able to follow a given problem or a set of problems over a period of time." The current arrangement often required Kissinger to make comments in a very short space of time on a given paper, and without the necessary context about how the decisions and positions were developed: "It is like being asked in the middle of a chess game to suggest a move without having been in a position to study the development of the game or being allowed to explain the rationale for the suggestion."[60] Bundy agreed that Kissinger's preference for a more informal role was the right decision, "…in light of the way you work and the way life goes down here." He did suggest, however, that in order for Kissinger to "follow a given problem or a set of problems over a period of time," it would either necessitate " . . . permanent membership in the Government, or, alternatively, relatively complete detachment, except as specific problems become ripe for consultative treatment."[61]

By September 1961, however, Kissinger concluded that "I can no longer make a useful contribution." In a detailed letter to his former Harvard colleague and friend, Arthur M. Schlesinger, Kissinger outlined the reasoning for his decision and discussed his experience as a consultant to the National Security Council. His conclusion to recuse himself from government service originated in large part from his unsatisfactory experience as a consultant, which he described as being "Kafka-like." Most importantly, Kissinger felt marginalized, especially by Bundy: "I have not been asked to do anything . . . Anything I have offered to do has been rejected or ignored." Indeed, all of his contributions in the summer of 1961 were unsolicited. "Since I have no contact with the President, and next to no contact with Mac, my contribution to Berlin planning is that of a kibitzer shouting random comments from the side-lines." Though he was loath to admit it, Kissinger was convinced, "painful as this thought is to me . . . my contribution to national policy was infinitely greater when I was a private citizen than it has been since I joined the White House staff."[62] With this in mind, on October 19, 1961, Kissinger tendered his formal resignation.

Assuming the roles of an occasional and informal diplomat to the West German government of Konrad Adenauer and a sporadic advisor on matters of European and military matters, Kissinger nevertheless remained a consultant to the National Security Council until September 1962. The situation became increasingly untenable, however, as Kissinger's ambiguous relationship to the National Security Council often caused confusion as to what constituted his own personal views as a scholar and public intellectual and what represented the official position of the Kennedy administration. As he wrote to his White House confidant Arthur Schlesinger:

> I have been manipulated into an essentially fraudulent posture: I am being used, if at all, for window dressing and to sell policies in the formulation of which I have had no part and the substance of which sometimes makes me highly uneasy. I have never had an opportunity to present my views consistently, or to participate in the policy process in any serious manner. I have not the slightest notion what becomes of the memoranda I submit on my own. (Indeed, I have reason to doubt that they ever leave Mac's office.) Yet the outside world and many inside the government consider me a White House advisor and treat me accordingly.[63]

Bundy alluded to the difficult situation in a September 1962 letter in which Kissinger's ties to the National Security Council were formally severed by mutual consent. "My impression of your own position," Bundy wrote, "is that to hold a continuing appointment as Consultant places you in a somewhat ambiguous posture, and while I know how much effort you have given to walking a careful line, it is also true for us here that occasionally we are asked if your publicly stated opinions somehow reflect those of the White House." Despite the official dissolution of Kissinger's ties to the Kennedy administration, Bundy averred "we would of course continue to have the benefit of your public writings, which probably have more impact within the Government—let alone outside it—than what happens in most consulting arrangements, and also of course the White House doors will remain open to you whenever you have a particular point of view that you would like to register privately."[64] For his part, Kissinger concurred, and in October he wrote to Bundy, "as you know, I have long been concerned that my public statements about certain aspects of policy might be misconstrued as White House 'trial balloons.'"[65] The roles of Kissinger the government consultant and Kissinger the public intellectual were simply incompatible.

Unlike Kissinger's ad hoc consultations, other Center affiliates joined the Kennedy administration on a full-time basis, which made for a much smoother transition from academia to public service. Carl Kaysen, for example, a Center research associate and professor of economics at Harvard, joined the Kennedy administration in May 1961 at the invitation of McGeorge Bundy as a National Security Council staff member.[66] Henry Rowen, another Center research associate, joined the Defense Department as deputy assistant secretary for international security affairs in early 1961 following an invitation from Paul Nitze. In September 1966, Bowie also returned to the government, this time as counselor to the State Department in the Johnson administration, where he would remain until 1968. Of course, Kissinger himself would ultimately choose to become a full-time policy maker, leaving Harvard to join the Nixon administration as national security advisor in 1969.

## Project Camelot and Misgivings at the CFIA

By the mid-1960s, however, the relatively effortless and unproblematic relationship between academia and government that had characterized the first years of the decade had become seriously complicated, to such an extent that Schelling, then acting director in Bowie's absence, felt compelled to expound at length upon the Center's current and historical links to the federal government in his October 1966 annual report. This was prompted by two recent events that had raised questions about the appropriateness of close academic involvement in American foreign policy activities abroad, especially with regard to links between the academy and the CIA.

The first major crisis emerged from a project organized by the U.S. Army, the Department of Defense, and the Special Operations Research Office at American University, which was designed to utilize behavioral science research in the Army's limited war and counterinsurgency doctrines. By 1965 the project had been terminated amid a furor that embroiled not only American University and the Department of Defense but also the White House, the Chilean government, the State Department, and the academic community at large. Project Camelot, as it was known, derived from this joint effort to mobilize the expertise of sociologists, psychologists, political scientists, economists and mathematicians in order to "identify indicators of conditions and trends which, if continued, would probably lead to the outbreak of internal war," and provide the necessary intellectual tools and methods to preempt the expression of undesirable social processes.[67] Some defined this effort to ascertain a predictive model of social dislocation and potential communist takeover in a number of Latin American countries as a plot by the U.S. military to interfere in the affairs of independent nations in the Western hemisphere. The controversy surrounding Project Camelot fundamentally complicated the scholar-statesman relationship, and initiated a debate within both the U.S. government and the scholarly community about the nature and appropriate use of academic research.[68]

This dispute was compounded in early 1966 by the close relationship between the Michigan State University Vietnam Advisory Group (MSUG) and the CIA in Vietnam. Formed in 1955 by Wesley Fishel at the behest of South Vietnamese President Ngo Dinh Diem, the MSUG provided consultancy services to Diem and his new government and was involved in a plethora of administrative, economic, and public order programs. It transpired that CIA operatives were involved in both the activities of the MSUG "Police Team"— whose primary role was to provide advice and technical assistance on purchasing and using equipment that was mostly provided by the American government— and to organize, train, and manage the South Vietnamese internal security services, totaling over 60,000 personnel.[69]

Schelling also recalls the furor generated in 1964–65 by the news that CIS had received funding from the Central Intelligence Agency for a number of its projects, which led to dispersions being cast upon the CFIA. Although the Center never accepted CIA funds, the relatively uncomplicated relationship between intellect and power that had characterized the early 1960s was beginning to become more problematic in light of these events, and as such the Center was being drawn into a broader public debate regarding the appropriate role of the scholar in formulating American foreign policy.[70]

With regard to these developments, Schelling observed "the Center was bound to examine its own activities in the light of this public interest in the relation of government agencies to academic research." He was candid about the Center's relationship to the federal government, and divulged that individual Center members had "engaged in research contracted for by the Air Force, the Department of Defense, the Arms Control and Disarmament Agency, the Agency for International Development, the National Science Foundation, and the Senate Committee on Foreign Relations." The Fellows Program, of course, was also a principal source of the Center's connection to not only the United States government but also governments around the world. None of these working relationships would have surprised anybody who had followed the Center's activities during the previous eight years, since the details had been openly reported in the CFIA's annual reports.

Harvard's policies on government contracts forbade including any classified material in University-related contractual work, and according to Schelling the CFIA had always abided by this mandate as well as the provisos that "scholarly standards shall not be impaired, the right to publish or otherwise disseminate the fruits of research shall be respected, and Harvard will not disguise its research activities or the source of its financing."[71] Moreover, Schelling insisted that the Center engaged in research initiated by the U.S. government "only to the extent that the research interests of the Center and of the government coincide; and it will not become a servicing agency to the government or build up a research staff dependent on continual government contracting."[72] From Schelling's perspective, the Center's experience had always been positive, and he felt that it was in fact "remarkable that U.S. government agencies concerned with defense and foreign policy have learned to appreciate the value of academic inquiry in the social as well as in the physical and engineering sciences in a manner compatible with the standards of the academic community."[73]

The tumult of the post–Project Camelot fiasco demonstrated the extent to which a seemingly compromised academy might damage not only the integrity of scholarly independence but also the efficient conduct of American foreign policy. As the Vietnam War became increasingly unpopular during the late 1960s, the relationship between the academy and the U.S. government came to be seen as potentially corrupt. "When you got to the . . . deep cleavages about the Vietnam War," Bowie recalls of the change that occurred in the late 1960s, " . . . many scholars didn't want to have much to do with the government. So that nexus was broken."[74] The perceived complicity of university scholars in the conduct of that divisive war was increasingly seen as corrosive to academic independence, at best, and at worst as morally bankrupt. For the time being, however, the CFIA remained justifiably above the fray. But as the country and its campuses became increasingly radicalized during the course of the 1960s, the Center would not remain immune for long.

# Eight

# Protests and Violence at the CFIA

WRITING AT THE END OF 1968, ACTING CENTER DIRECTOR RAYMOND Vernon rightly noted that the CFIA had reached "a significant milestone" in its existence.[1] The Center's first decade had passed, which warranted evaluating its past activities and considering new goals. This assessment was complicated, however, in that "the normal difficulties of such an evaluation have been compounded by the tensions and needs of the setting within which we live."[2] In Vernon's estimation, some important changes—in both the international system and the attitudes of students on campus—had inexorably transformed the foundations upon which the Center had been established, rendering many of the early conceptions of the Center's role less germane in 1968 than in 1958. Vernon was certainly cognizant that the Center's associates had made remarkable contributions over the previous ten years, but he also recognized that the local and international contexts of the CFIA's undertakings had fundamentally changed and the various constituencies the Center served had new expectations and needs.

Indeed, the Center's second decade was both transitional and turbulent. While in its first decade the Center was by no means a halcyon and bucolic outpost of cloistered and unmolested intellectual contemplation, the ravages of a changing domestic and international political context—coupled with the shifting composition and scholarship of the Center's research staff—ensured that the second decade at the Center would be far more dynamic (for better and for worse) than the previous one. Sometimes change was directed peacefully from the inside, and at times it was forced violently from the outside, but whatever the stimulus, the CFIA's research agenda and relationships shifted significantly over the next fifteen years.

Locally, nowhere was change more palpable than among the student body itself. Certainly, by 1968 the University was not immune from the increasingly radicalized student population, a fact that had become a feature of university life throughout the United States and around the world. Vernon recognized that this development demanded the Center's attention, especially given the CFIA's involvement in studying international affairs: "Whereas it once seemed self-evident that a Center such as ours could live alongside the student body, concentrating principally upon the enrichment of the disciplines that contributed to an understanding of international affairs rather than upon a direct interchange with the student body itself, the wisdom of that kind of specialization is no longer quite so clear."[3] In addition to the increasingly vocal student demands for a greater voice in the decision-making processes of their institutions, the more radical student movements from within Harvard and beyond targeted the Center with insinuations and even violence.

## Engaging Students

There is no question that one of the most significant challenges faced by the Center as it began its second decade resulted from the increasingly strident verbal and physical attacks on the Center by students and outsiders associated with radical organizations such as the Students for a Democratic Society (SDS) and its militant offshoot, the Weathermen. SDS had emerged as a campus organization in the fall of 1964, and by 1968 the Harvard chapter had established an activist resume that demonstrated its intention to remain a force for change at the University. Another local student organization, the November Action Committee (NAC), was also devoted to raising awareness about the CFIA's supposedly nefarious activities. These were but three in a complex network of politicized student groups operating on the Harvard campus by 1968, many of which were often more radical factions of the original SDS, and subject to influence from local activists. Amid the radicalism of the late 1960s, these groups sought to abolish the CFIA, and some were willing to go to great lengths to affect its demise.

When Bowie returned to the CFIA in the fall of 1968 following a two-year sabbatical in the Johnson administration, important modifications in the Center's program were soon evident. He recognized, as had Vernon, that the Center had never been simply a static, conservative institution, and he was quick to point out in his 1969 annual report that the Center had always adapted to the exigencies of its members and constituencies. He was also keen to demonstrate the ways in which the Center had evolved in the previous year. Bowie highlighted, for example, an increasing emphasis on the nature of the international system itself and the place of the United States in that system. Such an investigation, he observed, would both complement existing areas of inquiry and benefit from insights garnered by the extant core research fields.[4]

## The Graduate Student Associate Program

Perhaps the biggest change in the Center's operations, however, was the decision to engage more formally and directly with the Harvard student body. Despite graduate students' informal participation in some Center activities, "heretofore, the Center impact on students has been indirect, through the teaching by its faculty members in their respective departments; the Center itself has not sponsored or conducted any teaching." In 1968–69, therefore, the decision was made to formalize graduate student involvement with the Center by establishing the Graduate Student Associate (GSA) program, which provided a student cadre from across academic departments with material and intellectual assistance.[5] Undergraduate students were also encouraged to participate in the Center's activities by attending various noncredit seminars.[6]

Bowie invited his former research assistant (and future Center Director) Joseph Nye to lead the Center's efforts in reaching out to graduate and undergraduate students. Nye recalls that the general feeling in the Center at the time was that "the world of student life was changing and that [we needed] to pay more attention to it." For one thing, "there was a feeling that as [Students for a Democratic Society] and the antagonism toward the Vietnam War was growing, that that was creating a divide." Indeed, through their increasingly violent attacks on the Center and its staff, discussed below, students were demanding that the Center pay more attention to them.[7]

One of the first graduate students to formally join the Center in the summer of 1969 was another future Center Director, Jorge I. Domínguez. He recalls that the decision to incorporate graduate students into the Center's activities was both "strategic and tactical." Strategically, he remembers, "there was the notion that adding graduate students as partners was a good thing [on its own merits], and it was good for the Center to support research done by younger scholars in the making." Tactically, the Center leadership also recognized that, as Domínguez puts it, "the revolution had broken out by the end of the 1960s." In this regard it was clear that from the outside at least "the Center looked small, elitist, old; the very antithesis of what the revolution was about, and so frankly adding some younger-looking bodies to the Center was a good idea."[8] As a young graduate student, Domínguez found the GSA program attractive because of "the people, the seminars, the possibilities for discussion, and the practical element of physical space." Indeed, Center affiliation was as desirable for the participating students as it was efficacious for the CFIA.[9]

## Hey, Hey, CFIA, How Many Coups Did You Pull Today?

Despite the Center's efforts to respond to student needs, the CFIA soon found itself at the center of the student protest maelstrom. The NAC began its campaign against the CFIA in October 1968, when members organized a Center "tour" that was billed as "a demonstration to explain why the Center should be closed."[10] The Center responded magnanimously, perhaps in an effort to disarm the students' claims of secrecy and unaccountability, by announcing that Center staff and faculty would be available to answer any questions the students might have about the CFIA and its research. Nye promised that Center affiliates would "be delighted to meet with people and give them information. The Center is an interesting place, and we have nothing to hide."[11] The NAC was not inclined to have their tour co-opted by the CFIA leadership, however, and as one member announced: "we aren't interested in hearing what they're doing. But we just expected [sic] to see imperialist facilities," although they did recognize that, anthropologically, "having living imperialists on hand will be nice."[12]

By 1969 the situation dramatically escalated. At around noon on September 25, 1969, approximately twenty to thirty people rushed the Center's offices at 6 Divinity Avenue declaring their intention to "close the place down." During a rampage through the building, the intruders "forced virtually all of the 30-odd students, faculty, and employees in the building to leave. When some of those present attempted to argue, they were struck, pushed to the floor, or kicked." Among those who were physically assaulted by the protesters was advisor to the Fellows Program, Ben Brown. The *Crimson* reported that Brown "was the most seriously injured, requiring several stitches to close a gash over his ear." In addition to attacking Center staff and affiliates, pulling down bookcases, and tearing phones from their sockets, the protestors also daubed graffiti on the walls, shouted violent threats and obscenities, and threw rocks through windows.[13] Though the assailants claimed to be members of SDS, witnesses at the Center and the SDS leadership at Harvard claimed they were in fact members of the Weathermen, a violent faction that had split from SDS the previous June.[14] This proved to be the case when in December 1969 three members of the Weatherman faction were convicted of charges ranging from assault and battery to disturbing the peace.[15]

The indignities perpetrated against Brown did not end with a bloody ear. A leaflet defending three members of the Weathermen indicted for the attack called for a demonstration against their trial "for attacking the C.F.I.A., the gold plated pig sty." This particularly acerbic handout, "Weathermen vs. the Pigs," confidently declared:

> The people who run the C.F.I.A. are hired killers. They write reports for the
> government on how to keep a few Americans rich and fat by keeping most
> people poor and starving. You might think these vicious pimps would rush off to
> Vietnam to fight since they dig the war so much. But these are smart pigs. They
> prefer to stay at Harvard while Black people from Roxbury and white working
> kids from Dorchester and Jamaica Plain are sent off to die.

Ben Brown bore the brunt of the pamphlet's invective and was singled out as epitomizing the "hired killers" who roamed the halls of 6 Divinity Avenue. When not "[sitting] on his ass drinking sherry and pinching his secretary . . . Ben gets paid a lot to fight communism and the people of the world." In conclusion, wrote the authors, "racist teachers are pigs. Professors who help the government are pigs. Rich people are pigs. Isn't there A Pig You'd Like to Get!"[16]

## Debating the CFIA: Inside and Out

For the next two years the Center continued with little success to try and engage the radical elements of the student body. In the aftermath of this violent disruption, for example, Bowie, Vernon, and Nye met with *Crimson* reporter Richard Hyland, who himself was apparently an NAC member.[17] Their interview was part of a special *Crimson* issue that focused on the charges made against the CFIA. Hyland's report of the meeting was subsequently published in the newspaper, and Vernon responded with the Center's account, providing a defense against Hyland's conclusion that "those of us who support wars of national liberation must oppose the Center for International Affairs."[18] The Center's response to Hyland's uncompromising description of the Center and its activities highlighted what Hyland had neglected to mention:

139

*In brief, there isn't any Center line of policy, nor any Center brand of politics. According to your taste, you can try and pin a label on the Center by emphasizing the names of Bowie, or MacEwan, or Hoffmann or Bowles or Huntington. All have taken shelter and sustenance from the Center. But if you tried to pin a common label on any two of them, at least one would chew off the pin.*[19]

Vernon's rebuttal went on to point out that "Hyland's Center for International Affairs, that stout arm of the imperialist military-industrial complex, is a fantasy; it simply doesn't exist." In order to demonstrate the veracity of this claim, Vernon argued, one had to only look at some of the work that had been produced under CFIA auspices over the last five years, including two pertinent examples of Gene Sharp's studies on nonviolent action and a seminar on the Dominican Republic sponsored by Huntington that featured strong condemnations of the recent U.S. intervention in that country. Indeed, given the Center's support for scholars whose work was often avowedly anticapitalist and even anti-American, Vernon's rebuttal noted, "as the running dog of a sinister international conspiracy, the real Center would be in very deep trouble indeed."[20] Portraying the CFIA as a ferment of radical scholarship was without question overwrought, but the underlying point was valid.

Stanley Hoffmann more directly denounced the NAC's activities against the CFIA. Hoffmann viewed the charges against the Center of complicity in U.S. imperialism as nothing more than an attack on academic freedom: "To be sure, such freedom has often been abused, or used to shelter misdeeds." He also accepted that "there is an urgent need to reexamine the responsibility of social scientists and to revise the relations of universities or university agencies with public policy." Nevertheless, Hoffmann not surprisingly objected to the methods used by the radical student organizations such as the NAC:

*But it is not up to a fanaticized band of vigilantes of any persuasion to decide which activities are allowed to continue and which places must be shut down. Should one be indifferent in this instance, who knows who will be struck next? Tactics such as those of the NAC can only delay necessary change, and whatever worthy aims they have can never be served by means that are a grotesque mix of truculence and terror.*[21]

These exchanges on the pages of the *Crimson*, in conjunction with the increasingly vociferous student attacks on the Center, revealed a deeper debate taking place within the CFIA itself. One member of the Center's research staff,

Arthur MacEwan, objected to being included in Vernon's defense of the Center as a "token radical" in a letter to the *Crimson* a few days later.[22] He opined that his inclusion in Vernon's list of representative Center associates "is less than convincing to those who are familiar with the autocratic decision structure of the Center (in which we play no part whatsoever), or to those who know that Vernon's list of government apologists runs in the dozens while he runs out of house radicals at two."[23] He derided modern development policy, stimulated by social science research at the CFIA and at universities across the United States, as inherently opposed to equality and fundamental reform:

> *A thorough elaboration of this view of modern social science and its impact on the poor countries should provide a focus of attention for those who oppose the operations of the Center. We would also hope that Vernon and other directors of the Center, should they choose to defend further their function, will concentrate on these fundamental issues rather than dwelling smugly on isolated good deeds.*[24]

141

Conversely, in an unattributed letter to the *Crimson* dated October 31, 1969, another writer who appears to be a member of the Center's research staff provided a spirited defense of the CFIA's role in stimulating radical scholarship. "From my own experience and from that of many colleagues, I say categorically that the CFIA supports radical and critical scholarship and will continue to do so in the future."[25] In contrast to MacEwan and Bowles' criticism of the Center's "token radicalism," this writer suggested that while "radical scholars will form only a part of the CFIA," this was not a nefarious conspiracy to silence voices for change at the CFIA, as student opponents of the Center claimed. Rather, it was a function of "the individual ideas and temperaments of the men who study politics and economics in contemporary America." In addition, he pointed out that the Center was far from an anomaly at Harvard when it came to housing a rather limited amount of conceivably radical academics. Indeed, in his view the CFIA compared favorably to many other American universities: "the proportion of radical scholars (there are many more than the recently cited figure of two) to conventional ones in the CFIA is as high as it is in any of the Harvard Departments, and it is certainly higher in the CFIA than it is in the political science departments of any other American university."[26] In his analysis, the CFIA in fact had a vital role to play in supporting and stimulating radical scholarship at Harvard. According to the author, "in short, the Center for International Affairs is a necessary condition for systematic and sustained radical analyses of American foreign policy here at Harvard; again, to diminish it is to diminish our radical future."[27]

The debate continued unabated and the *Crimson* continued to publish both attacks and defenses of the CFIA and the nature and role of social science research in general. In response to the criticism that social science research in the United States was overreliant on government funds and restricted by "traditional" topics of inquiry, one observer retorted, "the ideal institution is one which is orthodox enough to get sufficient financial support from a variety of sources and unorthodox enough to recognize the need for diversity in its output."[28] As far as the CFIA was concerned, he contended, there were certainly areas in which the Center should cultivate more diverse opinions. Ultimately, in his view, while the Center undoubtedly had a number of shortcomings:

> [It] should be able to stand scrutiny from the left as well as the right and from scholars as well as policy makers. None should try to make it over in his own image, since that would diminish its value for all. Even more than in the past, the Center should be a place where conservatives argue with radicals, economists with political scientists, and scholars with policy makers. We should nourish and protect it because such places are hard to come by.[29]

## The CFIA and "American Imperialism": The DAS and the Fellows Program

Amidst the discourses that were taking place on the pages of the *Crimson*, the situation continued to escalate in and around 6 Divinity Avenue as student protestors focused their rancor toward the ongoing war in Vietnam against the CFIA. On April 9, 1970, for example, a Center visiting committee meeting was disrupted by around two hundred demonstrators who reportedly lined the meeting-room walls chanting, Bull-Shit! Bull-Shit! Bull-Shit! "We know that the Center created the Vietnam War," one student responded when asked why they interrupted the meeting.[30] After the meeting Bowie and a number of other visiting committee members were pursued through Harvard Square and surrounded for twenty minutes as they tried to leave in a taxi.[31] One month later about one hundred and fifty students staged a "mill-in" at the Center. In contrast to recent events, however, this was a peaceful gathering, and protesters were even provided with sandwiches and milk.[32]

Eventually, during the course of 1970 two student activist groups circulated pamphlets that purported to outline a definitive case against the CFIA and its affiliates. Their demands, however, were not mitigated by their transition to rhetoric over violence. In its indictment of the Center's activities, the Harvard-

Radcliffe November Action Committee (H-R NAC) announced, "even a hasty sketch of the history and projects of the Center reveals why such 'research in the social sciences' must be stopped." According to the authors, the Center was complicit in "[producing] ideas which maintain the international power of the United States at the expense of the majority of the world's people." This was tantamount to "academic imperialism," and as such the Center had been rightfully subjected to the ire of student protesters.[33]

The H-R NAC's case rested almost entirely on the supposed intrigues and machinations of the DAS and the Fellows Program. In short, the student groups alleged that the DAS enabled American economic and political domination of third world countries. According to the H-R NAC, the governments that received DAS support, the relationship between the DAS and the U.S. government, and the policies that DAS advisors in developing countries recommended, all served to "[illustrate] the supportive role the DAS plays in American imperialism."[34] In an attempt to validate their accusations, the authors of the H-R NAC report highlighted the fact that DAS advisors actively rendered economic advice to a number of insalubrious regimes throughout the underdeveloped world, including Indonesia under General Suharto. Indeed, the DAS was further portrayed as a proxy of the U.S. government. Although the authors conceded that the DAS operated independently of the U.S. State Department, they nevertheless concluded that in essence the "DAS and the U.S. government are working toward the same basic ends—a stable, capitalist third world dominated by American interests." Furthermore, they placed the DAS in a network of American governmental, corporate, and philanthropic organizations that collaborated to further the goals of U.S. foreign policy in the postcolonial world.[35] In this regard the DAS was a critical adjunct of an American-led scheme to impose liberal-democratic capitalism upon the third world in the ongoing ideological struggle with the Soviet Union and its allies.

While DAS advisors generally advocated liberal-democratic-capitalist-style economic reforms, members of the DAS rejected the notion that they were simply engaged in a government-sponsored attempt to apply American-style capitalism throughout the developing world. "It was not [just conceived] in a foreign policy context of how do you stop communism. [It] was implicit that if you had successful development—economic and hopefully political at some point—then you would create stable societies that wouldn't go communist; but the whole focus of the work was how do you get good economic analysis so people would have decent economic reforms," noted Dwight Perkins—a DAS advisor and future director of its successor organization, the Harvard Institute for

143

International Development.[36] Indeed, Gustav Papanek, who was the director of the DAS in 1965, had been fired from his post in the U.S. Agency for International Development in 1953 as the new Eisenhower administration came into office. He was accused of harboring "socialistic tendencies," which he acknowledges was true: during his time as an undergraduate at Cornell University, Papanek had been president of the Student League for Industrial Democracy, which was a self-declared organization of "Democratic Socialists."[37]

There were some in the CFIA, however, who agreed with the students that the DAS was abdicating its responsibilities to the people of the developing world. Arthur MacEwan, an assistant professor of economics and a research associate of the CFIA from 1968 to 1973, supported the goals—if not always the tactics—of the student demonstrators. As a development economist he chided what he saw as single-minded growth-oriented development models employed by the DAS at the expense of social justice and redistributive economic reform models. Although such policies had merit, MacEwan contends, they often required supporting military dictatorships (e.g., Pakistan) and making compromises with corrupt elites that were anathema to the interests of the majority.[38]

Another pamphlet published at the time was devoted entirely to a denunciation of the DAS and its purported complicity in a concerted program of American imperialism. "Underdeveloping the World: Harvard and Imperialism" elaborated the case against the DAS: "It is because of its supportive role in this process of subjugation and exploitation that Harvard's Development Advisory Service (DAS) must be condemned."[39] They placed the DAS within a nexus of agencies, institutions, governments, and policies dedicated to preserving international capitalism and, in particular, the interests of American investments overseas. DAS advisors "help create and maintain a system in which international business can best function. They play their role in imperialism."[40] In their assessment of DAS advisory programs in Pakistan, Indonesia, and Ghana, the authors concluded, "whatever the intent, the function of DAS advice is to support governments that are friendly to foreign business interests, but repressive to their own people."[41]

The DAS frequently countered these criticisms and tried to defend its choice of host governments. In an undated draft letter written in response to its critics, the Advisory Service defended itself against these claims of unethical relationships as well as widespread lies and innuendo. "We have always made a moral or value judgment . . . there are limits beyond which the DAS, as other parts of the university, is not willing to go." They also outlined three

144

criteria for considering invitations: Could DAS advisors be influential? What was the extent of repression in the given country? Did the proposed host government demonstrate a commitment to "growth and equity"? Although they acknowledged that it was often difficult to apply these criteria, they nevertheless stood by their record:

> There rarely is agreement within the DAS on countries that are "satisfactory." We have ended three projects that most of us considered beyond the pale in these terms and there are more than a dozen countries where, for the same reasons, we decided not to work . . .We will be concerned about repression, whether it is exercised in the name of religion or "the people," in the name of opposing "Godless Communism" or filthy capitalism . . . On the one basic issue we clearly agree with our critics. We are reform-mongers as an institution. We do not see the Third World as divided into many wholly civil capitalist governments, all threatened by imminent and desirable revolution and a few wholly good revolutionary societies. Rather we see that nearly all countries have a mixed economy. We are prepared to work with governments of this great mixed group so long as they fall within some very broad limits of decency.[42]

In addition to the numerous crimes supposedly perpetrated by the DAS, the H-R NAC also indicted the Fellows Program as an accessory to American imperialism in the third world. "Research done by the Fellows is in reality information for protecting the status quo, i.e. to keep the United States on the top and to keep capitalism growing."[43] In the view of the H-R NAC, the past and present positions of Fellows Program alumni—including the class of 1970–71—demonstrated the extent to which the Center chose Fellows who were actively engaged in military, economic, and diplomatic efforts to augment the power of the United States and its allies at the expense of underdeveloped countries. In conclusion, the H-R NAC report surmised, "it would therefore seem clear that what is billed as neutral social sciences at Harvard is in fact working against the interests of the people of the Third World. The CFIA instead serves the Kissingers and the Rostows and in doing so perpetuates the mechanism that has created the war in Southeast Asia."[44]

It is true that the majority of CFIA Fellows were from countries allied to the United States, but this does not prove a conspiracy against the interests of the developing world. In addition, the Center leadership constantly strove to find participants from developing countries who would enrich the Center's research.[45] It is likewise true that since its inception the Fellows Program

145

had included members of the U.S. military. But again this in itself does not demonstrate that their contributions to the CFIA were indicative of a nefarious link between the Center and the military-industrial complex. Of course, many of the Center's military Fellows had been involved in one way or another in the American effort in Vietnam, but it would have been especially difficult in the midst of wartime to have found senior military officers who had not been in some way engaged in the prosecution of the Vietnam War. Arguably, the Center would have been remiss toward its basic mandate—to study contemporary problems and issues in international relations—had it not provided a forum for diplomats and professional military officers who had some experience in that war, however unpopular it might have been.

146

Conversely, MacEwan points to the Fellows Program as "the clearest manifestation of a continuing connection to policy, and a very explicit effort to influence policy." The program's involvement in training foreign diplomats and its often understated role in acculturating these government officials to the assumptions and objectives of U.S. foreign policy meant that ultimately the effort was indicative of "universities operating as an extension of the government." It was this interrelationship between the academy and the government that opponents of the CFIA deemed to be inappropriate.[46]

## The CFIA and the War in Vietnam

Whatever the merits of the protest movement's indictments of the Fellows Program and the DAS, the notion that the CFIA was a bastion of support for the Vietnam War—let alone instrumental in its inception and prosecution—was a delusion. As in all other aspects of the Center's research agenda, there was no single Center position on the policy issues of the day, and individual scholars were always free to pursue their research without the Center leadership imposing topics or boundaries. One reason why the Center attracted such negative attention from student activists was the work of Samuel Huntington, who was one of the few CFIA members who, at least initially, supported the American war effort.

Most famously, Huntington chaired the Vietnam subcommittee of the Southeast Asia Development Advisory Group as a consultant to the Johnson administration from 1966 to 1969.[47] He prepared for the State Department a report on the war and U.S. policy, which he subsequently adapted into an article for *Foreign Affairs*.[48] The original report supported the effort to defeat the North Vietnamese and the National Liberation Front (NLF) but questioned the Johnson administration's methods. He called for a politics of "accommodation" in South Vietnam, "in which all significant political groups can participate," including the NLF where necessary. Huntington also advocated a more realistic appreciation for the political conditions within South Vietnam, in which local religious and ethnic allegiances were often paramount.[49] The original report was reportedly so contrary to the Johnson administration's policies in South Vietnam that it was immediately shelved by the White House. Indeed, one administration official apparently noted that "if this study is right, then everything we're doing is wrong."[50] Huntington's call for "accommodation" was largely ignored, however, when a *Foreign Affairs* article based on his original report appeared in July 1968. This disregard was largely because Huntington suggested that the NLF's appeal to the rural South Vietnamese peasantry could be undermined through the employment of "forced-draft urbanization." Such rhetoric was seized upon by many on the Harvard campus, and Huntington was subsequently excoriated. As Robert Putnam later noted, "in the super-heated climate of the times, these passages . . . made him a highly visible target for the anti-war movement."[51]

147

For the most part, however, the CFIA was far from an uncritical intellectual supporter of the federal government and the war effort in Vietnam, as these student protestors alleged. Seven months before the publication of this pamphlet linking the Center to the prosecution of the war in Vietnam, for example, a number of CFIA faculty members along with other senior scholars at Harvard embarked on a trip to Washington, D.C. to meet with their erstwhile colleague, Henry Kissinger, at the White House. This remarkable meeting was widely reported at the time, and demonstrates the extent to which there was no consensus on the issue of the Vietnam War at the CFIA. As documented by the *Crimson*, Schelling organized the group, which included such consummate Harvard "inners and outers" as Richard Neustadt, Francis M. Bator, George Kistiakowsky, Paul Doty, and Ernest May. In addition to Shelling and Doty, Seymour Martin Lipset also attended from the CFIA. It is important to note that their involvement in this endeavor was as individuals and not as Center representatives.

The decision to confront their former colleague, as well as other members of the executive and legislative branches of government, was occasioned by President Nixon's announcement to the nation on April 30, 1970, that the United States and South Vietnam were about to embark on military operations inside Cambodia. As Francis Bator insisted prior to their meeting with Kissinger, the group's intention was to "tell them to get the hell out of Cambodia, stop the idiot bombing, and reaffirm the road being taken in the past to withdraw all troops."[52]

Schelling recalls that the group essentially informed Kissinger that "we were no longer colleagues; we would no longer work with him or talk with him, we had no confidence in him or his administration, and that if we wanted to be influential we would work through senators and congressmen rather than the White House." In essence, he remembers there were "twelve of us boycotting the executive branch."[53] Schelling later related to *Crimson* reporter Mike Kinsley: "We had a very painful hour and a half with Henry, persuading him we were all horrified not just about the Cambodia decision, but what it implied about the way the President makes up his mind. It was a small gain to be had at enormous political risk. [Kissinger] refused to reply on-the-record, therefore he had our sentiments heaped upon him, sat in pained silence, and just listened."[54]

As the group prepared to leave Washington following the conclusion of their meetings, Kinsley was asked to call the *Crimson* office to enquire about the situation at Harvard. He was informed that the CFIA had just been "trashed" by a group of around five hundred students who were on their way to Harvard Square to protest the war. As if to illustrate how mundane such news had become, Lipset apparently replied "I don't leave anything important there anymore. I just hope Schelling remembered to take his stuff out before he came down here yesterday."[55] Apparently the professors' own activism had done little to ameliorate the anger of student protestors who continued to hold the CFIA responsible for the war.

## "The Case for Abolishing the CFIA"

In another effort to mitigate the attacks of radicals, the Center published a pamphlet in September 1970. "Questions and Answers about the Center for International Affairs" was a booklet that addressed some of the accusations student groups had leveled against the CFIA over the previous two years. The publications denied any links between the CFIA and the CIA and pointed out that of ninety-nine books published by the Center only one dealt with Southeast Asia and only one addressed counterinsurgency methods.[56] The Center emphasized that it had never been involved in classified research, nor were CFIA members subject to any pressure from the federal government to respond to the exigencies of U.S. foreign policy. In response to the frequent assertions of imperialism directed against the Fellows Program, the Center cited its inclusion of Fellows from socialist countries and defended the participation of military officers, since their significant experience was relevant to many questions in international affairs. With regard to another target of student radicals, the Center made it clear that the DAS "makes special efforts to ensure that its overseas advisers are independent of the influence of the US government and of foreign investors . . . The DAS teams are international in their composition. No financing of overseas DAS projects comes from the US government or private firms." In addition, the Center argued:

> *DAS advisers often provide assistance in preparing argumentation helping the government being advised to oppose particular US foreign assistance and trade policies and practices. Thus, when analysis has shown that trade with Communist countries would be beneficial, advisers have so advised a host government . . . The DAS has no policy line, either favorable or unfavorable, toward current US government policies or the interests of foreign investors.*[57]

149

Despite publishing this pamphlet, a collection of activists from the Students for a Democratic Society (SDS), the University Action Group (UAG), and the November Action Committee (NAC) denounced the CFIA and its activities again in December 1970. The students own provocatively named pamphlet purported to outline a comprehensive exposé of the Center's complicity in a broader program of U.S. political repression and economic imperialism:

> *Here at Harvard, the CFIA is a particularly blatant example of university complicity with U.S. economic penetration abroad at the expense of oppressed peoples. This pamphlet will attempt to show that the CFIA exists to provide technological and ideological resources for the formulation and implementation of a foreign policy more effective in serving U.S. financial interests; that it was conceived by men in business and government for that very purpose; and that since the Center's inception it has been a tremendous aid to the penetration and domination of the third world by U.S. business.*[58]

"The Case for Abolishing the CFIA" was seen by the students as their "ammunition" for a comprehensive and "militant campaign" to abolish the CFIA. This group's case rested in part upon the specious notion that since some of the key participants in the Center's founding would later occupy important positions in the U.S. foreign policy establishment, then by design the Center must have been devised as an instrument of U.S. foreign policy. McGeorge Bundy, former FAS Dean and future national security advisor to Presidents Kennedy and Johnson, was rightly named as a progenitor of the CFIA, along with Henry Kissinger and Dean Rusk, former president of the

Rockefeller Foundation and future secretary of state in the Kennedy and Johnson administrations. Rusk had long been a State Department official, but his involvement in the foundation of the CFIA was negligible, despite the authors' claims, and prior to 1961 both Kissinger and Bundy had very little government experience. Bowie's involvement, of course, was instrumental, and there is no question that his experience in government service influenced his decision to accept Bundy's invitation to direct the CFIA. He did not, however, conceive of the Center as an appendage of the State Department or the National Security Council. Rather, Bowie always envisioned the CFIA as first and foremost an independent academic research center.

Nevertheless, the group assailed the Center for its involvement in academic research on counterinsurgency warfare, political and economic development, and even linked the CFIA to the March 1964 military coup in Brazil through the personage of former U.S. Ambassador to Brazil and former member of the CFIA Faculty Advisory Committee, Lincoln Gordon.[59] As in the case of previous student protests, the DAS and the Fellows Program were again singled out as particularly odious examples of the Center's complicity in a comprehensive program of U.S. political and economic imperialism in the developing world. In the final analysis, according to the authors, "CFIA researchers know what their research and advice will be used for and they make political decisions affecting the lives and conditions of masses of people every step of the way. They are technicians of imperialist foreign policy and we want to stop them from doing what they do."[60] While opposing the kinds of violent action perpetrated by more extreme groups against the CFIA, these students felt that the Center would have to be the subject of continued strikes, sit-ins, picketing, and petitions in order to ensure its abolition.

## Bombing the CFIA and Bombing North Vietnam

Others, however, were not willing to wait for the cumulative effect of student pamphleteering and protesting to persuade the Harvard administration to abolish the CFIA. In the early morning hours of October 14, 1970, a bomb exploded in a third floor office of 6 Divinity Avenue. The blast ripped through the ceiling and adjacent walls, causing significant damage to offices and the Center's library. Approximately twenty minutes prior to the 1:02 a.m. explosion, the Harvard University Police, the Cambridge Police, and the *Boston Globe* all received an anonymous warning: "This is not a joke. Remember the Brooklyn courthouse and California. Get the janitor out of the building."[61] The blast caused an estimated

150

$25,000 worth of damage to the building and destroyed three offices. The Center's librarian, Maury Feld, announced later that the bomb had caused "miraculously negligible" damage to the Center's collection of books.[62] There was no loss of life in the incident, although police and fire officials were on the first floor of the building at the time of the explosion.[63]

Members of the Center's faculty had already taken to storing important papers at home, though as DAS Director Gustav Papanek remarked, "you can always take papers home, but the real damage has been the general suspicion that has been engendered."[64] Indeed, Feld would later report, "although the bomb was directed at the Center as a whole, the library area was the natural place to plant it because it is both conspicuous and vulnerable: it is open at all times, and people circulate freely." He also noted that "for a week and a half before the bombing, suspicious-looking persons had been observed, taking notes on the names of office doors and loitering about."[65] When the Center library reopened on October 26, all library patrons were subject to a screening process prior to being granted access, a new pass system was introduced for access to the building, and a guard was placed at the front door.[66] The president of the University, Nathan Pusey, also responded to the incident in a press release on the day of the attack. He deplored the bombing as "a senseless attack upon the entire university," and condemned the act as a rejection "of the very foundations of civilization, not only for a university but for all society."[67]

The protests against the CFIA would continue for almost another year and a half, until the student activism began to diminish in conjunction with the abatement of the war in Vietnam. With the exception of another "rampage" through 6 Divinity Avenue in April 1972, the violent protests that had characterized agitation against the Center since the late 1960s waned, and the CFIA continued to operate despite the best efforts of the SDS and the Weathermen to close the Center down.[68]

It is difficult in retrospect to comprehend the animosity with which more radical elements of the student protest movement regarded the activities of the CFIA. The fact that before the student protests members of the Center referred to the institution as the 'CIA' may have led to some confusion. Indeed, once the unfortunate similarity to the other CIA became a liability, the letter "f" was added to the Center's abbreviated moniker. More seriously, on one hand, student antagonism derived in part from a lack of understanding of the CFIA's actual relationship to the policy-making community. Huntington himself recalls of that period:

151

*The general intellectual environment in Cambridge was—I wouldn't want to say hostile—but it was certainly skeptical and often quite antagonistic. And in part that was due to the misconception that we were out there promoting war ... some people at the Center obviously supported the [Vietnam War] and supported various other military involvements of the United States. But it was always as individuals.*

Ultimately, he argues, "most of the images and ideas that people had about the Center were totally misguided. It was really a very quiet place to go and do academic research and participate, most importantly, in discussions and seminars."[69] While there is no question that Center research staff often played a key role in transmitting the insights of their scholarship to policy makers, there was no guarantee that their views and opinions would always find a receptive ear in Washington. Moreover, Center associates were primarily academics and intellectuals, and as such their work was addressed to the broader academic community rather than government agencies.

On the other hand, MacEwan suggests that the Center was in many ways the logical target of student (and indeed faculty) disaffection with the ongoing war in Vietnam. He recalls that despite the relative lack of research emanating from the CFIA on the subject of the war, the Center nevertheless "was viewed as an important backdrop to the policies that were being developed in relation to the war." In particular, the CFIA, and other institutions like it, provided an "intellectual rationalization for what was going on," which in turn legitimated the war and the wider objectives of U.S. foreign policy. In addition, MacEwan notes that institutions such as the CFIA provided a locus for the frustrations of students and others for whom the war was distant and physically removed from their daily experience. As he suggests, "you look for local things to vent on. . . . so [the CFIA] gave local content to people's opposition to the war and became the focal point." In many ways, then, the Center was an available and accessible symbol that represented a surrogate for the U.S. government.[70]

Despite a lull in student protests directed at the CFIA, a third major incident in April 1972 vindicates MacEwan's analysis. In response to the renewal of American bombing raids against North Vietnam during the North's 1972 Easter Offensive, approximately two hundred students left a demonstration in Harvard Square and ransacked the CFIA. According to the *Boston Globe*, "demonstrators broke into the center using the staffs of their banners as battering rams, and raced through the three-storey [sic] building, overturning desks, files, and bookcases. In less than 10 minutes, the inside of the center was in ruins." A small fire was set in the office of CFIA research associate (and future CNN political correspondent) William Schneider. According to a statement by the party responsible for leading the demonstration, "the center has long participated in planning and implementing America's genocidal war against the people of Indochina. As long as the United States continues to devastate Indochina, the American antiwar movement will continue to seek ways to express its solidarity with the victims of our government's policies."[71] In this regard, as MacEwan argues, the Center represented the closest available symbol of U.S. foreign policy, and as such yet again became the focus of student anger and frustration at the policies of the American government.

Ultimately, Bowie had long recognized this as well. As early as 1970 he contended, "these attacks, while disturbing, should be kept in perspective. They clearly have been the work of a very small group of militants, whose real target, as stated in their manifestoes, is the University and the wider society. Most students, including the great part of the critical or disenchanted, have either opposed these actions or dissociated themselves from them." This did not mean, however, that the CFIA could be complacent about the disillusionment that was felt by many students on the Harvard campus. It was clear, he affirmed, that "many moderate students are out of sympathy with United States foreign policy or have little or no interest in foreign affairs." As Bowie argued, however, it was likely that future decades would present equally difficult and significant challenges in international affairs, and in this regard it was an essential role of the CFIA and the University at large to "help students attain the knowledge for understanding and responding to those challenges," despite their antipathy to the principles and assumptions of the current generation of leaders.[72] Although the Center ultimately emerged intact, the experience highlights the potency of late 1960s radicalism and the challenges it posed to the CFIA and its members.

## Nine

# The Challenges and Intellectual Trends of the Second Decade

THE FIRST DECADE OF THE CFIA'S EXISTENCE WAS CHARACTERIZED BY the gradual but nonetheless confident maturation of its objectives, methods, and intellectual output. The veritable surfeit of noteworthy contributions to the various issues under its purview from 1958–68 underlined the extent to which the Center had in many ways fulfilled Bowie's declared mandate of promoting and conducting "fundamental research on long-range problems of international affairs." Indeed, in the short space of ten years, affiliates of the Center had made pioneering contributions to the discussion of myriad pivotal contemporary issues. In subjects as diverse as nuclear arms control and economic development, the work of CFIA members had directly affected government policy in key areas, and shaped the terms of contentious academic debates across the country and around the world. Moreover, the Center's work had played a crucial role in the establishment of international relations as a viable and respected academic discipline.

The years 1968–72, however, had been the most turbulent and destabilizing in the Center's history. Most often, the challenges faced by the Center as an institution during this tumultuous period were external ones. Intellectually, however, there were also a number of important transformations taking place within the Center itself, changes that would lead to a number of far-reaching modifications in the CFIA's research agenda. In addition to the effects of the student protests, issues of reduced funding, changes in personnel, and transformations in the nature of international affairs all coalesced to test the Center's intellectual foundations. In addition, during this period the CFIA circumscribed the policy orientation of its research. In the immediate aftermath of the war in Vietnam this was hardly surprising, but it represented a significant departure from the previous decade.

This is not to say, however, that these challenges and changes were always negative for the CFIA. Intellectually, they stimulated modification and adaptation of the Center's research programs and motivated an extensive renovation of the assumptions, focus, and substance of the CFIA's scholarship. Initially, the three original core research programs had proven supple enough to assimilate a broad range of inquiries and perspectives, but as their primacy began to wane in the late 1960s, new programs had been initiated that impelled the CFIA forward into the 1970s. New approaches to familiar subjects also contributed to the advancement of knowledge and augmented the insights of the more traditional research programs. The growth of the Center's research portfolio during the 1970s was nothing short of prolific, and despite shortages in funding the CFIA remained a vigorous and productive institution. The infusion of new ideas and new scholars injected the Center with a sense of intellectual dynamism, even as it sustained its core of established research programs that continued to yield new findings.

## Catalysts of Change: The Cold War and Intellectual Competition

Internationally, according to then–Acting Director Raymond Vernon, the most important impetus for this changing environment was the dramatically shifting character of the cold war. The old assumptions that had characterized the cold war under Khrushchev and Eisenhower were becoming increasingly sterile and less dependable. The election of Richard Nixon to the presidency of the United States on the promise of ending the seemingly intractable war in Vietnam (and the appointment of former Center faculty member Henry Kissinger as his national security advisor) augured a fundamental change in the way the United States conducted its foreign relations. Furthermore, the promise of détente with the Soviet Union and its allies portended dramatic implications for the conduct of the cold war in Europe and Asia. As Vernon wrote in the Center's annual report in 1968 "there has scarcely been a time in modern history when the future of international relations has been less clear." Whatever else could be said of the terrifying logic of the bipolar struggle in 1958, with the palpable dangers of mutually assured destruction and the escalating nuclear arms race, "one could perhaps observe a certain pattern which at least seemed to offer the hope of durability and continuity."[1] In this analysis, then, the predictability of rival political, military, and economic power blocs, and the stultifying but familiar patterns of American and Soviet diplomacy, provided a comprehensible paradigm within which to study and respond to the exigencies of Soviet-American relations. The initial endeavors of the CFIA, Vernon noted, had been premised upon the imperatives of the international situation as it had existed in 1957, but in 1968 "the setting for international affairs that existed a decade ago has, however, been nearly erased."[2]

The nature of academic inquiry was also evolving, Vernon noted, but the Center was uniquely equipped to adapt to new questions and methodologies. Trends toward interdisciplinary investigation were intensifying, and Center associates had long been attuned to this form of research. At the same time, specialization within academic disciplines was also increasing, and the CFIA was equally well-placed to benefit from developments in scholarship, which promised "an even stronger and more important role for an institution such as the Center, prepared without inhibition to draw on the disciplines or straddle them if necessary to achieve understanding."[3]

Another function of this seemingly paradoxical trend toward grow-ing specialization coupled with the increased emphasis on interdisciplinary research was the emergence at Harvard of several new institutions, which were also "examining some of the problems with which the Center has long been concerned." The Committee on Latin American Studies (which later became the David R. Rockefeller Center for Latin American Studies) and the Institute of Politics at the John F. Kennedy School of Government were both founded during the first decade of the CFIA's existence, and in many ways their emergence threatened to undermine the Center's predominance as Harvard's focal point for international affairs research. Vernon remained sanguine that the Center would continue to thrive in this increasingly competitive atmosphere, since the CFIA had always projected a broader scope of inquiry, and had never limited itself to a single geographic or analytical focus. Indeed, greater competition also meant greater possibilities for cooperation, which could only enrich the collective intellectual output. The expectation that a new building complex to be constructed near the banks of the Charles River in Cambridge would afford the CFIA new neighbors—other area studies centers and the Kennedy School of Government—gave further cause for optimism.[4]

Despite the myriad challenges confronting the Center in 1968, Vernon confidently predicted that the CFIA as an organic and flexible community of scholars was alert to the potential difficulties it faced and would successfully navigate the transition from the first decade to the second. Indeed, the very strengths that had contributed to its growth over the previous ten years would assure its continued vitality and dynamism in the future.

## Facilities and Finances

Other changes were beginning to manifest themselves in that year, however, which would have an equally significant impact on the future of the Center. For one thing, as the Center expanded its operations over the course of the first decade it had by necessity become a far more scattered and expansive institution, both intellectually and physically. One of the implications of this diffusion was that the Center's activities and associates were spread among a number of different buildings in the vicinity of 6 Divinity Avenue. For all the shortcomings of the Center's physical space on Divinity Avenue, the premises had the virtue of facilitating the kind of unplanned and impromptu circulation of ideas that often engendered innovation. Now, however, as Bowie lamented in 1969, "one consequence [of diffusion] has been to hamper this spontaneous interaction and to make the Center less cohesive and stimulating than it would be if it were located in a single building."[5]

Perhaps more importantly, the decade-long financial support of the major foundations was beginning to wane, and as Bowie intimated, the Center would have to begin to look elsewhere for the bulk of its funding. From 1958 to 1969, he reported that 70 percent of the Center's income had come from the foundations, with the Ford Foundation providing almost half of the CFIA's overall financial capital. This compared with just 13.2 percent from the University and the Center's endowment, with the balance coming mostly from individual government agencies such as the Department of Defense and USAID for specific contracted research. The prospect of a reduction in foundation spending on international affairs was therefore viewed with a certain degree of apprehension. As Bowie mused, "we are convinced that the needs for research and training in the international field are as great as or greater than in the past. It would be most regrettable if the capacities which have been created at Harvard and elsewhere to serve these needs were allowed to wither from lack of essential resources."[6]

By June 1970, for example, Bowie reported that the Center's most recent five-year grant from the Ford Foundation had expired. The CFIA had relied heavily on this funding for the previous ten years, and in its absence it was becoming more difficult to secure financial support from both private and governmental sources. Bowie reported, for example, that "according to one estimate, the total of private grants of $10,000 or more for 'international studies' has declined from a high of $50 million in 1966 to only about $7.5 million in 1969. Federal support for foreign affairs research has fallen from a peak of $40.6 million in 1967 to about $33 million in 1969," and, ominously for the Center, the most precipitous cuts in federal funding were evident in the State Department, USAID, and ACDA.[7] The philanthropic foundations were increasingly diverting their funding toward domestically oriented social, cultural, and educational programs, and largely eschewed international studies by the early 1970s. The CFIA would now have to rely on private contributions and individual grants to a far greater extent in order to fund its programs over the coming decade.

## Personnel

Another important catalyst for change at the CFIA in evidence by 1969 was the beginning of a notable transformation in personnel. Edward Mason retired from the University at the end of the 1968–69 academic year and consequently resigned his position on the Center's executive committee, although he would remain a consultant to the DAS, which he had created in 1962. In addition, Henry Kissinger left the CFIA and the University to become President Nixon's national security advisor. Though this was not apparent at the time of his departure, his absence from Harvard would become permanent in 1973, and he would remain in government service until 1977.[8] Alex Inkeles also left Harvard in 1971 to become the Margaret Jacks Professor of Sociology and Education at Stanford University. He had been an integral part of the Center since 1961, and his research on the social and cultural aspects of development in modern industrial societies and developing countries was among some of the most groundbreaking work conducted at the CFIA during the first decade.

Three years later at the end of 1972, Bowie resigned his post as Center Director after fifteen years to "have time for writing and other activities."[9] As he reflected upon his tenure, Bowie lauded the many achievements of the previous decade and a half and looked forward to the continued challenges and changes that in his view would require the constant and vigorous application of intellect. He was adamant that the CFIA remain as relevant and engaged as it had been for the previous fifteen years, despite the twin challenges of reduced funding and the rapidly transforming international system. As he prepared to depart, Bowie remarked with characteristic sagacity:

> *Fifteen years have reinforced my own conviction that programs like that of
> the Center are indispensable. In that period, it has become apparent that the
> problems of international order are even more complex, the pace of change more
> rapid, and the scope of change much broader than we had earlier realized. The
> capacity to cope must still rest on fundamental knowledge and analysis which
> governments are not equipped to provide. For that need, I see no alternative to
> mobilizing the intellectual resources of the universities. It is essential that these
> problems continue to attract the interest of first-rate minds and the substantial
> funding required by their importance and urgency.*[10]

Nevertheless, the Center remained in capable hands, as Bowie was quick to point out. Raymond Vernon, who had been associated with the Center since 1960, took over the directorship with Samuel Huntington taking on the role of associate director. Indeed, notwithstanding the aforementioned losses in personnel, the continuing presence of Schelling, Vernon, Huntington, Hoffmann, Doty, Nye, Lipset (and of course Bowie himself, who remained an active participant in the Center's activities) ensured that the Center retained a largely stable and prosperous intellectual core, along with numerous longstanding research associates and affiliates.

In addition, the CFIA had assembled an excellent administrative staff that provided stability and purpose as the Center evolved. Benjamin Brown continued in his role as advisor to the Fellows Program, a position he had held since 1961. His association with the Center began in 1960 after two years as vice president of the American University in Beirut. Brown was initially the executive secretary, but he also provided steady leadership wherever it was needed at the CFIA, including administering Center programs and even the Center itself temporarily in 1978. Former vice president of the Carnegie Endowment, Lawrence Finkelstein, was secretary to the Center in the fall of 1969, and in this capacity he served as the Center's business manager and steward of the Center's financial and administrative needs. Maury Feld also continued in his role as Center librarian, a position he had held since the inception of the CFIA in 1958.

## "Twice-Removed from Policy Concerns"

Amid the many challenges the Center faced in the post-Vietnam period, one posed a particularly important question regarding the Center's identity. Though it was always conceived to be an academic research center, there is no question that during the first decade the Center conducted a far greater degree of its research with an eye toward policy. By 1968, however, this concern with policy making had come to be regarded by many in American society as an abdication of responsibility on the part of academics and intellectuals. With regard to the Vietnam War, many (especially on the Left) believed America's academics were culpable, either in their failure to speak out against the war or in their intellectual justifications for what many regarded to be a tragedy. In the aftermath of the war, the Center's ties to the policy-making community would never again be as far-reaching as during the 1960s.

As Arthur MacEwan astutely points out, another reason for this withdrawal from the policy sphere was the fact that Republican administrations were in office from 1969 to 1977.[11] Center associates had traditionally been drawn to the Democratic administrations of Kennedy and Johnson; predictably, Huntington, Nye, and indeed even Bowie all entered government service under the Democratic Carter administration.[12] Two new developments—the migration of the DAS to a University-wide initiative in 1974 and the creation of the Center for Science and International Affairs in 1978—further curtailed the Center's involvement in policy-making roles. Indeed, the first director of the CSIA, Paul Doty, recalls that because of its significant policy orientation, the PSIA "was not very comfortable in the Faculty of Arts and Sciences, with its more academic outlook."[13] In addition, a new generation of scholars arrived and many original core faculty members departed, severing many of the personal ties between the CFIA and the Washington foreign policy establishment.

The extent of this elision is evident in Huntington's 1976 observation that the Center was "twice-removed from policy concerns."[14] He compared the CFIA with independent research institutions such as the RAND Corporation, the Brookings Institution, and the Council on Foreign Relations, "which focus almost exclusively on public policy issues, but which attempt to deal with those issues in greater analytical and historical depth than they can normally be treated in government." Huntington argued that University research centers were different, however, and the CFIA was somewhere between the two. If academic institutions were primarily concerned with issues "almost entirely of a theoretical, historical, and scholarly nature," then "the Center for International Affairs has carved out a niche for itself somewhere to the policy side of this latter group of institutions."[15]

Some members of the Center's visiting committee questioned the CFIA's apparent withdrawal from avowedly policy-relevant research. As one commit-tee member asked of the Center's purpose in 1973: "Is it to conduct research on long-term questions of policy significance? Or is it to conduct pure research aimed at theoretical knowledge in international relations? If it is the former—as I believe it should be—then a much more obvious test of policy recommendations must be applied to all Center projects."[16] The Center's shift toward more theoretical research was not entirely unwelcome. In his response to the visiting committee's suggestion for imposing policy-relevance tests, Center faculty member Jorge I. Domínguez wrote to Huntington: "it views the Center as if it were no more than a research arm of the U.S. government, perhaps as an addition or alternative to Brookings." This, in his view, was not the appropriate model for the CFIA. Rather, Domínguez argued, "I prefer to define the Center as an independent institution concerned with fundamental research on international affairs . . . that research may or may not have immediate policy relevance . . . this is principally an academic institution, and it should be judged accordingly."[17] The Center's ambiguous relationship to policy had attracted a great deal of criticism during the student protests of the late 1960s; now the CFIA was attracting criticism from its own visiting committee for not being sufficiently policy oriented.

## A New International Order, a New Intellectual Order

There is no question, however, that the very real world of international affairs had an effect on the research conducted by the Center. Vernon assumed the directorship of the CFIA in January 1973 amid tectonic shifts in the suppositions that had heretofore underpinned the Center's research agenda. Indeed, Vernon's outlook had not changed significantly since his earlier time as acting director five years before: "For anyone who is concerned with the course of international affairs, these are times of extraordinary confusion."[18] The problem remained an epistemological one, Vernon thought, in that "some of the bedrock propositions that represented the conventional wisdom of the 1950's and 1960's have lost their solidity and persuasiveness. The elaborate structure of analysis and policy based on that conventional wisdom will no longer serve." This problem was exacerbated as far as the CFIA was concerned because " . . . not much in the way of guiding assumptions has yet taken the place of the earlier framework."[19]

Vernon was confident, however, that the Center's research staff shared a number of assumptions upon which the continued progress of the CFIA could be predicated. First, he was certain of a consensus that "the shrinkage of space and the growth of contact among the nations of the globe will surely continue. As a result, the opportunities for cooperation and the occasions for conflict among nations will also grow." What was new about this development,

Vernon averred, was that in the past this "prognosis would conjure up visions of generals and diplomats, maneuvering and countermaneuvering to press their national advantages against the others." Now, he contended, the traditional concerns of military officials and ambassadors were yielding to other domestic considerations with international implications such as "income distribution, employment discrimination, inflation, lagging regions, social services, ethnic identity, and the quality of the environment." Moreover, how nations chose to resolve these issues had potential repercussions for their neighbors: "more and more," he observed, "the line of demarcation between national affairs and international affairs has lost its meaning."

Vernon also noted that the primacy of the state in international affairs was gradually being eroded by the proliferation of intergovernmental and nongovernmental international institutions such as the World Health Organization (WHO) and the International Monetary Fund (IMF).[20] One of the cumulative effects of these developments had particular implications for research centers such as the CFIA: "Paradoxically, the decline in the distinction between domestic and international affairs and the penetration of national institutions into the economies of their neighbors may well have been responsible in part for reducing the general interest in the formal study of international affairs."[21] With all this in mind, Vernon expected that under his tenure of leadership the CFIA would begin—or rather continue—to address these issues and explore their impact on international affairs.

Indeed, as Vernon indicated, the Center had already begun to expand its purview over the course of the previous five years. The CFIA was embarked on an evolutionary process to inculcate the realities of the changing international system into its research program. Indeed, an emerging nexus of new and innovative research initiatives was in evidence by as early as 1969. The work of Seymour Martin Lipset, the George D. Markham Professor of Government and Sociology, exemplified the new directions that were increasingly apparent at the Center as the new decade began. Lipset had already conducted pioneering research on social mobility in industrial societies, and his 1960 study *Political Man: The Social Bases of Politics* was a landmark comparative study on the social and political dynamics of democracy.[22] By the mid-1960s Lipset had turned his discerning eye toward the materializing student protest movements with his 1965 study *The Berkeley Student Revolt*, and in 1969, together with Philip G. Altbach, he edited a collection of essays entitled *Students in Revolt*.[23] The United States was not the only subject of research, however, and by 1972 the Center was hosting a growing number of scholars who were working on comparative studies of student attitudes and protest movements ranging from Latin America to India to Africa. By 1974 this remarkably fertile project, sponsored by the CFIA and the Hazen Foundation, had produced twelve books, four bibliographies, and a profusion of articles.[24]

In addition to research on the dynamics of student protest movements, Lipset also embarked on a larger project, together with a number of Center research associates, oriented toward producing "long-range comparative studies of the place of intellectuals and universities in their political societies."[25] In conjunction with the Carnegie Commission on Higher Education, Lipset and his collaborators conducted a questionnaire-based study of sixty thousand professors, designed to elicit insights into the relationship between politics and intellectuals in a number of developed countries. This research was further expanded in 1972 when Lipset joined with Harvard sociology professor Daniel Bell. Funded by a grant from the National Endowment for the Humanities, Bell and Lipset inaugurated a new study and research seminar on intellectual behavior and social organization in Great Britain, France, Japan, and the United States.[26]

## International Order and Transnational Relations

In the fall of 1969 the Center also initiated a new program on international order, led by Nye, who had just completed work on his study *Peace in Parts: Integration and Conflict in Regional Organization*.[27] In many ways, this project represented the recrudescence of an earlier proposal Bowie had included in the Center's original research agenda. The program on international order was designed "to study questions of international organization as they are affected by shifting patterns of international relationships . . . The conditions for international order cannot fail to evolve in response to rapidly changing relationships among nations, institutions, private organizations and transnational movements which comprise the international system." The significance of this program derived in large part from its attention to the role of nonstate actors in international affairs, and their interaction with both each other and the international governmental organizations.

Center Research Associate Karl Kaiser had already begun a theoretical analysis of this subject and had published "Transnational Politics: Towards a Theory of Multinational Politics" in the German journal *Politische Vierteljahresschrift* in 1969 that was subsequently printed in *International Organization* two years later. Kaiser highlighted the theoretical inadequacy of international relations theory in relation to the reality of the international system, in which the predominance of state actors was increasingly being eroded by the growing autonomy of nonstate actors. Kaiser presented a theoretical model that sought to remedy this deficiency by identifying three possible conduits of multinational politics: "multibureaucratic decisionmaking, integration, and transnational politics."[28] The last received the majority of his attention. In his 1971 article "Transnational Relations as a Threat to the Democratic Process," Kaiser was also the first to emphasize the potential difficulty posed by this manifestation of international politics: "The intermeshing of decisionmaking across national frontiers and the growing multinationalization of formerly domestic issues are inherently incompatible with the traditional framework of democratic control."[29] His work was an early articulation of what would become one of the most intellectually profitable endeavors ever undertaken by the CFIA.

The first major undertaking convened by the new International Order program was a three-day gathering of scholars in the summer of 1970. Interdisciplinary in scope, the meeting's focus was to plan and discuss a forthcoming volume to be published as a special issue in the summer of 1971 by the journal *International Organization*. As editor of this project, Nye was joined by Robert Keohane of Swarthmore College, and the two presided over a series of discussions that "covered the dynamics of transnational processes, transnational actors as international organizations, transnational processes with respect to representative international issues, and transnational processes and values."[30]

The program got off to an auspicious start, attracting seventeen scholars from around the United States to contribute to the initial *International Organization* volume. In addition, the program attracted funding from the Carnegie Endowment for International Peace, the Ford Foundation, and the Fund for Peace. This collection of essays was subsequently published as *Transnational Relations and World Politics* and remains a benchmark for scholars investigating the contours and implications of transnational actors in international affairs.[31]

This resulting collection of essays challenged the conventional notion that the state was the dominant actor in international affairs, and Nye recalls that "the Center played a very important role in making that possible" by providing an intellectual space that removed the boundaries among academic disciplines and departments.[32] Keohane and Nye employed the term "transnational interactions" to describe "the movement of tangible or intangible items across state boundaries when at least one actor is not an agent of a government or an intergovernmental organization."[33] The volume considered a wide range of actors who might conceivably engage in "transnational interactions," and contained essays on the roles of multinational corporations, philanthropic foundations, revolutionary groups, the Roman Catholic Church, labor organizations, airlines, and even agencies involved in exploration and resource management of the oceans or outer space. The authors demonstrated the validity of the approach by utilizing this expansive conception of transnational actors and their roles in international affairs and by addressing central questions pertaining to the relationship of these movements and organizations with both governments and one another.

Armed with these innovative and probing essays, Keohane and Nye speculated that the "classic state-centric paradigm" of international affairs was inadequate. They questioned the supposition of those who privileged the state in their analysis of international relations, and highlighted the ways in which states were subject to pressure—and sometimes competition—from nonstate transnational actors. "We seek to challenge basic assumptions that underlie the analysis of international relations"; in their view a "world-politics paradigm" had not only significant academic import but also policy formulation implications.[34]

The size and scope of the International Order program grew exponentially over the coming year, and it soon rivaled the three original research initiatives in both size and ability to attract research associates. The Nye and Keohane volume spawned a study group that met to discuss further aspects of transnational relations, including the role of foreign correspondents and the development of Concorde. The program's vitality was further bolstered by scholars from outside Harvard—including Alan Henrikson from the Fletcher School of Law and Diplomacy, Harrison Wagner from the University of Texas, Peter Evans from Brown University, and John Ruggie from the University of California at Berkeley[35]—and it continued to succeed in attracting funding from a number of foundations, including the Ford Foundation, the Johnson Foundation, and the Inter-University Consortium for World Order Studies.[36]

In 1974 the program evolved again, due in large part to a grant from the Rockefeller Foundation. It retained the most salient features of the earlier project but was recast under the rubric of "Transnational Processes and Institutions" under the leadership of Nye, Huntington, and Vernon. This program reorientation enabled the CFIA to subsume a number of related activities under the joint leadership of these three faculty members, which brought a greater degree of coherence to the Center's efforts in the rapidly emerging field of transnational relations. According to that year's annual report, "starting from the common premise that interstate harmony, political development, and the equitable allocation of economic resources are desirable political goals, this project analyzes the effect transnational actors have on the capacity of societies, individually and collectively, to achieve such objectives." Under the auspices of this new guise, Huntington assumed responsibility for leading the investigation into the role of transnational actors in national development, Nye led the Center's endeavors in interstate harmony and conflict, and Vernon took control of overseeing the economic aspects of the question.[37] The project continued to attract visiting scholars from around the country and from abroad, including researchers from Denver, Washington state, New York state, and Northern Ireland. The Center also embarked upon a new study that sought to unravel the various international and transnational processes that had instigated the recent oil crisis.[38] The Center published its findings in a special issue of *Daedalus* in 1975, which was subsequently published in book form the following year.

This new enterprise was one of the most significant and productive activities initiated by the CFIA since its inception in 1958. It vindicated the ways in which the Center nurtured innovative research agendas, and justified the Center's interdisciplinary, and consolidating, approach to individual and group research:

> The ... transnational program serves as a paradigm of the generative nature
> of Center research. It was notable for the variety of research interests it
> comprised, its members working on such subjects as the internal problems of
> the European Community, the nature of East-West economic relations, and
> the interaction of the industrialized and developing worlds. The three main
> participants, who also directed the program, Professors Huntington, Nye,
> and Vernon, discovered that their originally independent research interests,
> respectively, political modernization, supranational economic agencies, and
> multinational corporations, converged on the problem of transnational actors ...
> This convergence, rather than narrowing the nature of the subject, provided the
> participants with a conceptual focus encompassing an expanding number of
> international phenomena.[39]

The following year was exceptional in the number of monographs that came to fruition under the auspices of this program. Huntington, along with Michel Crozier and Joji Watanuki, published *The Crisis of Democracy*, which derived from a report to the Trilateral Commission on the governability of democracies. This famous study explored what the authors perceived to be a general pessimism surrounding the continued sustainability of democratic forms of government in the United States, Japan, and Western Europe. This pessimism was a function of the myriad social, political, cultural, and economic challenges that assailed democracies on a constant basis. In the authors' words, "this combination of challenges seems to create a situation in which the needs for longer-term and more broadly formulated purposes and priorities, for a greater overall coherence of policy, appear at the same time that the increasing complexity of the social order, increasing political pressures on government, and decreasing legitimacy of government make it more and more difficult for government to achieve these goals."[40]

168

That same year, Nye and Keohane completed their second collaborative manuscript, *Power and Interdependence: World Politics in Transition,* which presented a new theoretical approach to international relations that integrated the authors' accumulated insights into the role and influence of transnational actors. They challenged the dominant realist paradigm of international relations and sought to elucidate the impact of increasing interdependence on international affairs. In addition, they hoped to provide an understanding of the cause and nature of change in international regimes, or the rules, organizations, and institutions by which international politics are conducted.[41] Nye and Keohane then applied their conceptual framework to two arenas in which interdependence and transnational relations were inextricably linked with the construction and alteration of international regimes: international financial mechanisms and the issue of "free seas."

In contrast to realist assumptions about the primacy of the state, the primacy of force, and the primacy of military affairs, they posited an alternative model of international affairs dubbed "complex interdependence." Nye and Keohane's alternative theory suggested that relations between and among states are often conducted through "multiple channels," and not just by governments and their direct representatives. This included both "nongovernmental elites" and transnational organizations of various types. Secondly, military and security affairs are not necessarily the prevailing or most dominant issue with which states are concerned. Finally, they challenged the realist claim that "force is a usable and effective instrument of policy." According to Nye and Keohane, there are circumstances in which force might not be a "usable and effective" policy among or between members of alliances, cohabitants of geographic regions, or adversaries, usually in situations of complex interdependence.[42]

As the Center's annual report asserted in 1976, these studies were "little more than the tip of the iceberg." The program continued to prosper throughout the 1970s, and in addition to facilitating the completion of monographs, articles, dissertations, and working papers, the CFIA also hosted a wide array of conferences, workshops, symposia, and study groups, all of which contributed to a flourishing and lively debate on the role and influence of transnational actors in international affairs.[43]

## The Program for Science and International Affairs

The Program for Science and International Affairs was initiated in 1973 as a result of a seven-year Ford Foundation grant under the leadership of the Mallinckrodt Professor of Biochemistry and longtime arms control advocate, Paul Doty. It not only revived the Center's pioneering research program on nuclear arms control but also expanded the CFIA's research in international security issues. This multidisciplinary program integrated insights from the natural, social, and behavioral sciences, "with particular attention to the interaction of technology and politics." As the program's first annual report stated in 1974, "its major focus is the study and understanding of arms control and disarmament and the part these can play in reducing the dependence on force in world politics."[44]

In addition to the immediate restoration of the Harvard-MIT Joint Arms Control Seminar, the Program for Science and International Affairs also instituted a joint Harvard-MIT Faculty Seminar on International Technology, which at the outset focused on the technology implications of the oceans in international politics: fishing rights, oil and natural gas exploration, and the rights of developing nations. The PSIA also developed a relationship with Harvard's Institute of Politics in the form of a seminar series on détente and arms control.

The program quickly garnered a reputation for both the quality of its research and for its new scholarly journal, *International Security*. By 1976 the program was beginning to think beyond the confines of arms control and a more expansive research agenda began to take shape. PSIA addressed issues of security in Europe and the Middle East, and offered a popular Harvard College course called "Technology, War and Peace." A pilot project was also initiated that brought journalists to Harvard from around the world in order to provide an immersion program in issues related to arms control and international security.[45]

The following year the Ford Foundation provided four million dollars to help transform the PSIA into a research center in its own right, to be housed in the John F. Kennedy School of Government upon its completion in September 1978. In addition to the continued emphasis on nuclear arms

169

control and disarmament, the new center also set out to address related issues such as "the benefits and risks attendant to the growing use of nuclear materials in power generation, the international competition for energy resources and the likelihood of conflict stemming from this competition, and the impact of national sciences policies on international efforts to deal with global problems."[46] From its origins in the Harvard-MIT Joint Arms Control Seminar, the CSIA would become the second major CFIA initiative, after the DAS, to become an institution at Harvard. In many ways its departure represented the last remnant of the Center's original core research program, but its success was testament to both the validity and continued relevance of Bowie's vision and the faculty and research associates that had produced such a remarkable torrent of literature on the subject of arms control almost twenty years before.

## The Twentieth Anniversary: Optimistically Pessimistic

In 1978 the Center's acting director, Benjamin Brown, reflected upon the twentieth anniversary of the founding of the CFIA.[47] In recounting the evolution of the Center's research programs over the previous two decades, he highlighted the CFIA's many contributions to both scholarship and the University. In the context of the original research agenda, Brown noted, the Center's research output had been especially significant in both quantity and substance. He recognized, however, that the challenges of the second decade had undermined many of the assumptions and principles upon which the Center's research agenda was based, necessitating modifications and transformations in the Center's programs. One thing had not changed, however, Brown observed: "The basic commitment was, and is, to investigate underlying processes of change in international affairs."[48] Ultimately, he contended, despite the many challenges the Center had faced in the previous ten years, the CFIA continued to thrive. "It shows none of the telltale signs of aging, the flabby tone and sluggish responses that warn of institutional decay. On the contrary, it is bursting with energy and ideas."

The twentieth anniversary report certainly vindicated Brown's optimism, and demonstrated the continued vitality of an institution that had weathered the storms of the last decade and was seeking new avenues of inquiry in an uncertain age. But it was also clear to Brown, as it was to many others, that the CFIA's once well-defined and well-balanced research agenda was now far more diffuse and variegated.

*The Center's program is more differentiated, more nuanced than it was two decades, or even one decade ago. It reflects the world as we perceive it today. Seen as a whole, the program is also less structured than before. This is perhaps not the best time for the hedgehog, who seeks to know a big thing. It is preeminently a time for foxes, who know many things.*

*Yet recurringly, an institution like the Center must seek a thematic structure in some sort of conceptual framework, however tentative it must be in the uncertain state of our art and times. The very search itself helps to fix boundaries, locate critical issues, and define priorities. It helps us to know and declare what we at the Center collectively are, and what we intend.*[49]

Despite the lack of such thematic structures, Brown was confident that the CFIA would endure and continue to contribute to the study of international affairs. "The Center's flexibility, its capacity for innovation, and the multiple strengths that it has developed in responding to profound and persistent change equip it to play a significant role in what promises to be a new flowering of international studies at Harvard and generally throughout the country in the years ahead."[50]

The Center's "capacity for innovation" was nowhere more evident than during the second decade. In addition to Lipset's project on student protestors and intellectuals, and Nye and Keohane's program on transnationalism, the scope and promise of the 1970s research agenda was broad and invigorating. The Center's work on international conflict resolution, begun in 1976 with a grant from the Lilly Endowment, was indicative of this new and innovative approach to international relations. Under the leadership of Harvard Law School professor Roger Fisher, the Center tackled problems as seemingly intractable as the conflict in Northern Ireland, apartheid in South Africa, and Muslim-Christian relations in Lebanon. The so-called Devising Seminar provided a focal point for cross-cultural and interdisciplinary appraisals of such issues and brought together participants from around the world to discuss the myriad sources of discord that perpetuated some of the world's most intransigent conflicts. The seminar provided a forum for possible solutions and approaches to conflict resolution, and proved to be a remarkably inventive and flexible tool.[51]

The Arab-Israeli conflict formed the focus of another Center seminar led by the Richard Clarke Cabot Professor of Social Ethics Herbert C. Kelman. Kelman probed the numerous facets of this conflict in conjunction with a number of visiting associates and collaborators, and his pioneering work on the social and psychological aspects of the Middle East conflict produced some of the most perceptive, sensitive, and important contributions to the potential resolution of this internecine conflict.[52] The Center also began to address the implications of America's oil dependency—brought into sharp relief following the first oil crisis in 1973 and compounded by the 1979 Iranian revolution. Jorge I. Domínguez's Latin American Seminar and the Center's North-South International Relations Seminar further expanded the purview of the CFIA's research agenda, demonstrating the extent to which the Center had broadened its horizons since 1958. The Center remained actively engaged in the study of American foreign policy, however, under the guise of various workshops, seminars, and programs concerned with aspects of the U.S. role in the world and its relationships with allies and adversaries alike.

## The Klitgaard Report

Despite Brown's certitude in the CFIA's continued relevance and significance at the University and beyond, another challenge emerged at the end of the decade, this time from within the University itself. The expanded scope of the Center's research programs that he saw as a strength were just as likely to be viewed by some as a liability. In 1979 Harvard undertook a comprehensive investigation of international and area studies at the University. The resulting report became known as the Klitgaard Report after its author, Robert Klitgaard, an associate professor of public policy at the John F. Kennedy School of Government who was also serving as a special assistant to President Bok. The CFIA was by no means the only international research center under scrutiny, but the Center did attract some of the most scathing criticism.

In general terms, Klitgaard identified two major problems that potentially undermined Harvard's international efforts and therefore in his view warranted a closer examination by the University administration. In the first place, he noted a lack of coordination across the University, which in turn inhibited the effectiveness of Harvard's international programs and research centers. In addition, Klitgaard concluded that the level of planning at most of the University's research centers was woefully inadequate. Klitgaard's interviews with faculty members who were engaged in both researching and teaching international issues at Harvard revealed something quite striking: "how little they [the faculty] seemed to have thought about the objectives of their institutions, the priorities for the next few years, and even the most immediate concrete needs."[53] In essence, the basic problem was that "in a word, few of Harvard's international activities have well-specified objectives and plans, and across activities there are few functioning mechanisms for coordination or the establishment of priorities."[54]

This unorganized condition was particularly troubling in the context of Harvard's desire to maintain its preeminence in the field, Klitgaard argued, especially given the abiding importance of international studies at home and abroad. The University would need to address some fundamental questions regarding its efforts in international and area studies in order to remedy these shortcomings.

> *Harvard's international activities are a national resource, in some cases a world resource. But in a time of downward trends in external support for such activities, and at a time where growing global interdependence suggests to some that Harvard should become more truly a world university, it is worthwhile to reconsider the current, atomistic, uncoordinated system. How do the varied activities serve the central purposes of the University? Are there opportunities for strengthening, coordinating, or combining (or recasting, deemphasizing, or eliminating) certain international activities?*[55]

Klitgaard's remarks echo the many challenges Vernon had identified ten years before about the CFIA, and Klitgaard's pessimism seemed to illustrate that the Center and its institutional colleagues had not in fact resolved many of these problems. For example, Klitgaard recognized what many within the CFIA had observed at the beginning of the decade: the desiccation of financial support from the major philanthropic foundations was an unfortunate external contributor to the situation in which Harvard's international research centers now found themselves. Klitgaard went further, however, and suggested that the relatively easy access to research funds in the 1960s—coupled with the relatively uncomplicated international milieu—had led to a degree of intellectual and financial complacency among the University's research centers:

> *Many of the international research centers evolved in a time when money was plentiful and the intellectual agendas relatively clear. Under such circumstances, systematic planning and management was not essential. Fifteen or twenty years later, most observers note a change in the external environment. Funds and enrollments are in decline. In most areas of international research, the previous, rather straightforward views of the intellectual problems have given way to perceptions of increasing complexity, even confusion.*[56]

Klitgaard was optimistic, however, that his study might compel donors to reconsider their reluctance to fund international programs by demonstrating that the effort was still important, and the University was responding to the real and perceived shortcomings of its research endeavors. "Nationally, a University-wide review might have an important effect on the policies of governmental agencies and philanthropies—particularly when . . . so many national reviews and attempts to rethink international studies are underway."[57]

It was in this context that the CFIA came under inspection. Klitgaard began his assessment by acknowledging the Center's many achievements in the previous twenty years: "The Center for International Affairs, founded in 1958, has been called a powerhouse of international research. It has ranged widely and deeply . . . Indeed, in some respects the Center was key to the founding of both arms control and economic development as subfields of academic inquiry."[58] This success was seen as a function of several factors that allowed the Center to maintain its preeminence at the University and beyond:

174

> In the 1960's, the Center could be characterized with a string of descriptors: a clear mission with a strong link to U.S. policy, great people in relatively large numbers, intellectual novelty and coherence, no competition elsewhere at Harvard, relative isolation within the University (especially from students), and an exclusive focus on research.[59]

By the end of the 1970s, however, based on his interviews with those around the Center and the University, Klitgaard argued that the situation had dramatically reversed, to the detriment of the CFIA and its research output:

> Today, it would be an exaggeration but one with a point to turn those descriptors around. The Center no longer has a clear mission and an increasing amount of its work is not linked to U.S. policy. It has a distinguished staff, but according to some the numbers are not as great. Where there is intellectual novelty, some believe there is also a lack of coherence. Along some dimensions CFIA now has competitors: CSIA, HIID, and the revitalized School of Government. The Center itself has displayed an increasing interest in graduate students, undergraduates, and continuing education.[60]

The notion that the CFIA now lacked a clear institutional and intellectual identity was a recurring theme in comments made by Center affiliates interviewed by Klitgaard. For example, one unidentified member of the CFIA remarked, "our problem here at the CFIA is clear to me each fall, when I try to explain to our Fellows what it is we do here. We are not addressing the central issues of foreign policy, but doing lots of fragmented stuff, interesting work here on the Middle East, there on multinationals, but it doesn't cohere. We need a grand scheme."[61] For Klitgaard, comments such as these represented a pattern among CFIA members, who often articulated a "widespread, though certainly not unanimous, sense of the need for a more coherent intellectual agenda." According to Klitgaard's interlocutors, such comments stood in vivid contrast to their perceptions of the CFIA in the previous decade, when the Center possessed a more articulate and manageable core research agenda.[62] In addition, Klitgaard noted the occasionally pessimistic appraisals contained in the CFIA's annual reports in the 1970s, especially those of Vernon and Brown in 1972 and 1978, respectively. Based on these assessments, Klitgaard proffered that as the Center's purview had expanded:

175

> *what was gained in vitality was lost in coherence and collegiality. Each new field of investigation was a full-time occupation for somebody. The right hand no longer knew, or always seemed so much to care, what the left hand was doing. Outsiders, and some insiders, described the Center as more supermarket than specialty shop. A former colleague, returning after some years, summed up his impressions in a pun that echoed Yeats. "Things fall apart. The Center will not hold."[63]*

The CFIA's fortune seemingly stood in sharp contrast to that of one of its most thriving progeny, the CSIA. According to Klitgaard, the CSIA "is widely seen as a successful institution. A relative newcomer founded only in 1973, it has already attained national stature."[64] Its avowed policy orientation, integrated research agenda, emphasis on science and technology, and "sheer volume of output" apparently distinguished the CSIA from its erstwhile parent institution, and in this regard it stood out as a success during a period when similar institutions were seen to be in decline.[65]

The situation was not entirely negative for the CFIA, however, and Klitgaard proposed a number of ways in which the Center might refocus its efforts. In one way, the CFIA might function as "the catalyst for innovations across the University's international activities" in that it might provide "a possible (desirable, optimal) vehicle for stimulating area centers, focusing the University's resources on pressing world problems, and/or creating new educational opportunities for students from around the globe."[66] Klitgaard was confident that circumstances at the CFIA were ripe for a redoubling of efforts to maintain its continued relevance at the University and beyond. Huntington's return from service in Washington—and his acceptance of the Center's directorship—augured well for a renewal of the Center's original focus on major issues in international affairs. Klitgaard implied that Huntington's government service, coupled with that of Nye who had also recently returned to the CFIA after a period in Washington, might revitalize the Center's policy orientation. In addition, Klitgaard cited the recent move to new facilities at Coolidge Hall on Cambridge Street, coupled with a gradual turnover in senior members of the research staff, as evidence of the Center's "perceived need and the capability to strike out in some new directions."[67]

With this in mind, Klitgaard suggested five possible institutional and intellectual directions that the Center might follow over the coming years. First, the Center could simply strengthen its extant programs and priorities, eschewing fundamental change in favor of reinforcing its current agenda. In this scenario the CFIA could identify two or three discrete subjects to explore in greater depth. Implicit in this suggestion was that the Center ought to return to the spirit of its foundational program and exert a greater degree of effort toward a smaller number of topics. Klitgaard further speculated that the Center might expand its teaching responsibilities, possibly by offering a course in the recently created Core Curriculum.[68]

His second alternative for development required an even greater degree of specialization. In this model, Klitgaard imagined that the Center's research agenda would reflect the research interests of the Center Director, thereby becoming "a proprietary research organization" dealing with one single issue or topic. This might involve, for example, exclusively studying political development or U.S. foreign policy.[69] In contrast, Klitgaard's third model envisaged the Center becoming "in part the facilitator and entrepreneur of research projects involving various of the area centers."[70] This incubator model would capitalize on the proximity engendered by the recent migration of many area research centers to Coolidge Hall. In principle, the Center's broad focus and experience in managing a wide variety of individual, group, and interdisciplinary research would enable it to facilitate cooperation among the various centers and expedite contacts that might otherwise languish in bureaucratic and intellectual inertia. Klitgaard further anticipated that increased collaboration among the various research centers under the CFIA's administrative hand could invigorate teaching at Harvard College, possibly resulting in new and innovative courses for the curriculum.[71] Klitgaard recognized, however, that this last model had potential pitfalls: "if the CFIA were perceived as a sort of super-center trying to order the others about, the results might be bitter. The catalytic and entrepreneurial role envisioned here would require a delicate touch—and additional resources, so that the game were not zero-sum."[72]

Klitgaard's fourth proposal was even more ambitious. He envisioned the CFIA acting as the focal point of a broader University-wide effort to tackle "mankind's most important problems." In this regard he mused that "the Center would be given encouragement (via resources and appointments) to mount two or three major research efforts on world problems." He was well aware of the many institutional challenges such an undertaking would pose, so much so that he doubted whether it would even be worth seriously considering such a development.[73]

Klitgaard's final suggestion was that the CFIA become "Harvard's training arm to the world." Specifically, the Center would cease to be predominantly a research institution and would instead capitalize on the early success of the Fellows Program. Klitgaard envisaged that this training program could take a number of forms, ranging from short, "topically oriented" executive programs for government officials, to graduate and postdoctoral training programs for foreign teachers and potential future leaders. Consistent with many of his other proposals, Klitgaard speculated that such a program would provide potential benefits in the teaching of Harvard's undergraduates.

These five proposals, though often couched with caution and realism, challenged the CFIA to evaluate its place in both the University and the world. Klitgaard's critique of the CFIA was not without merit, though in many ways he merely recapitulated the concerns articulated by Center affiliates over the course of the previous decade. He relied heavily on the Center's self-appraisals as contained in a number of annual reports, and much of his analysis would have come as no surprise to those who had observed the CFIA during the past ten years. His analysis and recommendations do, however, provide insight into the priorities of the University as the administration looked forward to the next decades. The need for an increased emphasis on teaching and training loom large in Klitgaard's assessment of the University's international research centers, and in this regard his report reflects the changing imperatives of an increasingly global university. Whatever the virtues of his proposals, the implications were clear for the CFIA: "Some of these roles would entail profound changes in the Center's mission—so profound, perhaps, as to be in effect an abolishment of the old CFIA and the creation of a new Center for International Affairs."[74]

## The CFIA Responds: Research is Our Business

The following year, new Center Director Samuel Huntington produced his own report on the CFIA. As far as the Center was concerned, "research is its business." Despite any proposals to orient the Center toward teaching and training, "whatever other activities the Center engages in are justifiable only in so far as they contribute to this overriding mission."[75] Although "over the years, the subjects of research at the Center have changed and in some measure diversified," Huntington was dedicated to the enduring principle derived from Bowie's 1958 injunction: the Center was ultimately concerned with "basic research in the fundamental problems of international affairs."[76]

In assessing the Center's contributions over the previous two decades, Huntington also responded to the criticisms and proposals set forth in the Klitgaard Report. He reiterated that the mandate of the Center had been and continued to be research in international affairs, and he was unambiguous in rejecting Klitgaard's suggestions about the CFIA's future development:

> The Center is not in the business and should not go into the business of doing good, "consciousness raising," training world leaders, organizing programs to solve the world nutritional problems, or coordinating the multifarious international activities that go on at Harvard—all of which were suggested as possible CFIA missions in the so-called Klitgaard Report. Conceivably the Center's research may have some secondary spill-over effects in terms of these missions. But they are not the reasons for the Center's existence, and they do not provide the criteria by which to judge the Center's success or failure. Those criteria instead must be the importance and quality of the Center's research, its originality, its relevance to critical issues, and its fecundity, i.e. its potential for opening up new paths of investigation. The other activities in which the Center engages should be shaped and sized so as to maximize their contribution to the primary research mission.[77]

Huntington also rebutted many of the criticisms presented in the Klitgaard Report. He stressed the extent to which the CFIA was already fulfilling the role of facilitator among the various international research centers through its research seminars, which spanned a large number of topics such as "The Japanese-American Relationship," and "North-South Relations." He also highlighted the CFIA's formative role in creating the Harvard Institute for International Development, the Center for Science and International Affairs, and, to a lesser extent, the Center for European Studies. In this regard the

Center had germinated the seeds of future endeavors that filled "important lacunai [*sic*] in Harvard's structure of research centers."[78]

The Center's role in teaching, although often indirect, was also touted by Huntington as a major contribution to the University. No doubt in response to Klitgaard's frequent allusions to the need for the CFIA to become more actively engaged in instruction at the University, Huntington highlighted the important role that the Center's research had played in enriching teaching across the faculties. Additionally, he emphasized the contributions of the Center's student programs to graduate and undergraduate scholarship and the extent to which the student body had been integrated into the CFIA over the previous decade.[79]

Huntington did recognize, however, that the Center faced certain challenges as it entered its third decade. For example, he identified a need within the CFIA to strike a better balance among the various disciplines and methodologies represented by the Center's research associates and faculty. Political scientists vastly outnumbered economists and sociologists on the Center's executive committee, for example, and Huntington was keen to redress this balance by appointing faculty working in international economics and sociology. Richard N. Cooper's arrival at the Center as the Maurits C. Boas Professor of International Economics the following year served in part to redress this imbalance. Huntington also alluded to the continuing financial pressures that threatened to inhibit the development of new research initiatives. The Center's operating costs—from faculty salaries to administration—continued to increase with no concomitant rise in income. Unless the Center could secure additional endowment funds, this trend would strain the Center's ability to support junior faculty members. Huntington was keenly aware of the need to alleviate the pressures on the Center's discretionary funds, which were increasingly directed toward overhead rather than research seminars, student programs, and promising research projects.

In addition, the constant specter of inadequate space continued to hinder the Center's development and growth, and Huntington bemoaned the fact that even after the move to Coolidge Hall the Center still lacked sufficient facilities for its activities. "The advantages achieved by integrating the various regional and international centers in Coolidge Hall have to be balanced against the dissipation that occurs within centers as they acquire satellite offices outside the building. Eventually, the centers in Coolidge Hall will almost certainly need more fundamental answers to the space problem. Either some occupants of Coolidge Hall will have to move out, or substantial additional funds will have to be raised to acquire or construct a new facility."[80] Indeed, by 1982 the Center reported that almost 40 percent of CFIA staff and associates were housed outside Coolidge Hall in two separate buildings.[81]

## Conclusion

After twenty-five years there can be no doubt that the CFIA had made an exceptional contribution to the development of international affairs as an academic discipline. The prodigious output of research papers, scholarly articles, and monographs had in many cases defined the contours of the field, and in some cases forged wholly new areas of inquiry, none more so than in the areas of arms control theory and development theory.

The first ten years can be understood as what Ben Brown called the "unitary" phase in the Center's development. This was a period in which Center scholars toiled in the context of a relatively stable international system, which was characterized by a seemingly enduring and intractable cold war, a clearly defined research agenda, and ample funding. Brown viewed the second ten years as the "eclectic" phase of the Center's development, in which the economic, political, and strategic foundations of the once reliable cold war were subject to domestic and international challenges that undermined the original guiding assumptions of the CFIA. The Center responded to these challenges by diversifying its research programs and expanding its purview and its constituencies.[82]

Brown's depiction of the Center's history deftly captures the dynamic and occasionally ambiguous evolution of the CFIA. At times implicit, and occasionally explicit, was the recognition that growth was not necessarily synonymous with progress. As Huntington noted in his 1982 biennial report on the Center's activities:

> It is clearly neither necessary nor desirable nor ultimately possible for the Center to continue to expand at the rates which it did between 1979 and 1982. Beyond a certain point the marginal returns from further expansion decrease significantly. Most importantly, the character of the Center as a center inevitably changes: at present the Center is still of a size where, during the course of an academic year and despite the heavy annual turnover in Fellows, visiting scholars, research associates and post-doctoral fellows, it is still possible for everyone to get to know everyone else. An increase in size much beyond the current level would make the Center more of a holding company for discrete

*research programs than the complex but interrelated whole of overlapping and reinforcing activities which, in my view, it ought to be.*[83]

The Center had certainly grown: by 1983 its operating budget was slightly over two million dollars. Expenditures had increased from $129,527 in 1958–59 to $2,016,222 in 1982–83.[84] From an original core faculty of four—the nucleus of what would become the Center's executive committee—by 1984 the Center boasted a sixteen-member executive committee, six faculty associates, twelve research fellows, eighteen Fellows, nineteen visiting scholars, forty-five research associates and affiliated researchers, six postdoctoral fellows, sixteen graduate student associates, twenty-three undergraduate associates, and thirty-nine staff members.[85]

As Brown observed in his candid report to President Bok in 1978, however, the Center's financial situation was not positive, and he feared that "continued weakness in this area threatens the Center's vitality."[86] Though Brown felt that the Center's financial issues could be resolved fairly easily, he also noted that sustained lack of funding had a subsidiary effect on the research program. As a result of the dearth in major funding for large-scale projects, the Center had instead fostered small-scale or individual research that had the result of fragmenting the research program: "The constructive effect of the critical mass that powered the breakthroughs in arms control, development/modernization, and transnational studies has to a large extent been lost."[87] Brown was confident that the Center would continue to prosper, but the question was whether or not it would retain the coherence of the first decade, or dissipate into a cluster of disparate individual research projects. He feared that "the program as a whole will be fragmented, and the Center as a collegial institution, a close-knit company of scholars pursuing a common enterprise, will decline." Disturbingly, Brown noted, "that tendency is evident now."[88]

This dramatic increase in size and scope—coupled with reductions in available funding—raised serious questions as the Center entered its third decade. Would it be possible to maintain the clarity of purpose that had illuminated much of the Center's earlier work? Would the Center continue to successfully manage the precarious balance between individual research and collaborative, interdisciplinary projects? How effectively would the Center navigate the vicissitudes of a rapidly evolving international system? How would the Center cope with losing two of its most intellectually and financially lucrative research programs, the DAS and the PSIA? How would increased competition for funds and research talent affect the CFIA in the coming decade? The challenges of the first two decades had, for the most part, been met with verve and resolve. It remained to be seen how effectively the Center would meet the challenges of the third decade.

# Harvard Studies in International Affairs

From 1958 to 1983 the Center published this numbered series.

1   *A Plan for Planning: The Need for a Better Method of Assisting Under-Developed Countries on Their Economic Policies.* Gustav F. Papanek, 1961.

2   *The Flow of Resources from Rich to Poor.* Alan D. Neale, 1961.

3   *Limited War: An Essay on the Development of the Theory and an Annotated Bibliography.* Morton H. Halperin, 1962.

4   *Reflections on the Failure of the First West Indian Federation.* Hugh W. Springer, 1962.

5   *On the Interaction of Opposing Forces under Possible Arms Agreements.* Glenn A. Kent, 1963.

6   *Europe's Northern Cap and the Soviet Union.* Nils Orvik, 1963.

7   *Civil Administration in the Punjab: An Analysis of a State Government in India.* E.N. Rai, 1963.

8   *On the Appropriate Size of a Development Program.* Edward S. Mason, 1964.

9   *Self-Determination Revisited in the Era of Decolonization.* Rupert Emerson, 1964. **Reprinted by UPA in 1984**.

10  *The Planning and Execution of Economic Development in Southeast Asia.* Clair Wilcox, 1966.

11  *Pan-Africanism in Action.* Albert Tevoedjre, 1965. **Reprinted by UPA in 1984**.

12  *Is China Turning In?* Morton H. Halperin, 1965. **Reprinted by UPA in 1984**.

13  *Economic Development in India and Pakistan.* Edward S. Mason, 1966.

14  *The Role of the Military in Recent Turkish Politics.* Ergun Ozbudun, 1966.

15  *Economic Development and Individual Change: A Social Psychological Study of the Comilla Experiment in Pakistan.* Howard Schuman, 1967.

16  *A Select Bibliography on Students, Politics, and Higher Education.* Philip G. Altbach, UMHE Revised Edition, 1970.

17  *Europe's Political Puzzle: A Study of the Fouchet Negotiations and the 1963 Veto.* Alessandro Silij, 1967. **Reprinted by UPA in 1984**.

18  *The Cap and the Straits: Problems of Nordic Security.* Jan Klenburg, 1968.

19  *Cyprus: The Law and Politics of Civil Strife.* Linda B. Miller, 1968.

20   *East and West Pakistan: A Problem in the Political Economy of Regional Planning*. Md. Anisur Rahman, 1968.

21   *Internal War and International Systems: Perspectives on Method*. George A. Kelly and Linda B. Miller, 1969.

22   *Migrants, Urban Poverty, and Instability in Developing Nations*. Joan M. Nelson, 1969.

23   *Growth and Development in Pakistan, 1955-1969*. Joseph J. Stern and Walter P. Falcon, 1970. **Reprinted by UPA in 1984**.

24   *Higher Education in Developing Countries: A Select Bibliography*. Philip G. Altbach, 1970.

25   *Anatomy of Political Institutions: The Case of Israel and Some Comparative Analyses*. Amos Perlmutter, 1970. **Reprinted by UPA in 1984**.

26   *The German Democratic Republic from the Sixties to the Seventies*. Peter Christian Ludz, 1970. **Reprinted by UPA in 1984**.

27   *The Law in Political Integration: The Evolution and Integrative Implications of Regional Legal Processes in the European Community*. Stuart Scheingold, 1971.

28   *Psychological Dimensions of U.S.-Japanese Relations*. Hiroshi Kitamura, 1971. **Reprinted by UPA in 1984**.

29   *Conflict Regulation in Divided Societies*. Eric A. Nordlinger, 1977 (2nd ed.). **Reprinted by UPA in 1984**.

30   *Israel's Political-Military Doctrine*. Michael I. Handel, 1973.

31   *Italy, NATO, and the European Community: The Interplay Foreign Policy and Domestic Politics*. Primo Vanicelli, 1974. **Reprinted by UPA in 1984**.

32   *The Choice of Technology in Developing Countries: Some Cautionary Tales*. Peter C. Timmer, Louis T. Wells, and David Morawetz, 1975.

33   *The International Role of the Communist Parties of France and Italy*. Donald L.M. Blackmer and Annie Kriegel, 1975. **Reprinted by UPA in 1984**.

34   *The Hazards of Peace: A European View of Détente*. Juan Cassiers, 1976. **Reprinted by UPA in 1984**.

35   *Oil and the Middle East War: Europe in the Energy Crisis*. Robert J. Lieber, 1976. **Reprinted by UPA in 1984**.

36   No records of this book.

37   *Climactic Change and World Affairs*. Crispin Tickell, 1977. **Reprinted by UPA in 1984**.

38   *Conflict and Violence in Lebanon: Confrontation in the Middle East*. Walid Khalidi, 1979.

39   *Diplomatic Dispute: U.S. Conflict with Iran, Japan, and Mexico*. Robert L. Paarlberg, Eul Y. Park, and Donald L. Wyman [undated]. **Reprinted by UPA in 1984**.

40    *Commandos and Politicians: Elite Military Units in Modern Democracies.* Eliot A. Cohen, 1978. **Reprinted by UPA in 1984.**

41    *Yellow Earth, Green Jade: Constants in Chinese Political Mores.* Simon de Beaufort, 1979. **Reprinted by UPA in 1984.**

42    *The Future of North America: Canada, the United States, and Quebec Nationalism.* Ed., Elliot J. Feldman and Neil Nevitte, 1979. **Reprinted by UPA in 1984.**

43    *The Dependence Dilemma: Gasoline Consumption and America's Security.* Ed., Daniel Yergin, 1980. **Reprinted by UPA in 1984.**

44    *The Diplomacy of Surprise: Hitler, Nixon, Sadat.* Michael I. Handel, 1981. **Reprinted by UPA in 1984.**

45    *Economic Sanctions.* Robin Renwick, 1981. **Reprinted by UPA in 1984.**

46    *Tutelary Pluralism: A Critical Approach to Venezuelan Democracy.* Luis J. Oropeza, 1983. **Reprinted by UPA in 1984.**

185

## Appendix Two

# Books Published Under the Auspices of the Center for International Affairs, 1960–1983

### 1960

*The Soviet Bloc,* by Zbigniew K. Brzezinski. Jointly with Russian Research Center. Harvard University Press.

### 1961

*The Necessity for Choice,* by Henry A. Kissinger. Harper & Brothers.

*Strategy and Arms Control,* by Thomas C. Schelling and Morton H. Halperin. Twentieth Century Fund.

*Rift and Revolt in Hungary,* by Ferenc A. Vali. Harvard University Press.

### 1962

*United States Manufacturing Investment in Brazil,* by Lincoln Gordon and Engelbert L. Grommers. Harvard Business School.

*The Economy of Cyprus,* by A. J. Meyer with Simos Vassiliou. Jointly with Center for Middle Eastern Studies. Harvard University Press.

*Entrepreneurs of Lebanon,* by Yusif A. Sayigh. Jointly with Center for Middle Eastern Studies. Harvard University Press.

*Communist China 1955–1959: Policy Documents with Analysis,* with a Foreword by Robert R. Bowie and John K. Fairbank. Jointly with East Asian Research Center. Harvard University Press.

### 1963

*In Search of France,* by Stanley Hoffmann, Charles P. Kindleberger, Laurence Wylie, Jesse R. Pitts, Jean-Baptiste Duroselle, and François Goguel. Harvard University Press.

*Somali Nationalism,* by Saadia Touval. Harvard University Press.

*The Dilemma of Mexico's Development,* by Raymond Vernon. Harvard University Press.

*Limited War in the Nuclear Age,* by Morton H. Halperin. John Wiley & Sons.

*The Arms Debate,* by Robert A. Levine. Harvard University Press.

### 1964

*Africans on the Land,* by Montague Yudelman. Harvard University Press.

*Counterinsurgency Warfare,* by David Galula. Frederick A. Praeger, Inc.

*People and Policy in the Middle East,* by Max Weston Thornburg. W. W. Norton & Co.

*Foreign Aid and Foreign Policy,* by Edward S. Mason. Jointly with Council on Foreign Relations. Harper & Row.

*Public Policy and Private Enterprise in Mexico,* edited by Raymond Vernon. Harvard University Press.

*How Nations Negotiate,* by Fred Charles Iklé. Harper & Row.

*Shaping the Future,* by Robert R. Bowie. Columbia University Press.

## 1965

*China and the Bomb,* by Morton H. Halperin. Jointly with East Asian Research Center. Frederick A. Praeger, Inc.

*Communist China and Arms Control,* by Morton H. Halperin and Dwight H. Perkins. Jointly with East Asian Research Center. Frederick A. Praeger, Inc.

*Democracy in Germany,* by Fritz Erler (Jodidi Lectures). Harvard University Press.

*Pan-Africanism and East African Integration,* by Joseph S. Nye, Jr. Harvard University Press.

*Problems of National Strategy,* edited by Henry A. Kissinger. Frederick A. Praeger, Inc.

*The Rise of Nationalism in Central Africa,* by Robert I. Rotberg. Harvard University Press.

*The Troubled Partnership,* by Henry A. Kissinger. Jointly with Council on Foreign Relations. McGraw-Hill Book Co.

## 1966

*Arms and Influence,* by Thomas C. Schelling. Yale University Press.

*Containing the Arms Race,* by Jeremy J. Stone. M.I.T. Press.

*Deterrence before Hiroshima,* by George H. Quester. John Wiley & Sons.

*Export Instability and Economic Development,* by Alasdair I. MacBean. Harvard University Press.

*Germany and the Atlantic Alliance,* by James L. Richardson. Harvard University Press.

*Planning without Facts: Lessons in Resource Allocation from Nigeria's Development,* by Wolfgang F. Stolper. Harvard University Press.

*Political Change in a West African State,* by Martin L. Kilson. Harvard University Press.

## 1967

*Africa and United States Policy,* by Rupert Emerson. Prentice-Hall.

*Contemporary Military Strategy,* by Morton H. Halperin. Little, Brown & Co.

*Elites in Latin America,* edited by Seymour M. Lipset and Aldo Solari. Oxford University Press.

*Europe's Postwar Growth,* by Charles P. Kindleberger. Harvard University Press.

*Foreign Policy and Democratic Politics,* by Kenneth N. Waltz. Jointly with Institute of War and Peace Studies, Columbia University. Little, Brown & Co.

*Party Systems and Voter Alignments,* edited by Seymour M. Lipset and Stein Rokkan. Free Press.

**1967** *(continued)*

*Pakistan's Development,* by Gustav F. Papanek. Harvard University Press.

*The Rise and Decline of the Cold War,* by Paul Seabury. Basic Books.

*Student Politics,* edited by Seymour M. Lipset. Basic Books.

*Sino-Soviet Relations and Arms Control,* edited by Morton H. Halperin. Jointly with East Asian Research Center. M.I.T. Press.

*Strike a Blow and Die: A Narrative of Race Relations in Colonial Africa,* by George Simeon Mwase. Edited and introduced by Robert I. Rotberg. Harvard University Press.

**1968**

*Agrarian Socialism* (revised edition), by Seymour M. Lipset. Doubleday Anchor.

*Aid, Influence, and Foreign Policy,* by Joan M. Nelson. Macmillan.

*The Brazilian Capital Goods Industry, 1929–1964,* by Nathaniel H. Leff. Jointly with Center for Studies in Education and Development. Harvard University Press.

*Development Policy: Theory and Practice,* edited by Gustav F. Papanek. Harvard University Press.

*Economic Policy-Making and Development in Brazil, 1947–1964,* by Nathaniel H. Leff. John Wiley & Sons.

*German Foreign Policy in Transition,* by Karl Kaiser. Oxford University Press.

*International Regionalism,* by Joseph S. Nye, Jr. Little, Brown & Co.

*Korea: The Politics of the Vortex,* by Gregory Henderson. Harvard University Press.

*The Precarious Republic: Political Modernization in Lebanon,* by Michael Hudson. Random House.

*Political Order in Changing Societies,* by Samuel P. Huntington. Yale University Press.

*Revolution and Counterrevolution: Change and Persistence in Social Structures,* by Seymour M. Lipset. Basic Books.

*The TFX Tangle: McNamara and the Military,* by Robert J. Art. Little, Brown & Co.

*Turmoil and Transition: Higher Education and Student Politics in India,* edited by Philip G. Altbach. Lalvani Publishing House (Bombay).

*Student Politics & Higher Education in the United States: A Select Bibliography,* by Philip G. Altbach. United Ministries in Higher Education.

*Student Politics in Bombay,* by Philip G. Altbach. Asia Publishing House.

*Political Development in Latin America: Instability, Violence, and Evolutionary Change,* by Martin C. Needler. Random House.

**1969**

*The Process of Modernization: An Annotated Bibliography on the Sociocultural Aspects of Development,* by John Brode. Harvard University Press.

*Students in Revolt,* edited by Seymour M. Lipset and Philip G. Altbach. Houghton Mifflin.

*Taxation and Development: Lessons from Colombian Experience,* by Richard M. Bird. Harvard University Press.

## 1970

*Agricultural Development in India's Districts: The Intensive Agricultural Districts Programme,* by Dorris D. Brown. Harvard University Press.

*Authoritarian Politics in Modern Society: The Dynamics of Established One-Party Systems,* edited by Samuel P. Huntington and Clement H. Moore. Basic Books.

*Europe's Would-Be Polity,* by Leon Lindberg and Stuart A. Scheingold. Prentice-Hall.

*Korean Development: The Interplay of Politics and Economics,* by David C. Cole and Princeton N. Lyman. Harvard University Press.

*The Logic of Images in International Relations,* by Robert Jervis. Princeton University Press.

*Lord and Peasant in Peru: A Paradigm of Political and Social Change,* by F. LaMond Tullis. Harvard University Press.

*Peace in Europe,* by Karl E. Birnbaum. Oxford University Press.

*Protest and Power in Black Africa,* edited by Robert I. Rotberg and Ali A. Mazrui. Oxford University Press.

*Revolution and Counterrevolution: Change and Persistence in Social Structures* (revised edition), by Seymour M. Lipset. Anchor.

## 1971

*Nuclear Diplomacy,* by George H. Quester. Dunellen.

*Defense Strategy for the Seventies,* by Morton H. Halperin (revision of *Contemporary Military Strategy*). Little, Brown & Co.

*Development Policy II: The Pakistan Experience,* edited by Walter P. Falcon and Gustav F. Papanek. Harvard University Press.

*Higher Education in India,* edited by Amrik Singh and Philip Altbach. Oxford University Press (Delhi).

*Higher Education in Transitional Society,* by Philip G. Altbach. Sindhu Publications (Bombay).

*International Norms and War between States: Three Studies in International Politics,* by Kjell Goldmann. Läromedelsförlagen (Sweden) and Swedish Institute of International Affairs.

*The Kennedy Round in American Trade Policy,* by John W. Evans. Harvard University Press.

*The Myth of the Guerrilla,* by J. Bowyer Bell. Blond (London) and Knopf (New York).

*Passion and Politics,* by Seymour M. Lipset with Gerald Schaflander. Little, Brown & Co.

*Peace in Parts: Integration and Conflict in Regional Organization,* by Joseph S. Nye, Jr. Little, Brown & Co.

*Political Mobilization of the Venezuelan Peasant,* by John D. Powell. Harvard University Press.

*Sovereignty at Bay: The Multinational Spread of U.S. Enterprise,* by Raymond Vernon. Basic Books.

*Studies in Development Planning,* edited by Hollis B. Chenery. Harvard University Press.

## 1972

*The Boundary Politics of Independent Africa,* by Saadia Touval. Harvard University Press.

*Latin American University Students: A Six Nation Study,* by Arthur Liebman, Kenneth N. Walker, and Myron Glazer. Harvard University Press.

*Peasants Against Politics: Rural Organization in Brittany, 1911–1967,* by Suzanne Berger. Harvard University Press.

*The Politics of Land Reform in Chile, 1950–1970: Public Policy, Political Institutions, and Social Change,* by Robert R. Kaufman. Harvard University Press.

*Transnational Relations and World Politics,* edited by Robert O. Keohane and Joseph S. Nye, Jr. Harvard University Press.

## 1973

*The Politics of Nonviolent Action,* by Gene E. Sharp. Porter Sargent Publishers, Inc.

*System 37 Viggen: Arms, Technology, and the Domestication of Glory,* by Ingemar Dörfer. Universitetsforlaget (Oslo).

## 1974

*The Andean Group: A Case Study in Economic Integration among Developing Countries,* by David Morawetz. M.I.T. Press.

*Becoming Modern,* by Alex Inkeles and David H. Smith. Harvard University Press.

*Big Business and the State: Changing Relations in Western Europe,* edited by Raymond Vernon. Harvard University Press.

*Economic Nationalism and the Politics of International Dependence: The Case of Copper in Chile, 1945–1973,* by Theodore Moran. Princeton University Press.

*Kenya: The Politics of Participation and Control,* by Henry Bienen. Princeton University Press.

*Land Reform and Politics: A Comparative Analysis,* by Hung-chao Tai. University of California Press.

*Organizing the Transnational: The Experience with Transnational Enterprise in Advanced Technology,* by M. S. Hochmuth. Harvard University Press.

*University Students and African Politics,* by William John Hanna. Africana Publishing Company.

## 1975

*East Africa and the Orient: Cultural Synthesis in Pre-Colonial Times,* by H. Neville Chittick and Robert I. Rotberg. Africana Publishing Company.

*Economic Policymaking in a Conflict Society: The Argentine Case,* by Richard D. Mallon and Juan V. Sourrouille. Harvard University Press.

*New States in the Modern World,* edited by Martin Kilson. Harvard University Press.

*Politics and the Migrant Poor in Mexico City,* by Wayne A. Cornelius. Stanford University Press.

*Revolutionary Civil War: The Elements of Victory and Defeat,* by David Wilkinson. Page-Ficklin Publications.

## 1976

*The Arabs. Israelis, and Kissinger: A Secret History of American Diplomacy in the Middle East,* by Edward R. F. Sheehan. Reader's Digest Press.

*The International Politics of Natural Resources,* by Zuhayr Mikdashi. Cornell University Press.

*No Easy Choice: Political Participation in Developing Countries,* by Samuel P. Huntington and Joan M. Nelson. Harvard University Press.

*The Oil Crisis,* edited by Raymond Vernon. W. W. Norton & Co.

*The Politics of International Monetary Reform: The Exchange Crisis,* by Michael J. Brenner. Ballinger Publishing Co.

*Social Change and Political Participation in Turkey,* by Ergun Ozbudun. Princeton University Press.

*Perception and Misperception in International Politics,* by Robert Jervis. Princeton University Press.

## 1977

*Bankers and Borders: The Case of American Banks in Britain,* by Janet Kelly. Ballinger Publishing Co.

*The Military and Politics in Modern Times: On Professionals, Praetorians, and Revolutionary Soldiers,* by Amos Perlmutter. Yale University Press.

*Political Generations and Political Development,* edited by Richard J. Samuels. Lexington Books.

*Power and Interdependence,* by Robert O. Keohane and Joseph S. Nye, Jr. Little, Brown & Co.

*Shattered Peace: The Origins of the Cold War and the National Security State,* by Daniel Yergin. Houghton Mifflin.

*Soldiers in Politics: Military Coups and Governments,* by Eric Nordlinger. Prentice-Hall.

*Storm Over the Multinationals: The Real Issues,* by Raymond Vernon. Harvard University Press.

*The Nation, the State and the International System: The Case of Modern Greece,* by Andreas I. Psomas.

## 1978

*Cuba: Order and Revolution in the Twentieth Century,* by Jorge I. Domínguez. Harvard University Press.

*Commodity Conflict: The Political Economy of International Commodity Negotiations,* by L. N. Rangarajan. Cornell University Press and Croom Helm.

*Israel: Embattled Ally,* by Nadav Safran. Harvard University Press.

*Defending the National Interest: Raw Materials Investments and U.S. Foreign Policy,* by Stephen D. Krasner. Princeton University Press.

## 1979

*Access to Power: Political Participation by the Urban Poor in Developing Nations,* by Joan M. Nelson. Princeton University Press.

*The Quest for Self-Determination,* by Dov Ronen. Yale University Press.

*The Rational Peasant: The Political Economy of Rural Society in Vietnam,* by Samuel L. Popkin. University of California Press.

*Enhancing Global Human Rights,* by Jorge I. Domínguez, Nigel S. Rodley, Bryce Wood, and Richard Falk. McGraw-Hill.

*Gandhi as a Political Strategist,* by Gene Sharp. Porter Sargent Publishers, Inc.

## 1980

*American Spectator Special Issue,* edited and co-authored by Stephen P. Rosen.

*The Civic Culture Revisited,* edited by Sidney Verba with Gabriel Almond. Little, Brown & Co.

*The Collapse of Welfare Reform: Political Institutions, Policy and the Poor in Canada and the United States,* by Christopher Leman. M.I.T. Press.

*East-West Trade and the Communist Bloc: Japan and the Soviet Union,* by Stephen Sternheimer. Sage Publications.

*Energy and Security,* edited by Joseph S. Nye, Jr., and David A. Deese. Ballinger Publishing Co.

*The Fall of France, Volume I,* edited by Stanley Hoffmann. Center for European Studies, Harvard University.

*Insurrection or Loyalty: The Breakdown of the Spanish American Empire,* by Jorge I. Domínguez. Harvard University Press.

*L'Election du Parlement European au suffrage universel directe,* edited by Panayotis Soldatos with G. Rossignol. CEDE (Montreal).

*Legislative-Executive Relations and the Politics of United States Foreign Economics Policy 1929–1979,* by Robert Pastor. University of California Press.

*Palestinian Society and Politics,* by Joel S. Migdal et al. Princeton University Press.

*The Quebec Referendum: What Happened and What Next?,* by Elliot J. Feldman and Jerome Milch. University Consortium for Research on North America.

*Social Power and Political Freedom,* by Gene Sharp. Porter Sargent Publishers, Inc.

*Standing Guard: The Protection of Foreign Investment,* by Charles Lipson. University of California Press.

*State-Owned Enterprises in the Western Economies,* by Raymond Vernon with Yair Aharoni. Croom Helm.

*Suffer the Future: Policy Choices in Southern Africa,* by Robert I. Rotberg. Harvard University Press.

*U.S. Foreign Economic Policy, 1929–1976,* by Robert Pastor. University of California Press.

*The War Ledger,* by Jacek Kugler with A.F.K. Organski. The University of Chicago Press.

*Conflict and Compromise in South Africa,* edited by Robert I. Rotberg with John Barrett. Lexington Books.

## 1981

*American Politics: The Promise of Disharmony,* by Samuel P. Huntington. Harvard University Press.

*Bureaucrats and Politicians in Western Democracies,* by Robert D. Putnam et al. Harvard University Press.

*The Caribbean: Its Implications for the United States,* by Jorge I. Domínguez and Virginia R. Dominguez. Foreign Policy Association Headline Series, No. 253.

*Comparative Government: Politics of Industrialized and Developing Nations,* by Jorge I. Domínguez et al. Houghton Mifflin.

*Corporation and National Development in Latin America,* by Howard J. Wiarda. Westview Press.

*Corpus of Early Arabic Sources for West African History,* edited by Nehemia Levtzion with J.F.P. Hopkins. Cambridge University Press.

*The Dilemma of American Ideals and Institutions in Foreign Policy,* by Samuel P. Huntington. American Enterprise Institute.

*The Dominican Republic: Profile of a Caribbean Crucible,* by Howard J. Wiarda with Michael Kryzanek. Westview Press.

*Duties Beyond Borders,* by Stanley Hoffmann. Syracuse University Press.

*Economists in Government: An International Comparative Study,* by Kozo Yamamoto and Ryutaro Komiya. Duke University Press.

*The European Communities in Action,* edited by Panayotis Soldatos with D. Lasok. Bruylant (Brussels).

*The Fall of France, Volume II,* edited by Stanley Hoffmann. Center for European Studies, Harvard University.

*The Fifth Republic at Twenty,* edited by Stanley Hoffmann with William Andrews. State University of New York Press.

*On the Autonomy of the Democratic State,* by Eric Nordlinger. Harvard University Press.

*A Practical Guide to the Conduct of Field Research in the Social Sciences,* by Elliot J. Feldman. Westview Press.

*Regional Issues in Energy Development: A Dialogue of East and West,* edited by Christopher Leman. Jointly with University Consortium for Research on North America.

*Security with the Persian Gulf II: Sources of Interstate Conflict,* by R. S. Litwak. Gower Publishing Company for International Institute for Strategic Studies (London).

*Technocracy vs. Democracy: The Comparative Politics of International Airports,* by Elliot J. Feldman and Jerome Milch. Auburn House.

*Towards a Certain Future: The Politics and Economics of Southern Africa,* by Robert I. Rotberg. David Philip (Capetown).

*Weak States in the International System,* by Michael Handel. Harvard University Press.

## 1982

*Chinese Communist Negotiating Styles,* by Lucian Pye. Oelgeschlager, Gunn & Hain.

*The Civil War in Lebanon: A Bibliographic Essay,* by Nawaf Salam. Center for Arab and Middle Eastern Studies, The American University of Beirut.

**1982** *(continued)*

*Cuba: Internal and International Affairs,* edited by Jorge I. Domínguez. Sage Publications.

*The Eastasia Edge,* by Kent E. Calder with Roy Hofheinz, Jr. Basic Books.

*Economic Issues and Political Conflict: U.S.–Latin American Relations,* edited by Jorge I. Domínguez. Butterworths.

*Food in the Global Arena,* by Robert Paarlberg with Raymond F. Hopkins and Mitchel B. Wallerstein. Holt, Rinehart, and Winston.

*Global Insecurity: A Strategy for Energy and Economic Renewal,* by Daniel Yergin. Houghton Mifflin.

*The International Monetary System Under Flexible Exchange Rates,* edited by Richard N. Cooper et al. Ballinger Publishing Co.

*Learning from the Japanese Experience,* by Ezra Vogel et al., edited by Chong-Yah Lim. Maruzen Asia.

*Mexico's Political Economy: Challenges at Home and Abroad,* edited by Jorge I. Domínguez. Sage Publications.

*The Politics of Canadian Airport Development: Lessons for Federalism,* by Elliot J. Feldman and Jerome Milch. Duke University Press.

*The Strategic Imperative: New Policies for American Security,* edited by Samuel P. Huntington. Ballinger Publishing Co.

*U.S. Interests and Policies in the Caribbean and Central America,* by Jorge I. Domínguez. American Enterprise Institute Special Analyses Series.

## 1983

*China Turned Rightside Up: Revolutionary Legitimacy in the Peasant World,* by Ralph Thaxton. Yale University Press.

*Conventional Deterrence,* by John J. Mearsheimer. Cornell University Press.

*Economics of Development,* by Dwight H. Perkins with Malcolm Gillis, Michael Roemer, and Donald Snodgrass. W. W. Norton & Co.

*Living with Nuclear Weapons: A Report by the Harvard Nuclear Study Group,* by Paul Doty, Stanley Hoffmann, Samuel P. Huntington, Joseph S. Nye, and Scott D. Sagan. Bantam Publishing Co.

*Poder, Luta, e Defesa: Teoria e Pratica da Acao Nao-Violenta [Power, Struggle, and Defense: Theory and Practice of Nonviolent Action],* by Gene Sharp. Edicoes Paulinas (Sao Paulo).

*Soviet Intervention in Third World Conflict: Patterns and Prospects,* by Neil MacFarlane. Graduate Institute of International Affairs (Geneva).

*The Soviet Union in India's Security Perspective,* by Robert Litwak. International Institute for Strategic Studies (London).

*Two Hungry Giants: The United States and Japan in the Quest for Oil and Ores,* by Raymond Vernon. Harvard University Press.

*What is Strategic Thought?,* by Hisahiko Okazaki. Chuokoron SHA (Tokyo).

# Government Service of CFIA Faculty Members

The following is an illustrative list of Center executive committee members from 1958 to 1983 who served in various presidential administrations and government agencies.

**Robert R. Bowie,** personal assistant to General Lucius Clay, the Military Governor of American Occupied Germany, (1945–46); principal legal advisor to John J. McCloy, high commissioner to Germany (1950–52); director of the Policy Planning Staff (1953–55), assistant secretary of state for planning (1955–57); counselor to the Department of State (1966–68); CIA deputy director for intelligence (1977–79).

**Benjamin H. Brown,** deputy secretary-general of the U.S. Mission to the United Nations (1947–53).

**Hollis B. Chenery,** economic advisor to President McNamara, World Bank (1970–72); vice president for developmental policy, World Bank (1972–82).

**Richard N. Cooper,** senior staff economist, Council of Economic Advisers (1961–63); deputy assistant secretary of state for international monetary affairs (1965–66); undersecretary of state for economic affairs (1977–81); chair, National Intelligence Council (1995–97).

**Paul M. Doty,** special assistant to the president for national security, member of the President's Science and Arms Control Advisory Committees (1959 consultant, 1960 became full member).

**Samuel P. Huntington,** consultant, policy planning council, Department of State (1967); chair, council on Vietnamese studies, Southeast Asia development advisory group (1966–69); member, presidential task force on international development (1969–70); coordinator of security planning for the National Security Council (1977–78); member, commission on integrated long-term strategy (1986–88); member, advisory board, Federal Emergency Management Agency (1980–91); member, commission on the reduction and protection of governmental secrecy (1995–97).

**Alex Inkeles,** social science research analyst, division of U.S.S.R. intelligence, Office of Strategic Services, (1942–45); Department of State (1945–46).

**Henry A. Kissinger,** consultant to the Operations Research Office (1951); consultant to the director of the Psychological Strategy Board (1952); consultant to the Operations Coordinating Board (1955); consultant to the Weapons Systems Evaluation Group of the Joint Chiefs of Staff (1959–60); consultant to the National Security Council (1961–62); consultant to the U.S. Arms Control and Disarmament Agency (1961–68); consultant to the Department of State (1965–68); assistant to the president for national security affairs (1969–75); Secretary of State (1973–77); chair of the national bipartisan commission on Central America (1983–84).

**Edward S. Mason,** deputy to the assistant secretary of state for economic affairs, Department of State (1945); economic consultant, Department of State (1946–47); chief economic advisor, Moscow Conference (1947); member of materials policy commission, (1951–52).

**Joseph S. Nye, Jr.,** deputy to the undersecretary of state (1977–79); assistant secretary of defense for international security affairs (1994–95).

**Gustav F. Papanek,** deputy chief, program planning for South & Southeast Asia, technical cooperation administration, Department of State (1951–53).

**Dwight Perkins,** member, academic advisory board, national council on U.S.-China trade (1974–78); consultant to permanent subcommittee on investigations, U.S. Senate (1974–79); member, program advisory committee, Overseas Development Council (1983–present).

**Robert Putnam,** staff, National Security Council (1978); member, president's council on service and civic participation (2003–05); occasional consultant, Department of State and Central Intelligence Agency (1975–85), World Bank (1992–98), White House (1995–present), British government agencies (2002–present), and Irish Taoiseach (2001–present).

**Edwin O. Reischauer,** U.S. Ambassador to Japan (1961–66).

**Thomas C. Schelling,** Bureau of the Budget (1945–46); the Marshall Plan in Copenhagen and Paris (1948–50); advisor to the White House and Executive Office of the President (1951–1953); occasional consultant, Department of Defense.

**Raymond Vernon,** statistician, Securities and Exchange Commission (1935–42); assistant director, trading and exchange division (1942–46); assistant chief, international resources division, Department of State (1946–48); deputy director, office of economic defense and trade policy (1951); staff, joint presidential-congressional commission on foreign economic policy (1953–54).

# Notes

## One  The Founding of the Center for International Affairs

1. From 1958 to 1983 the Center for International Affairs published a numbered series called the *Harvard Studies* (or *Occasional Papers*) *in International Affairs*. That series, included in Appendix One, ended with the publication of No. 46 in 1983. In addition, books by Center affiliates with other publishers, which are based in whole or in part on work done while affiliated with the Center, are recorded in Appendix Two. These books include either a general acknowledgment or the specific statement: "Published under the auspices of the Center for International Affairs, Harvard University."

2. Harvard University, Faculty of Arts and Sciences, Report on International Studies at Harvard Submitted to the Ford Foundation, April 1960, pp. 1–2. UAIII.29.60 Harvard University Archives.

3. Ibid., pp. 2–3. In many ways, the efforts of Archibald Cary Coolidge were instrumental in increasing the profile of international affairs at Harvard. Coolidge pioneered the inculcation of international issues through both his scholarship and his teaching as a member of the faculty in the History Department in the early twentieth century. His own interest in Slavic studies broadened the purview of the department, and he personally funded graduate student scholarships, library acquisitions, and even a colleague's salary. His influence was so significant that upon his passing one fellow faculty member lamented, "[His death] has snapped a link between [Harvard] and the world of big affairs." Coolidge was also a crucial link between the academy and the government. He was a member of Wilson's "Inquiry," and a member of the American delegation to the Paris Peace Conference. Moreover, as the first editor of the journal of the Council on International Relations, *Foreign Affairs*, Coolidge played a central part in promulgating the study of international affairs in the United States. McCaughey, Robert A., *International Studies and Academic Enterprise: A Chapter in the Enclosure of American Learning* (New York: Columbia University Press, 1984). pp. 76–82.

4. See, for example, Gelfand, Lawrence E., *The Inquiry: American Preparations for Peace, 1917–1919* (New Haven: Yale University Press, 1963) and Knock, Thomas J., *To End All Wars: Woodrow Wilson and the Quest for a New World Order* (Princeton, NJ: Princeton University Press, 1995).

5. Cardozier, V.R., *Colleges and Universities in World War II* (Westport, CT: Praeger, 1993). p. 212.

6. U.S. Office of Education Wartime Commission, *Handbook on Education and the War: Based on Proceedings of the National Institute on Education and the War, at American University, Washington, D.C., August 28 through 31, 1942* (Washington, D.C.: Government Printing Office, 1943). pp. xiii–xiv.

7. External Research Staff, U.S. Department of State, *The Scholar and the Policy Maker: A Series of Talks Given at the Plenary Session of the Association for Asian Studies* (Washington, D.C.: U.S. Department of State, 1964). p. 22.

8. Berman, Edward H., *The Influence of the Carnegie, Ford, and Rockefeller Foundations on American Foreign Policy: The Ideology of Philanthropy* (Albany, NY: State University of New York Press, 1983). p. 5.

198

9. Ibid., p. 99. The prominent Harvard University historian and former intelligence official, William L. Langer, suggests in his autobiography, for example, that the foundations played a central role in the study of the Soviet Union in the United States during the immediate postwar years. Recalling the establishment of the Harvard Russian Research Center and the Columbia University Russian Institute, founded three years earlier, Langer attests: "Within a generation this country, hitherto so woefully ignorant of Russia, of Soviet institutions, objectives, and policies, developed an impressive number of scholars and officials conversant with these affairs, who produced a substantial literature on numerous aspects of Russian history and literature, on the revolutionary movement, and on the existing regime." Langer, William L., *In and Out of the Ivory Tower: The Autobiography of William L. Langer* (New York: Neale Watson Academic Publications, Inc., 1977). p. 231.

10. The 1954 Faculty Committee included these Harvard faculty members: Edward S. Mason, dean, Graduate School of Public Administration (Chair); Walter Bauer, M.D., Jackson Professor of Clinical Medicine; Kingman Brewster, Jr., professor of law; Merle Fainsod, professor of government; Rollin J. Fairbanks, lecturer on pastoral care; Bertrand Fox, director of research, Graduate School of Business Administration; V. O. Key, chair, Department of Government; Hugh R. Leavell, professor of public health practice; Frederick Mosteller, professor of mathematical statistics; Edwin B. Newman, chair, Department of Psychology; David E. Owen, chair, Department of History; Arthur Smithies, chair, Department of Economics; Samuel A. Stouffer, director, Laboratory of Social Relations; John W. M. Whiting, director, Laboratory of Human Development, Graduate School of Education.

In addition to Bundy, the 1956 Faculty Committee consisted of interested parties from the Department of Government (Rupert Emerson and Merle Fainsod), the Department of Economics (Edward S. Mason), the Department of History, (William Langer) and the Graduate School of Business Administration (Lincoln Gordon). This committee met over the course of two lunch meetings in 1956 to consider and conceptualize the framework of a potential future research center. A copy of the committee's report in the records of the Center for International Affairs, which are located in the Harvard Depository, indicates that the cover memorandum was dated February 10, 1956, although it is unclear when the committee actually met.

11. Center for International Affairs, Harvard University, *The First Two Years: 1958– 1960* (1960). p. 1.

12. Faculty Committee on Behavioral Sciences, Correspondence and Memoranda, Box 1, Memorandum from the Ford Foundation, "Individual Behavior and Human Relations," August 2, 1950, p. 1, in folder Behavioral Sciences Committee, Folder 2. UAI.10.545.7 Harvard University Archives.

13. Ibid., p. 1.

14. Ibid., p. 2.

15. These five universities were granted funds by the Ford Foundation to review the behavioral sciences in their institutions: University of Chicago, Harvard University, University of Michigan, University of North Carolina, and Stanford University. *The Behavioral Sciences at Harvard: Report by a Faculty Committee, June 1954* (Cambridge, 1954). p. 1.

16. Faculty Committee on Behavioral Sciences, Correspondence and Memoranda, Box 1, Memorandum from the Ford Foundation, "Self-Study Program," March [1953], p. 3, in folder Behavioral Sciences Committee, Folder 2. UAI.10.545.7 Harvard University Archives.

17. Faculty Committee on Behavioral Sciences, Correspondence and Memoranda, Box 1, "Memorandum Harvard University to the Behavioral Sciences Division, Ford Foundation," undated [1953], p. 4, in folder Behavioral Sciences Committee, Folder 2. UAI.10.545.7 Harvard University Archives.

18. Ibid., p. 4.

19. Ibid., p. 6.

20. Ibid., pp. 6–7.

21. *The Behavioral Sciences at Harvard.* p. 1.

22. Ibid., p. 4.

23. Ibid., p. 5.

24. Ibid., p. 3.

25. Faculty Committee on Behavioral Sciences, Correspondence and Memoranda, Box 1, "Department of Government," undated [1953], p. 3, in folder Behavioral Sciences Committee, Folder 2. UAI.10.545.7 Harvard University Archives.

26. Faculty Committee on Behavioral Sciences, Correspondence and Memoranda, Box 1, "Draft Recommendations—Department of Government," undated [1953], p. 1, in folder Behavioral Sciences Committee, Folder 2. UAI.10.545.7 Harvard University Archives.

27. Ibid., p. 1. Key was more circumspect about endorsing any serious effort in international relations: "The international field has a good deal of glamour about it, but it ranks low in substance." Faculty Committee on Behavioral Sciences, Correspondence and Memoranda, Box 1, "Department of Government," undated [1953], p. 8.

28. *The Behavioral Sciences at Harvard*, p. 43.

29. Ibid., p. 48.

30. As quoted in Leuchtenburg, William E., "The Historian and the Public Realm," *The American Historical Review* 97, no. 1 (February 1992). p. 10.

31. *The Behavioral Sciences at Harvard*, pp. 166–67.

32. Ibid., p. 168.

33. Ibid., p. 169.

34. Ibid.

35. Ibid., p. 463.

36. Ibid., p. 464.

37. Ibid., p. 465.

38. Ibid. There was no guarantee that the Ford Foundation would fund this, or any, of the recommendations of the 1954 Faculty Committee, despite their instrumental role in initiating the Behavioral Sciences study. As the Foundation stipulated in their letter of solicitation, "The Foundation gives no commitment in advance that it will provide financial support necessary to put recommendations into effect. However, it is anticipated that the reports will present important opportunities for implementation." Faculty Committee on Behavioral Sciences, Correspondence and Memoranda, Box 1, Memorandum from the Ford Foundation, "Self-Study Program," March [1953], p. 4.

39. The members of the visiting committee, appointed jointly by the Ford Foundation and Harvard University, included: George P. Murdock, professor of anthropology, Yale University (Chair); Dean A. Clark, M.D., director, Massachusetts General Hospital; R. Taylor Cole, professor of political science, Duke University;

Ernest R. Hilgard, dean, Graduate Division, Stanford University; William A. Mackintosh, principal and vice chancellor, Queens University; Robert K. Merton, professor of sociology, Columbia University; and W. Allen Wallis, professor of statistics and economics, University of Chicago, and director, Program of University Surveys of the Behavioral Sciences.

40. *The Behavioral Sciences at Harvard*, pp. 516–17.

41. Russian Research Center, Harvard University, *Five Year Report and Current Projects* (May, 1953). p. 8.

42. Committee on International and Regional Studies, Correspondence and Records, 1948–1955, Box 1, Letter from McGeorge Bundy to V. O. Key, November 5, 1953, p. 1, in folder 1953–54: International Affairs Program. UAIII.10.202.10 Harvard University Archives.

43. Robert Richardson Bowie, in an interview with the author, September 10, 2005.

44. Faculty of Arts and Sciences Dean, Letters, 1957–58, Box 12, "A Harvard Center for International Studies," undated [1956], p. 1, in folder Center for International Affairs. UAIII.5.55.26 Harvard University Archives.

45. Ibid., p. 4.

46. Ibid., p. 2.

47. The 1956 Faculty Committee anticipated that the majority of practitioners would be U.S. Foreign Service Officers and officials from various other U.S. agencies, whereas international students, government officials, and scholars would constitute the bulk of those involved with the Center.

48. Faculty of Arts and Sciences Dean, Letters, 1957–58, Box 12, "A Harvard Center for International Studies," undated [1956]. pp. 4–6.

49. Ibid., pp. 7–9.

50. Ibid., p. 9.

51. Faculty of Arts and Sciences Dean, Letters, 1957–58, Box 12, Memorandum from Milton Katz to Dean Griswold, Associate Dean Cavers, and M. Katz's Files, undated [1956], p. 1, in folder Center for International Affairs. UAIII.5.55.26 Harvard University Archives.

52. McFadzean, Andrew, "The Bigger Picture: Biography and/or History? Robert Bowie," *Australasian Journal of American Studies* 22, no. 2 (December 2003). pp. 43–44.

53. Robert Richardson Bowie, in an interview with the author, September 10, 2005.

54. Ibid.

55. Center for International Affairs History Pre-1970, Box 1, Letter from McGeorge Bundy to Robert R. Bowie, November 29, 1956, in folder Historical 1959, Bowie Correspondence, Harvard University Depository.

56. Center for International Affairs History Pre-1970, Box 1, Letter from Robert R. Bowie to McGeorge Bundy, December 8, 1956, in folder Historical 1959, Bowie Correspondence, Harvard University Depository.

57. Center for International Affairs History Pre-1970, Box 1, Letter from McGeorge Bundy to Robert R. Bowie, February 8, 1957, in folder History Pre-1970, Harvard University Depository.

58. Center for International Affairs History Pre-1970, Box 1, Letter from Don K. Price to Robert R. Bowie, October 26, 1956, in folder Historical 1959, Bowie Correspondence, Harvard University Depository.

59. Center for International Affairs History Pre-1970, Box 1, Letter from W. Barton Leach to Robert R. Bowie, undated [Received October 20, 1956], p. 1, in folder History Pre-1970, Harvard University Depository.

202

60. Ibid., p. 2.

61. Ibid., p. 3.

62. Ibid., p. 4. The double entendre of this statement may, or may not, be intentional.

63. Center for International Affairs History Pre-1970, Box 1, Letter from Robert R. Bowie to McGeorge Bundy, May 8, 1957, in folder History Pre-1970, Harvard University Depository.

## Two The Program of the Center for International Affairs

1. Robert Richardson Bowie, in an interview with the author, September 10, 2005.

2. Ibid.

3. Hereafter abbreviated as *Program*.

4. Robert Richardson Bowie, in an interview with the author, September 10, 2005.

5. Center for International Affairs, *The Program of the Center for International Affairs* 1958, p. 1. HUF.461.5158 Harvard University Archives.

6. Ibid., p. 2.

7. Ibid., p. 1.

8. Ibid., p. 3.

9. Ibid., p. 5.

10. Ibid., p. 8.

11. Ibid.

12. Ibid.

13. Ibid., p. 11.

14. Robert Richardson Bowie, in an interview with the author, September 10, 2005.

15. Ibid.

16. Center for International Affairs, *The Program of the Center for International Affairs*, p. 13.

17. Ibid., p. 9.

18. Ibid., p. 14.

19. Ibid.

20. Center for International Affairs, *The Program of the Center for International Affairs* Revised Draft [1958?], p. 12. HUF.461.5158.2 Harvard University Archives. The catalog of the Harvard University Archives speculates that this draft of the Center's program was completed sometime in 1958. I am inclined to believe that it was actually completed sometime in the fall of 1957, since I have found in Robert Bowie's Center files correspondence from that time period commenting on the draft.

21. Ibid., p. 12.

22. Ibid., p. 13.

23. Center for International Affairs History Pre-1970, Box 1, Memorandum from Robert R. Bowie to Henry A. Kissinger, March 26, 1959, p. 1, in folder Historical 1959, Bowie Correspondence, Harvard University Depository.

24. Committee on International and Regional Studies, Minutes 1946, "Minutes of the Meeting of the standing faculty committee on International and Regional Studies," October 22, 1946, p. 2. UAIII.10.202.A Harvard University Archives.

25. Ibid.

26. Committee on International and Regional Studies, Minutes 1946, "Minutes of the Meeting of the standing faculty committee on International and Regional Studies," December 12, 1946, p. 4. UAIII.10.202.A Harvard University Archives.

27. Committee on International and Regional Studies, Minutes 1946, "Minutes of the Meeting of the standing faculty committee on International and Regional Studies," May 26, 1948, p. 1. UAIII.10.202.A Harvard University Archives.

28. Center for International Affairs History Pre-1970, Box 1, "Emerson Proposes New International Center," *Harvard Crimson*, November 29, 1956, p. 1, in folder Historical 1959, Bowie Correspondence, Harvard University Depository. The very next day, Emerson received the support of the dean of the Graduate School of Public Administration, who reiterated the notion that some provision for undergraduate and graduate instruction ought to be considered in any discussion of a new international research center. Mason's enthusiasm was qualified, however, when he indicated that the director of any such center would invariably determine the nature of the institution. "Mason Declares Support of International Center," *Harvard Crimson*, November 30, 1956.

29. "Wanted: An International Center," *Harvard Crimson*, December 4, 1956.

30. Center for International Affairs History Pre-1970, Box 1, Letter from Rupert Emerson to McGeorge Bundy, December 13, 1957, p. 1, in folder Historical 1959, Bowie Correspondence, Harvard University Depository.

31. Center for International Affairs, *The Program of the Center for International Affairs* Revised Draft [1958?], p. 21.

32. Ibid., p. 24.

33. Center for International Affairs History Pre-1970, Box 1, Letter from Associate Dean David A. Cavers to Robert R. Bowie, October 24, 1957, pp. 1–2, in folder Historical 1959, Bowie Correspondence, Harvard University Depository.

34. Center for International Affairs History Pre-1970, Box 1, Letter from Dean Erwin Griswold to Robert R. Bowie, October 26, 1957, in folder Historical 1959, Bowie Correspondence, Harvard University Depository.

35. Center for International Affairs History Pre-1970, Box 1, Letter from Stanley H. Hoffmann to Robert R. Bowie, October 31, 1957, pp. 1–4, in folder Historical 1959, Bowie Correspondence, Harvard University Depository.

36. Ibid., p. 3.

37. Center for International Affairs History Pre-1970, Box 1, "Suggestions on Harvard Program," by Wallace Lampshire, November 5, 1957, p. 1, in folder Historical 1959, Bowie Correspondence, Harvard University Depository.

38. Center for International Affairs History Pre-1970, Box 1, Memorandum from Henry A. Kissinger to Robert R. Bowie, February 28, 1958, p. 1, in folder Henry Kissinger, Harvard University Depository.

39. Ibid., p. 2.

40. Center for International Affairs History Pre-1970, Box 1, "Observations on the Harvard Center for International Affairs" by Henry A. Kissinger, [Undated], in folder CFIA Governance, Harvard University Depository. pp. 9–13.

41. Ibid., pp. 13–14.

42. Ibid., pp. 14–15.

43. Center for International Affairs History Pre-1970, Box 1, Letter from Henry A. Kissinger to Robert R. Bowie, August 13, 1957, in folder History Pre-1970, Harvard University Depository.

44. *Report of the President of Harvard College and Reports of Departments, 1957-1958*, Official Register of Harvard University, Volume LVI, No. 22, August 31, 1959. p. 45.

45. Center for International Affairs History Pre-1970, Box 1, Letter from Dean Don Price to President Nathan Pusey, October 29, 1958, in folder Space 56–66, Harvard University Depository.

204

46. Center for International Affairs History Pre-1970, Box 1, Letter from Robert R. Bowie to A. D. Trottenberg, November 24, 1958, in folder Space 56–66, Harvard University Depository.

47. Center for International Affairs History Pre-1970, Box 1, "A Proposal for the International Studies Building," March 2, 1959, in folder Space 56–66, Harvard University Depository.

48. Robert Richardson Bowie, in an interview with the author, September 10, 2005.

49. Thomas C. Schelling, in an interview with the author, September 9, 2005.

50. Faculty of Arts and Sciences Dean, Letters, 1957–58, Box 12, Letter from Mc-George Bundy to Robert R. Bowie, March 10, 1958, pp. 1–2, in folder Center for International Affairs. UAIII 5.55.26 Harvard University Archives.

51. Center for International Affairs History Pre-1970, Box 1, Letter from Dean McGeorge Bundy to Robert R. Bowie, February 8, 1957, in folder History Pre-1970, Harvard University Depository.

52. Ibid.

53. Ibid.

54. Robert Richardson Bowie, in an interview with the author, September 10, 2005.

55. From 1958 to 2007, the Center for International Affairs has had seven faculty directors who have held this professorship: Robert R. Bowie (1958–72), Raymond Vernon (1973–78), Samuel P. Huntington (1978–89), Joseph S. Nye (1989–92), Robert D. Putnam (1993–96), Jorge I. Domínguez (1996–2006), and Beth A. Simmons (2006–present).

56. The Center for International Affairs was renamed the Weatherhead Center for International Affairs in 1998 in gratitude for the endowment established by Albert and Celia Weatherhead and the Weatherhead Foundation.

57. Robert Richardson Bowie, in an interview with the author, September 10, 2005. Bowie also recollects that his model for the Fellows Program derived in part from the Nieman Fellowship Program at Harvard, which was established in 1938 as a midcareer program for journalists.

58. Ibid.

59. Ibid.

60. Ibid.

61. *Report of the President of Harvard College and Reports of Departments, 1960–1961,* Official Register of Harvard University, Volume LIX, No. 26, August 31, 1962. p. 45.

62. Ibid.

63. Ibid., p. 46.

205

### Three    The First Two Years and the Evolving Role of the Fellows Program

1. Center for International Affairs, *The First Two Years*, p. 3.

2. Ibid.

3. Ibid., p. 16.

4. Ibid., pp. 5–6.

5. Ibid., p. 5.

6. Thomas C. Schelling, in an interview with the author, September 9, 2005.

7. Alex Inkeles, in an email correspondence with the author, June 21, 2006.

8. Joseph S. Nye, Jr., in an interview with the author, June 7, 2006.

9. Samuel P. Huntington, in an interview with the author, May 19, 2006.

10. Ibid.

11. Jorge I. Domínguez, in an interview with the author, June 22, 2006.

12. Joseph S. Nye, Jr., in an interview with the author, June 7, 2006.

13. Jorge I. Domínguez, in an interview with the author, June 22, 2006. Domínguez recalls that these experiences greatly influenced the way in which he perceived his own role as the Center Director from 1996 to 2006.

14. Karl Kaiser, in an interview with the author, April 19, 2006.

15. Samuel P. Huntington, in an interview with the author, May 19, 2006.

16. Ibid.

17. Jorge I. Domínguez, in an interview with the author, June 22, 2006.

18. Center for International Affairs, *The First Two Years*, p. 17.

19. Once the program was underway the Fellows' term of association with the Center was settled at nine months, or one academic year.

20. "U.S. Denies Harvard Talk Led to Shift by Dulles." *New York Times*, October 4, 1958. p. 7.

21. Center for International Affairs, *The First Two Years*, p. 20.

22. Thomas C. Schelling, in an interview with the author, September 9, 2005.

23. Samuel P. Huntington, in an interview with the author, May 19, 2006.

24. Karl Kaiser, in an interview with the author, April 19, 2006.

25. Morton H. Halperin, in an interview with the author, March 19, 2006.

26. Jorge I. Domínguez, in an interview with the author, June 22, 2006.

27. Samuel P. Huntington, in an interview with the author, May 19, 2006.

28. Center for International Affairs, *The First Five Years: 1958–1963* (1963). p. 39.

29. Center for International Affairs, Harvard University, *Eighth Annual Report: 1965–66* (1966). p. 21.

30. Ibid., p. 40.

31. Ibid., p. 41.

32. Joseph S. Nye, Jr., in an interview with the author, June 7, 2006.

33. In 1963–64 alone, for example, the Center welcomed a staggering list of visiting dignitaries from the United States including former Secretaries of State Acheson and Herter, director of the Central Intelligence Agency, Allen Dulles, as well as former ambassador to India and Harvard economics professor John Kenneth Galbraith. The Center also hosted fifteen other luminaries from Europe, Asia, and Africa, including the retiring NATO secretary-general, Dirk Stikker, the Indian ambassador to the United States, B. K. Nehru, the British ambassador to the United States, David Ormsby-Gore, and Shintaro Fukushima, president of the *Japan Times*. Center for International Affairs, Harvard University, *Seventh Annual Report: 1963–64* (1964). p. 25.

34. Center for International Affairs, Harvard University, *Twelfth Annual Report: 1969–70* (1970). p. 48.

35. Center for International Affairs, Harvard University, *Tenth Annual Report: 1967–68* (1968). p. 27.

36. Center for International Affairs, *Eleventh Annual Report*, p. 30.

37. Ibid., pp. 30–31.

38. Center for International Affairs, *Twelfth Annual Report*, pp. 43–44.

39. Ibid., p. 44.

40. Ibid., p. 45.

41. Ibid., p. 46.

42. Ibid.

43. Ibid., p. 47.

44. Ibid., p. 48.

45. Ibid.

## Four  The Evolving Role of Europe

1. Center for International Affairs, *The First Two Years*, p. 12.

2. Hoffmann, Stanley, et al., *In Search of France* (Cambridge, MA: Harvard University Press, 1963).

3. Center for International Affairs, *The First Two Years*, p. 12. Only one chapter focused explicitly on the ramifications of France's recent history and national trauma on French foreign policy.

4. Hoffmann et al, *In Search of France*, p. ix.

5. Center for International Affairs, *The First Two Years*, p. 12.

6. Hoffmann et al, *In Search of France*, p. x.

7. Karl Kaiser, in an interview with the author, April 19, 2006. Kaiser's own book, published under the joint auspices of the CFIA, the Twentieth Century Fund, and the Royal Institute of International Affairs, was a product of the aborted German

study. Kaiser, Karl, *German Foreign Policy in Transition: Bonn Between East and West* (London: Oxford University Press, 1968).

8. Stanley Hoffmann, in an email correspondence with the author, September 19, 2006.

9. Brzezinski, Zbigniew K., *The Soviet Bloc: Unity and Conflict* (Cambridge, MA: Harvard University Press, 1960).

10. *Communist China 1955–1959: Policy Documents with Analysis* (Cambridge, MA: Harvard University Press, 1962).

11. Center for International Affairs, Harvard University, *Sixth Annual Report: 1963–64* (1964). p. 1.

12. Karl Kaiser, in an interview with the author, April 19, 2006.

13. Fritz Erler's lectures were subsequently published in Erler, *Democracy in Germany* (Cambridge, MA: Harvard University Press, 1965).

14. Center for International Affairs History Pre-1970, Box 1, CFIA funding proposal to the Ford Foundation, May 8, 1964, p. 42, in folder [Unmarked], Harvard University Depository.

15. Ibid., p. 43.

16. Ibid., pp. 43–44.

17. Ibid., p. 47.

18. Center for International Affairs, Harvard University, *Seventh Annual Report: 1964–65* (1965). pp. 11–13.

19. Center for International Affairs, Harvard University, *Ninth Annual Report: 1966–67* (1967). pp. 16–17.

20. Vernon, Raymond, *Sovereignty at Bay: The Multinational Spread of U.S. Enterprises* (New York: Basic Books, Inc., 1971). p. v.

21. Center for International Affairs, *Tenth Annual Report*, pp. 20–21.

22. Center for International Affairs, *Twelfth Annual Report*, p. 32.

23. Stanley Hoffmann, in an email correspondence with the author, September 19, 2006.

### Five   The Role and Control of Force

1. Center for International Affairs, *The First Five Years* (1963), p. 20.

2. Ibid.

3. Hans Morgenthau, writing in the *American Political Science Review*, noted that *Nuclear Weapons and Foreign Policy* had achieved "spectacular popular success, quite unprecedented for works of this kind." Morgenthau was quick to add that "this popular success has tended to obscure the extraordinary intellectual merits of the book," which he saw as its "fusion of political and military thinking and development of a coherent doctrine of limited war." Morgenthau, Hans, Review

of *Nuclear Weapons and Foreign Policy*, by Henry Kissinger. *The American Political Science Review* 52, no. 3 (September 1958). p. 842. Paul Nitze, Bowie's predecessor as director of the State Department's Policy Planning Staff and a participant in the Council on Foreign Relations discussions that led to Kissinger's book, was less kind and wrote a famously savage review of *Nuclear Weapons and Foreign Policy* that would embitter their relationship for decades. Isaacson, *Kissinger*, pp. 89–90. Nevertheless, the book went on to win the Woodrow Wilson Prize in 1958 for the best contribution to the fields of government, politics, and international affairs.

4. Kissinger, Henry A., *Nuclear Weapons and Foreign Policy* (New York: Harper & Bros. for the Council on Foreign Relations, 1957). p. 111.

5. Morton H. Halperin, in an interview with the author, March 19, 2006.

6. Center for International Affairs, Harvard University, *Fourth Annual Report: 1961–62* (1962). p. 17.

7. Center for International Affairs, *The First Two Years* (1960), p. 11.

8. Center for International Affairs, Harvard University, *Eighth Annual Report: 1965-66* (1966). p. 15.

9. Ibid., p. 24.

10. Ibid.

11. Ibid., pp. 24–25.

12. Thomas C. Schelling, in an interview with the author, September 9, 2005.

13. Carl Kaysen, in an interview with the author, March 15, 2006.

14. Paul Doty, in an interview with the author, August 8, 2006.

15. Sims, Jennifer E., *Icarus Restrained: An Intellectual History of Nuclear Arms Control, 1945–1960* (Boulder, CO: Westview Press, Inc., 1990). p. 19.

16. *Daedalus* ("Special Issue: Arms Control") 89, no. 4 (Fall 1960). p. 675.

17. Carl Kaysen, in an interview with the author, March 15, 2006.

18. Bowie, Robert R., "Basic Requirements of Arms Control," *Daedalus* 89, no. 4 (Fall 1960). pp. 720–22.

19. Kissinger, Henry A., "Limited War: Conventional of Nuclear? A Reappraisal," *Daedalus* 89, no. 4 (Fall 1960). p. 810.

20. Ibid., p. 816.

21. Schelling, Thomas C., "Reciprocal Measures for Arms Stablilization," *Daedalus* 89, no. 4 (Fall 1960). p. 894.

22. Ibid., p. 904.

23. Schelling, Thomas C. and Halperin, Morton H., *Strategy and Arms Control* (New York: The Twentieth Century Fund, 1961). p. ix. Halperin, Schelling, and Henry Rowen attended the seminar.

24. Papers of Bernard Taub Feld, 1943–1990, Box 3, Series II: Subject and Correspondence Files, "Letter from Thomas C. Schelling to Bernard Feld," [undated], p. 1, in folder 19, Summer Study on Arms Control, MC 167, Institute Archives and Special Collections, MIT Libraries, Cambridge, Massachusetts.

25. Ibid., p. 2.

26. Papers of Bernard Taub Feld, 1943–1990, Box 2, Series II: Subject and Correspondence Files, "Letter from Thomas C. Schelling to Bernard Feld," October 6, 1960, p. 2, in folder F 15 – AAAS Comm TP of AL, MC 167, Institute Archives and Special Collections, MIT Libraries, Cambridge, Massachusetts.

27. Morton H. Halperin, in an interview with the author, March 19, 2006.

28. *Daedalus* 89, no. 4 (Fall 1960), p. 677.

29. Brennan, Donald G., "Setting and Goals of Arms Control," *Daedalus* 89, no. 4 (Fall 1960). p. 693.

30. Thomas C. Schelling, in an interview with the author, September 9, 2006.

31. Brennan, Donald G., ed., *Arms Control, Disarmament, and National Security* (New York: George Braziller, 1961). pp. 9–10.

32. Thomas C. Schelling, in an interview with the author, September 9, 2006.

33. Morton H. Halperin, in an interview with the author, March 19, 2006. It is important to note, however, that the Eisenhower administration had also been sympathetic to arms control and had initiated policies that were designed to reduce the threat of nuclear war, such as his "open skies" proposal and his famous "Atoms for Peace" speech, delivered to the United Nations on December 8, 1953. At the same time, the Eisenhower administration had undertaken a series of policies designed to create a framework of deterrence, such as the Polaris submarine-launched ballistic missile (SLBM), which provided the United States with a second-strike capability, and the "massive retaliation" doctrine that was introduced by Dulles in January 1954.

34. Papers of Max Millikan, Box 2, "Memorandum from Morton H. Halperin," September 12, 1960, p. 1, in folder 63, CIS Arms Control, MC 188, Institute Archives and Special Collections, MIT Libraries, Cambridge, Massachusetts.

35. Ibid.

36. Center for International Affairs, CFIA Joint Arms Control Seminar, Box 1, "Joint Seminar on Arms Control First Annual Report, 1960–61" June 1961, pp. 1–2, in folder [unmarked]. UAV.462.1142.5 Harvard University Archives.

37. Ibid., p. 2.

38. Ibid., pp. 2–3.

39. Sims, *Icarus Restrained*, p. 19.

40. Ibid., p. 27.

41. Ibid., p. 29.

42. Ibid.

43. Ibid., p. 35.

44. Center for International Affairs, CFIA Joint Arms Control Seminar, Box 1, "Joint Arms Control Seminar: Abstract of Discussion, 4 October 1960, pp. 1–3, in folder Arms Control Seminar—Minutes of the Sessions, 1960–61. UAV.462.1142.3 Harvard University Archives.

45. Center for International Affairs, CFIA Joint Arms Control Seminar, Box 1, "Joint Arms Control Seminar: Abstract of Discussion, 12 December 1960," pp. 1–6, in folder Arms Control Seminar—Minutes of the Sessions, 1960–61. UAV.462.1142.3 Harvard University Archives. The Pugwash Conferences were named after the first such conference between scientists that took place in Pugwash, Nova Scotia in July 1957.

46. Center for International Affairs, CFIA Joint Arms Control Seminar, Box 1, "Joint Arms Control Seminar: Abstract of Discussion, 24 October 1960," p. 5, in folder Arms Control Seminar—Minutes of the Sessions, 1960–61. UAV.462.1142.3 Harvard University Archives.

47. Center for International Affairs, CFIA Joint Arms Control Seminar, Box 1, "Joint Arms Control Seminar: Abstract of Discussion, 22 May 1961," pp. 1–5, in folder Arms Control Seminar—Minutes of the Sessions, 1960–61. UAV.462.1142.3 Harvard University Archives.

48. Center for International Affairs, CFIA Joint Arms Control Seminar, Box 1, "Joint Seminar on Arms Control First Annual Report, 1960–61" June 1961, p. 22, in folder [unmarked]. UAV.462.1142.5 Harvard University Archives.

49. Ibid., p. 4.

50. Schelling and Halperin, *Strategy and Arms Control*, p. 1.

51. Thomas C. Schelling, in an interview with the author, September 9, 2006. Schelling recalls that "the Twentieth Century Fund found a printer who said he could do the book in six weeks, and so within two weeks after inauguration day we had copies of the book and we distributed several hundred copies around Washington. And…people like Mac Bundy, and Walt Rostow, and Harry Rowen, Abram Chayes…who were now at the level of White House advisor, or assistant secretary or deputy assistant secretary, they all knew the book, [and] they all would ask for twenty copies and distribute them."

52. Morton H. Halperin, in an interview with the author, March 19, 2006.

53. Center for International Affairs, CFIA Joint Arms Control Seminar, Box 1, "Joint Arms Control Seminar: Minutes of the Fourth Session, November 20, 1961," pp. 1–4, in folder Arms Control Seminar—Minutes of the Sessions, 1961–62. UAV.462.1142.3 Harvard University Archives.

54. Center for International Affairs, CFIA Joint Arms Control Seminar, Box 1, "Joint Arms Control Seminar: Minutes of the Second Session, October 22, 1962," p. 5, in folder Arms Control Seminar—Minutes of the Sessions, 1962–63. UAV.462.1142.3 Harvard University Archives.

55. Morris, Charles R., *Iron Destinies, Lost Opportunities: The Arms Race Between the U.S.A. and the U.S.S.R., 1945–1987* (New York: Harper & Row Publishers, 1960). p. 134.

56. Thomas C. Schelling, in an interview with the author, September 9, 2006.

57. Center for International Affairs, CFIA Joint Arms Control Seminar, Box 1, "Joint Arms Control Seminar: Minutes of the Eleventh Session, April 22, 1963," pp. 1–2, in folder Arms Control Seminar—Minutes of the Sessions, 1962–63. UAV.462.1142.3 Harvard University Archives.

58. Ibid., pp. 2–4.

59. A December meeting was attended by the Israeli ambassador to the United Nations, Gideon Rafael, and Raymond Garthoff, the deputy assistant secretary for politico-military affairs at the U.S. State Department, and both participated in a discussion on Soviet military strategy. In addition to government officials, the seminar also hosted a number of guests from the RAND Corporation and numerous other universities and independent research centers. The Center also benefited from the insights of military personnel such as General Glenn Kent of the Office of Defense Research Engineering. These names of attendees are all taken from the files of Center for International Affairs, CFIA Joint Arms Control Seminar, Box 1, in folder Arms Control Seminar—Minutes of the Sessions, 1963–64. UAV.462.1142.3 Harvard University Archives.

60. Center for International Affairs, CFIA Joint Arms Control Seminar, Box 1, "Joint Arms Control Seminar: Minutes of the First Session, October 19, 1964, pp. 1–2, in folder Arms Control Seminar-Minutes of the Sessions, 1964–65. UAV.462.1142.3 Harvard University Archives. Schelling's position on this issue may in large part reflect his own intellectual development, since by this time he was becoming increasingly interested in issues of organized crime and segregation.

61. Center for International Affairs History Pre-1970, Box 1, "Summary of the Visiting Committee Meeting," March 5, 1971, p. 2, in folder Various Historical Documents, Harvard University Depository.

62. Center for International Affairs, Harvard University, *Fourteenth Annual Report: 1971–72* (1972). pp. 28–29.

63. Center for International Affairs, Harvard University, *Fifteenth Annual Report: 1972–73* (1973). p. 31.

64. Center for International Affairs, Harvard University, *1973–74 Annual Report* (1974). p. 22.

65. Huntington, Samuel P., and Nye, Joseph S., Jr., eds., *Global Dilemmas* (Lanham, MD: University Press of America and the Center for International Affairs, 1985). p. 60.

66. May, Ernest R., "Ideas about Military Strategy" in Lyons, Gene M., ed., *The Role of Ideas in American Foreign Policy* (Hanover, NH.: University Press of New England, 1971). p. 28.

67. Ibid., p. 45.

68. Ibid.

69. Schelling, Thomas C., "What Went Wrong with Arms Control?" *Foreign Affairs* 64 (Winter 1985/86). p. 223.

70. Thomas C. Schelling, in an interview with the author, September 9, 2006. John McNaughton was perhaps the most important link between Schelling and the Defense Department. Schelling had originally been offered the position of deputy for arms control to then–assistant secretary of defense for international security affairs, Paul Nitze. Schelling turned down the offer, but recommended his friend and Harvard Law School professor John McNaughton. McNaughton would later succeed Nitze as assistant secretary of defense, and became a direct link between Schelling and Secretary of Defense McNamara.

71. Levine, Robert, *Still the Arms Debate* (Brookfield, VT: Dartmouth Publishing Company, 1990). p. 11.

72. Ibid., p. 127.

73. Newhouse, John, *Cold Dawn: The Story of SALT* (Washington, D.C.: Pergamon-Brassey's, 1989). pp. 49–50.

74. Ibid., pp. 112–13.

## Six    Development and Modernization

1. Center for International Affairs, Harvard University, *The First Two Years: 1958–1960* (1960). pp. 6–7. The other two scholars responsible for these studies were Montague Yudelman, an agricultural economist from South Africa, and George B. Baldwin, a member of the Harvard advisory group in Tehran.

2. Edward S. Mason, *Foreign Aid and Foreign Policy* (New York: Harper & Row, 1964).

3. Center for International Affairs, Harvard University, *Seventh Annual Report: 1964–1965* (1965). pp. 3–4.

4. Center for International Affairs, Harvard University, *Sixth Annual Report: 1963–1964* (1964). p. 7.

5. One member of the Chenery team, Arthur MacEwan, a CFIA research associate and assistant professor of economics, remembers that Chenery's project "became the center of the young leftists in the Department of Economics." Arthur MacEwan, in an interview with the author, March 22, 2007.

6. Center for International Affairs, Harvard University, *Ninth Annual Report: 1966–1967* (1967). p. 8.

7. Center for International Affairs, Harvard University, *Twelfth Annual Report: 1969–1970* (1970). p. 6.

8. Ibid., p. 6.

9. Ibid., p. 11.

10. Gustav Papanek, in an interview with the author, May 5, 2006. Papanek notes the extent to which DAS members contributed to the academic life of the University: "A number of faculty members who served as DAS consultants did some of their research on the basis of their DAS work. An example is Louis Wells at the Harvard Business School and his work on negotiating with foreign investors in raw materials. Some faculty members started with DAS in overseas assignments and were later recruited by Harvard for faculty positions. Maurice Kilbridge was an advisor in the 1950s in Pakistan, and he later was dean of the Graduate School of Design; Hollis Chenery, also in Pakistan in the 1950s, later was professor of economics."

11. Center for International Affairs, *Twelfth Annual Report*. pp. 11–12.

12. Center for International Affairs, Harvard University, *Fifteenth Annual Report: 1972–1973* (1973). p. 24.

13. Center for International Affairs, Harvard University, *Thirteenth Annual Report: 1970–1971* (1971). pp. 7–8.

14. Center for International Affairs, Harvard University, *The First Two Years: 1958–1960* (1960). p. 8.

15. Alex Inkeles, in an email correspondence with the author, June 21, 2006.

16. Center for International Affairs, Harvard University, *The First Five Years: 1958–1963* (1963). p. 14.

17. Center for International Affairs, Harvard University, *Sixth Annual Report: 1963–1964* (1964). pp. 11–13.

18. For a sample of the questionnaire, see appendix A in Alex Inkeles and David H. Smith, *Becoming Modern: Individual Change in Six Developing Countries* (Cambridge, MA: Harvard University Press, 1974).

19. Ibid., p. 174.

20. Ibid., p. 192.

21. Center for International Affairs, *Sixth Annual Report* (1964). pp. 13–16.

22. Samuel P. Huntington, in an interview with the author, May 19, 2006.

23. Center for International Affairs, *Sixth Annual Report* (1964). p. 17.

24. Center for International Affairs, Harvard University, *Seventh Annual Report: 1964–1965* (1965). p. 9.

25. Center for International Affairs, Harvard University, *Eighth Annual Report: 1965–1966* (1966). pp. 8–10.

26. Center for International Affairs, Harvard University, *Ninth Annual Report: 1966–1967* (1967). pp. 10–11.

27. Center for International Affairs, Harvard University, *Tenth Annual Report: 1967–1968* (1968). p. 11.

28. Samuel P. Huntington, *Political Order in Changing Societies* (New Haven, CT: Yale University Press, 1968). pp. 1–2.

29. Ibid., pp. 4–5. This insight raised important implications for the effectiveness of foreign aid programs, especially those of the United States, since, as he pointed out, American foreign aid tended to conflate political stability with economic development. In fact, Huntington noted, the two goals are not necessarily reciprocal, and economic development might just as easily engender political instability.

30. Ibid., pp. 8–24.

31. Ibid., p. 397.

32. Ibid., p. 412.

33. Center for International Affairs, Harvard University, *Twelfth Annual Report: 1969–1970* (1970). p. 18.

34. Ibid., p. 20.

35. Center for International Affairs, Harvard University, *Thirteenth Annual Report: 1970–1971* (1971). p. 10.

36. Center for International Affairs, Harvard University, *Fourteenth Annual Report: 1971–1972* (1972). p. 20.

37. Center for International Affairs, Harvard University, *Fifteenth Annual Report: 1972–1973* (1973). p. 8.

38. Ibid., p. 13.

39. Center for International Affairs, Harvard University, *Fourteenth Annual Report: 1971–1972* (1972). p. 7.

40. Edward S. Mason, *The Harvard Institute For International Development And Its Antecedents* (University Press of America, 1986). p. v.

41. Ibid., p. 1.

42. Ibid., p. 13.

43. Development Advisory Service, Administrative and Project Records, 1958–1974, Box 1, Letter from Robert R. Bowie to F. F. Hill, March 28, 1962, p. 1, in folder DAS Background Notes, Reports, Memos, 1962–69. UAV 462.5095.6 Harvard University Archives.

44. Ibid., pp. 1–2.

45. Center for International Affairs, Harvard University, *Fourth Annual Report: 1961–1962* (1962). p.27.

46. Ibid., p. 26.

47. Mason's 1986 monograph, *The Harvard Institute For International Development And Its Antecedents*, remains the best and, to my knowledge, only history of the DAS and the HIID. Anybody interested in a fuller narrative account of the DAS and its activities should turn to Mason's treatment.

48. Development Advisory Service, Administrative and Project Records, 1958–1974, Box 1, *Fourth Annual Report on the Operations of the Development Advisory Service, July 1, 1965–June 30*, 1966, p. 1, in folder DAS Background Notes, Reports, Memos, 1962–69. UAV 462.5095.6 Harvard University Archives.

49. Center for International Affairs, Harvard University, *The First Five Years: 1958–1963* (1963). pp.34–35.

50. Gustav Papanek, in an interview with the author, May 5, 2006.

51. Mason, *The Harvard Institute For International Development And Its Antecedents*. p. 62.

52. Center for International Affairs, Development Advisory Service, Correspondence and Papers, 1969–1970, The Permanent DAS Group, November 15, 1968, pp. 1–6, in folder 1968–1972. UAV 462.1117.5 Harvard University Archives.

53. Gustav Papanek, in an interview with the author, May 5, 2006.

54. Center for International Affairs, Development Advisory Service, Correspondence and Papers, 1969–1970, Research and the Development Advisory Service, December 16, 1968, pp. 1–6, in folder 1968–1972. UAV 462.1117.5 Harvard University Archives.

55. Center for International Affairs, Development Advisory Service, Correspondence and Papers, 1969–1970, The DAS and the Disciplines/Professions, November 20, 1968, pp. 1–5, in folder 1968–1972. UAV 462.1117.5 Harvard University Archives.

56. Center for International Affairs, Development Advisory Service, Correspondence and Papers, 1969–1970, DAS Teaching, November 8, 1968, pp. 1–4, in folder 1968–1972. UAV 462.1117.5 Harvard University Archives.

57. Mason, *The Harvard Institute For International Development And Its Antecedents*. pp. 14–15.

58. Development Advisory Service, Administrative and Project Records, 1958–1974, Box 1, Draft Pamphlet, December 4, 1969, p. 18, in folder DAS Background Notes, Reports, Memos, 1962–69. UAV 462.5095.6 Harvard University Archives.

59. Mason, *The Harvard Institute For International Development And Its Antecedents*. p. 14.

60. Development Advisory Service, Administrative and Project Records, 1958–1974, Box 1, Draft Pamphlet, December 4, 1969, p. 18, in folder DAS Background Notes, Reports, Memos, 1962–69. UAV 462.5095.6 Harvard University Archives.

61. Dwight Perkins, in an interview with the author, August 7, 2006.

62. Development Advisory Service, Administrative and Project Records, 1958–1974, Box 1, Draft Pamphlet, December 4, 1969, p. 5, in folder DAS Background Notes, Reports, Memos, 1962–69. UAV 462.5095.6 Harvard University Archives.

63. Mason, *The Harvard Institute For International Development And Its Antecedents*. p. 17. The project ran from March 1954 to June 1970, which with hindsight Mason suggests "was about five years too long." Ibid. p. 3.

64. Gustav Papanek, in an interview with the author, May 5, 2006. Another important factor was the change in administration in the United States: "In 1953 when the Pakistan project was first staffed, a number of able and experienced economists were available. After twenty years of Democratic administrations a Republican government has come into office. David Bell had served in the Truman White House; Emile Despres had been in the Treasury or Federal Reserve, I believe; [said Papanek, who himself had been in the aid program for Asia]."

65. Harvard Institute for International Development, Project and Research Records, 1960–1980, Subseries IV, Box 58, Harvard University Pakistan Advisory Group Project Report, January–June 1970, by Richard Gilbert [Draft], 1970, p. 51, in folder, Harvard University Pakistan Advisory Group Project Report, 1970, Gilbert. UAV 462.5010 Harvard University Archives.

66. Ibid., p. 51.

67. Ibid., p. 51.

68. Gustav Papanek, in an interview with the author, May 5, 2006.

69. Harvard Institute for International Development, Project and Research Records, 1960–1980, Subseries IV, Box 58, Harvard University Pakistan Advisory Group Project Report, January–June 1970, by Richard Gilbert [Draft], 1970, p. 52, in folder, Harvard University Pakistan Advisory Group Project Report, 1970, Gilbert. UAV 462.5010 Harvard University Archives.

70. Ibid., p. 55.

71. Ibid., p. 56.

72. Ibid., pp. 56–58.

73. Dwight Perkins, in an interview with the author, August 7, 2006.

74. Gustav Papenek, in an interview with the author, May 5, 2006.

75. Ibid.

76. Harvard Institute for International Development, Project and Research Records, 1960–1980, Subseries IV, Box 58, Report on Pakistan, November 25, 1969, in folder, Report on Pakistan, 1969, Papanek. UAV 462.5010 Harvard University Archives.

77. Center for International Affairs, Development Advisory Service, Correspondence and Papers, 1969–1970, Letter from Gustav Papanek to David Bell, April 28, 1967, pp. 1, in folder 1968–1972. UAV 462.1117.5 Harvard University Archives.

78. See for example, Latham, Michael E., *Modernization as Ideology: American Social Science and "Nation Building" in the Kennedy Era* (Chapel Hill, NC: The University of North Carolina Press, 2000), Engerman, David C., Gilman, Nils, Haefele, Mark H., and Latham, Michael E., eds., *Modernization, Development, and the Global Cold War* (Amherst and Boston, MA: University of Massachusetts Press, 2003), and Gilman, Nils, *Mandarins of the Future: Modernization Theory in Cold War America* (Baltimore: Johns Hopkins University Press, 2003).

79. Mason, *The Harvard Institute For International Development And Its Antecedents*. p. 60.

80. Ibid., p. 63.

81. Samuel P. Huntington, in an interview with the author, May 19, 2006.

## Seven   The Center's Relation to Policy

1. Robert Richardson Bowie, in an interview with the author, September 10, 2005.

2. Samuel P. Huntington, in an interview with the author, March 19, 2006.

3. Center for International Affairs, *The First Two Years* (1960), p. 16.

4. U.S. Congress, Senate Committee on Foreign Relations, *United States Foreign Policy: Ideology and Foreign Affairs (The Principal Ideological Conflicts, Variations Thereon, Their Manifestations, and Their Present and Potential Impact on the Foreign Policy of the United States)* (Washington, D.C.: U.S. Government Printing Office, 1960). p. v. In addition to Brzezinski, the report included contributions by numerous members of the Harvard faculty, such as Rupert Emerson, Stanley H. Hoffmann, William Polk, and Max W. Thornburg, in conjunction with insights gleaned from, among others, William Y. Elliott, Carl J. Friedrich, Merle Fainsod, and Benjamin Schwartz.

5. Ibid., p. vi.

6. Ibid., p. ix.

7. Brzezinski's *The Soviet Bloc: Unity and Conflict* (Cambridge, MA: Harvard Univer-

sity Press, 1960) was the first book published under the auspices of the CFIA in conjunction with the Russian Research Center. *Ideology and Foreign Affairs* was published by the Senate Committee on Foreign Relations a month before. Bowie saw Brzezinski's book as epitomizing two key aspects of the Center's mission. He feted Brzezinski's work as characterizing the Center's role in bringing together scholars involved in studying international affairs from different areas of the University, since Brzezinski was also a member of the Russian Research Center: "Thus the newer Center began its publication program in collaboration with another part of the University—a circumstance in keeping with its function as a point of convergence for the Harvard Community of Scholars." In addition, Bowie also highlighted Brzezinski's acknowledgment in the preface of *The Soviet Bloc* that the Center "has provided a unique forum for testing my hypotheses against the judgment and experience of senior foreign-policy officials from a variety of countries." In this regard, Brzezinski had reinforced the validity of the Fellows Program. Center for International Affairs, *The First Two Years* (1960), p. 13, 18.

8.  Ibid., p. 1.

9.  Thomas C. Schelling, in an interview with the author, September 9, 2005.

10. U.S. Congress, Senate Committee on Foreign Relations, *United States Foreign Policy: Ideology and Foreign Affairs*, p. 7.

11. Ibid., p. 79.

12. U.S. Congress, Senate Committee on Foreign Relations, *Hearings Before the Committee on Foreign Relations on the Formulation and Administration of United States Foreign Policy, 87th Congress, First Session, Part 2* (Washington, D.C.: U.S. Government Printing Office, 1961). p. 328.

13. Ibid., pp. 327–28. Fulbright seems to have been serious, since the *New York Times* ran a story on the CFIA's report after the release of the study by the Foreign Relations Committee. "Risk Seen in Hope for Freer Soviet," *New York Times*, January 17, 1960. p. 17.

14. Ibid., pp. 355–56. Brzezinski sent the Foreign Relations Committee clippings from the communist press that appeared in the aftermath of the study's publication in 1961.

15. Bowie, Robert R., "The North Atlantic Nations: Tasks for the 1960s: A Report to the Secretary of State, August 1960 by Robert R. Bowie." The report was declassified and published in 1991 in *Nuclear History Program: Occasional Paper* 7, (College Park, MD: Center for International Security Studies at Maryland School of Public Affairs, University of Maryland, 1991).

16. Ibid.

17. Ibid., p. 45.

18. Ibid., p. 47.

19. Ibid., p. xx.

20. Ibid.

21. Ibid.

22. For a more complete discussion of the tortured path and eventual failure of the MLF proposal, see Seaborg, Glenn T., with Benjamin S. Loeb, *Stemming the Tide: Arms Control in the Johnson Years* (Lexington, MA: Lexington Books, 1987).

23. This type of critique was perhaps most vociferously articulated by Noam Chomsky in his book, first published in 1969, *American Power and the New Mandarins* (New York: New Press, 2002).

24. John Kenneth Galbraith, in an interview with the author, April 19, 2003.

25. Ibid.

26. Memorandum, INR-Deirdre Henderson to Professor Lerner, Undated, "Camp David Meeting on Research Papers" folder, Department of State, 1960–1966, James C. Thomson Papers (JTP), Box 6. pp. 6–7. John F. Kennedy Library (JFKL).

27. Ibid., pp. 7–8.

28. Polk, William R., "Problems of Government Utilization of Scholarly Research in International Affairs," in Horowitz, Irving Louis, ed., *The Rise and Fall of Project Camelot: Studies in the Relationship between Social Science and Practical Politics* (Cambridge, MA: The MIT Press, 1967). p. 239.

29. As quoted in External Research Staff, U.S. Department of State, *The Scholar and the Policy Maker: A Series of Talks Given at the Plenary Session of the Association for Asian Studies* (Washington, D.C.: U.S. Department of State, 1964). p. 15. John King Fairbank had his own encounter with the vitriol of McCarthyism during the early 1950s, an experience that demonstrates the fragility of the association between academic intellectuals and the federal government. In his case, despite the advantages of engaging academic specialists in dealing with unfamiliar cultures deemed to be of national importance, the dynamics of the cold war ultimately subsumed expediency. In August 1951, the Harvard University history professor and renowned expert on China arrived in California with his family, prepared to embark upon a year-long sabbatical to Japan in order to research Japanese historiography of China. His application to enter Japan was denied by the U.S. Army, which administered Japanese visas during the period of American occupation. This denial stemmed from the fact that Fairbank's name had come before Senator Pat McCarran's Internal Security Act Subcommittee on August 9, 1951, during an investigation into supposed communist infiltration of the Institute of Pacific Relations (IPR), of

which he was a trustee. Two former communists also explicitly accused him of harboring communist proclivities in their testimony before the committee. In his defense, prominent public figures such as Secretary of State Acheson and Secretary of Defense Marshall sought to help Fairbank clear his name. Details can be found in Army Permit—Correspondence; Correspondence and Other Papers Relating to the McCarthy Era (1934), 1950–51, Box 1, John King Fairbank Papers. Harvard University Archives.

30. Gilboa, Eytan, *The Scholar and the Foreign Policy-Maker in the United States* (Unpublished Ph.D. Dissertation, Harvard University, Cambridge, MA, May 1974). p. 1. Harvard University Archives.

31. Ibid., p. 4.

32. Rosenau, James N., *International Studies and the Social Sciences: Problems, Priorities and Prospects in the United States* (Beverly Hills: Sage Publications, 1973). pp. 87–88.

33. External Research Staff, U.S. Department of State, *The Scholar and the Policy Maker*, p. 1.

34. Ibid., p. 2.

35. Ibid., p. 3.

36. Draft Notes, Proposed Policy Research Studies Program for Fiscal Year 1964, Undated, "Policy Research Studies Program" folder, INR Budget FY 64, Roger Hilsman Papers (RHP), Box 5, JFKL.

37. Quoted in Gilboa, *The Scholar and the Foreign Policy-Maker in the United States*, p. 6.

38. Zbigniew Brzezinski, in an email correspondence with the author, May 1, 2003.

39. Ibid.

40. This quote is taken from "Diplomacy for the 70s: A Program of Management Reform for the Department of State," a Department of State publication produced in 1970, as quoted in Gilboa, *The Scholar and the Foreign Policy-Maker in the United States*, p. 98.

41. Nisbet, Robert A. "Project Camelot: An Autopsy," in Philip Rieff, ed., *On Intellectuals: Theoretical Studies, Case Studies* (Garden City, NY: Doubleday and Company, Inc., 1969). p. 296. Gene M. Lyons has also highlighted the State Department's reticence in employing outside research, which he argues derived from "more than a matter of 'choice'; it was a matter of operating traditions, organizational developments and staffing patterns." Lyons, *The Uneasy Partnership: Social Science Research and the Federal Government in the Twentieth Century* (New York: Russell Sage Foundation, 1969). p. 179.

42. For an illustrative list of faculty members of the Center who served in a government capacity, see Appendix Three.

43. Memorandum, McGeorge Bundy to the President, July 13, 1961, "Chronological File 7/1/61–7/16/61" folder, McGeorge Bundy Correspondence, National Security Files (NSF), Papers of President Kennedy (PPK), Box 398A, JFKL.

44. Robert Richardson Bowie, in an interview with the author, September 10, 2005.

45. Thomas C. Schelling, in an interview with the author, September 9, 2005.

46. Letter, McGeorge Bundy to Robert E. Osgood, April 29, 1961, "4/25/61–4/30/61" folder, McGeorge Bundy Correspondence, Chronological File, NSF, PPK, Box 398, JFKL.

47. "Schelling to be Named State Dept. Consultant," *Harvard Crimson*, April 13, 1967.

48. "Schelling Rejects State Dept. Post, Will Stay Here," *Harvard Crimson*, May 19, 1967.

49. Letter, McGeorge Bundy to President John F. Kennedy, February 8, 1961, "1/61–2/61" folder, Memos to the President, McGeorge Bundy Correspondence, NSF, PPK, Box 405, JFKL.

50. Letter, McGeorge Bundy to Henry A. Kissinger, January 8, 1961, "Henry Kissinger, 5/61" folder, Meetings and Memoranda, Staff Memoranda, NSF, PPK, Box 320, JFKL.

51. Kissinger, Henry A., *The Necessity for Choice: Prospects of American Foreign Policy* (London: Chatto and Windus, 1960). p. 349.

52. Ibid., pp. 350–51.

53. Ibid., p. 351. Morton Halperin concurs with this assessment from Kissinger. "People in the government are too busy to change their minds. You've got to educate them before they get in. They don't have time. Moreover, the arguments that outsiders give you are almost irrelevant to you because you know it, the question is how you do it?" Morton H. Halperin, in an interview with the author, March 19, 2006.

54. Letter, McGeorge Bundy to Henry A. Kissinger, February 18, 1961, "Henry Kissinger, 5/61" folder, Meetings and Memoranda, Staff Memoranda, NSF, PPK, Box 320, JFKL.

55. Memorandum, A. Russell Ash to Mr. Bromley Smith, September 26, 1961, "B: NATO + Security Agreement" folder, Kissinger Series, NSF, PPK, Box 462, JFKL. See also Memorandum from Ash to Bundy, June 2, 1961, in the same folder.

56. Memorandum, McGeorge Bundy to the Director of Central Intelligence, May 29, 1961, "Henry Kissinger, 5/61" folder, Meetings and Memoranda, Staff Memoranda, NSF, PPK, Box 320, JFKL.

57. Letter, Henry A. Kissinger to McGeorge Bundy, April 5, 1961, "B: NATO +

Security Agreement" folder, Kissinger Series, NSF, PPK, Box 462, JFKL.

58. Letter, Henry A. Kissinger to McGeorge Bundy, May 5, 1961, "Henry Kissinger, 5/61" folder, Meetings and Memoranda, Staff Memoranda, NSF, PPK, Box 320, JFKL.

59. For Kissinger's thoughts on the Nuclear Test Ban Treaty see Memorandum, Henry A. Kissinger to McGeorge Bundy, September 6, 1961, "Kissinger Chronological File, 7/61" folder, Kissinger Series, NSF, PPK, Box 462, JFKL. For Kissinger's reactions to U.S. disarmament proposals see, Letter, Henry A. Kissinger to McGeorge Bundy, June 20, 1961, "Kissinger Chronological File, 7/61" folder, Kissinger Series, NSF, PPK, Box 462, JFKL.

60. This letter, dated June 5, 1961, was quoted verbatim in a long letter to Arthur Schlesinger in September 1961. Letter, Henry A. Kissinger to Arthur M. Schlesinger, Jr., September 8, 1961. "Kissinger, Henry 4/19/61–12/2/61" folder, Subject File, White House Files, Papers of Arthur M. Schlesinger Jr. (ASP), Box WH13, JFKL.

61. Memorandum, McGeorge Bundy to Henry A. Kissinger, June 8, 1961, "Chronological File 6/1/61–6/18/61" folder, McGeorge Bundy Correspondence, NSF, PPK, Box 398, JFKL.

62. Letter, Henry A. Kissinger to Arthur M. Schlesinger, Jr., September 8, 1961. "Kissinger, Henry 4/19/61–12/2/61" folder, Subject File, White House Files, ASP, Box WH13, JFKL. Kissinger felt that "I am in the position of a man riding next to a driver heading for a precipice who is being asked to make sure that the gas tank is full and the oil pressure adequate."

63. Letter, Henry A. Kissinger to Arthur M. Schlesinger, Jr., April 9, 1962. "Kissinger, Henry 8/3/61–6/4/63" folder, Subject File, White House Files, ASP, Box WH39, JFKL.

64. Letter, McGeorge Bundy to Henry A. Kissinger, September 14, 1962, "Henry Kissinger, 6/62–12/62" folder, Meetings and Memoranda, Staff Memoranda, NSF, PPK, Box 321, JFKL.

65. Letter, Henry A. Kissinger to McGeorge Bundy, October 3, 1962, "Henry Kissinger, 6/62–12/62" folder, Meetings and Memoranda, Staff Memoranda, NSF, PPK, Box 321, JFKL.

66. Carl Kaysen, in an interview with the author, March 15, 2006.

67. SORO, "Document Number 2", in Horowitz, ed., *The Rise and Fall of Project Camelot*, p. 54.

68. Center faculty member Alex Inkeles gave testimony to the Senate Subcommittee on Government Research of the Committee on Government Operations in the summer of 1966, convened in the aftermath of Project Camelot to investigate

"Federal Support of International Social Research and Behavioral Research." U.S. Congress, Senate Committee on Government Operations, Subcommittee on Government Research, *Federal Support of International Social Research and Behavioral Research* (Washington, D.C.: U.S. Government Printing Office, 1967). Earlier hearings had been held in 1965 in the House. See U.S. Congress, House Committee on Foreign Affairs, Subcommittee on International Organizations and Movements, *Behavioral Sciences and the National Security; Part IX, Winning the Cold War: The U.S. Ideological Offensive* (Washington, D.C.: U.S. Government Printing Office, 1965).

69. See Scigliano, Robert, and Fox, Guy H., *Technical Assistance in Vietnam: The Michigan State University Experience* (New York: Frederick A. Praeger Publishers, 1965) and Ernst, John, *Forging A Fateful Alliance: Michigan State University and the Vietnam War* (East Lansing, MI: Michigan State University Press, 1998).

70. Thomas Schelling, in an interview with the author, September 9, 2005. For a discussion of the CIS and its relationship to the CIA see Blackmer, Donald L.M., *The MIT Center for International Studies: The Founding Years, 1951–1969* (Cambridge, MA: MIT Center for International Studies, 2002). pp. 28–29, 175–79.

71. Center for International Affairs, *Eighth Annual Report* (1966), p. 2. I have found no evidence to suggest that this assertion was inaccurate.

72. Ibid., pp. 2–3.

73. Ibid., p. 3.

74. Robert R. Bowie, in an interview with the author, September 10, 2005.

## Eight   Protests and Violence at the CFIA

1. Vernon was acting director of the CFIA while Bowie was counselor at the U.S. Department of State from 1966 to 1968.

2. Center for International Affairs, *Tenth Annual Report* (1968), p. 1.

3. Ibid., p. 2.

4. Center for International Affairs, *Eleventh Annual Report* (1969), p. 2.

5. Graduate student associates were established "to permit closer association between graduate students working on their dissertations in fields of interest." Center for International Affairs, Harvard University, Eleventh Annual Report, 1968-69 (1969). p. 39.

6. Ibid., p. 3.

7. Joseph S. Nye, Jr., in an interview with the author, June 6, 2006. Nye remembers that, notwithstanding the violent demands of more radical students, the initiative to create the GSA program came from within the Center itself, with no

pressure from the Faculty of Arts and Sciences.

8. Jorge I. Domínguez, in an interview with the author, June 22, 2006.

9. Ibid.

10. "Radicals to be Welcomed at CFIA," *Harvard Crimson*, October 8, 1968.

11. Ibid.

12. Ibid.

13. "Band Invades, Violently Disrupts Center for International Affairs," *Harvard Crimson*, September 26, 1969.

14. Ibid. See also Letter to the Editor, "SDS Not Involved," *Harvard Crimson*, September 27, 1969.

15. "Mann Gets Year Sentence For Role in CFIA Action," *Harvard Crimson*, December 1, 1969.

16. Harvard Institute for International Development, Project and Research Records, 1960–1980, Subseries I, Box 8, "Weathermen Vs. The Pigs" flyer, in folder Attacks on Center and DAS 1969–70. UAV 462.5010 Harvard University Archives.

17. On the same day that his report on the Center was published by the *Crimson,* Hyland also wrote, "The only reason I wouldn't blow up the Center for International Affairs is that I might get caught. But the desire is there." "In Defense of Terrorism," *Harvard Crimson*, October 22, 1969.

18. "Can We Know the Dancer from the Dance?" *Harvard Crimson*, October 22, 1969.

19. "Vernon Defines the Role of the CFIA," *Harvard Crimson*, October 22, 1969.

20. Ibid. To support this claim, the Center's response highlighted their support for visits by European intellectuals such as Andreas Papandreou (a Greek socialist and future prime minister who criticized American involvement in Greece), Miguel Wionzeck, Helio Jaguaribe, and Celso Furtado (an influential left-wing Brazilian economist).

21. "Hoffmann Criticizes NAC 'Tour,'" *Harvard Crimson*, October 22, 1969.

22. "Token Radicals," *Harvard Crimson*, October 27, 1969. Although the letter is unattributed, Arthur MacEwan (then an assistant professor of economics and research associate of the CFIA who had been involved in strikes against Harvard led by SDS the previous spring) confirms that he wrote this letter in conjunction with Samuel Bowles. His name was included by Vernon in his article to illustrate the broad range of opinions hosted by the Center. See "Depts. Reaffirm Appointments," *Harvard Crimson*, July 29, 1969.

23. "Token Radicals," *Harvard Crimson*, October 27, 1969.

24. Ibid.

25. "The Radical Scholar and the CFIA Policy," *Harvard Crimson*, October 31, 1969.

26. Ibid.

27. Ibid.

28. "In Defense of the CFIA, Social Research and the Center," *Harvard Crimson*, October 31, 1969.

29. Ibid.

30. "The Mail: CFIA Disruption," *Harvard Crimson*, April 14, 1970.

31. "CFIA Demonstration Face Bowie's Charge of Rights Violation" *Harvard Crimson*, April 27, 1970.

32. "150 Students Take Part in CFIA Mill-In," *Harvard Crimson*, May 14, 1970.

33. Center for International Affairs, Leaflets, etc., *Harvard-Radcliffe November Action Committee: The CFIA* [1970?], p. 1. HUF.461.5004 Harvard University Archives.

34. Ibid., pp. 2–3.

35. Ibid., pp. 3–4.

36. Dwight Perkins, in an interview with the author, August 7, 2006.

37. Gustav Papanek, in an interview with the author, May 5, 2006.

38. Arthur MacEwan, in an interview with the author, March 22, 2007.

39. "Underdeveloping the World: Harvard and Imperialism," (n.p., n.d.). p. 1. My thanks to Arthur MacEwan for providing me with a copy of this publication.

40. Ibid., p. 6.

41. Ibid., p. 26.

42. Development Advisory Service, Administrative and Project Records, 1958–1974, Box 1, letter, unaddressed, undated, p. 4–5 and p. 13 in folder DAS Background Notes, Reports, Memos, 1962–69. UAV 462.5095.6 Harvard University Archives.

43. Center for International Affairs, Leaflets, etc., *Harvard-Radcliffe November Action Committee: The CFIA* [1970?], p. 6, HUF.461.5004 Harvard University Archives.

44. Ibid., p. 12.

45. Robert Richardson Bowie, in an interview with the author, September 10, 2005.

46. Arthur MacEwan, in an interview with the author, March 22, 2007.

47. Putnam, Robert D., "Samuel P. Huntington: An Appreciation," *PS: Political Science and Politics* 19, no. 4, (Autumn 1986). p. 842.

48. Huntington, Samuel P., "The Bases of Accommodation," *Foreign Affairs* 46 (July 1968). pp. 642–56.

49. Ibid.

50. Putnam, "Samuel P. Huntington: An Appreciation," p. 843.

51. Ibid.

226

52. "12 Professors Visit Capitol Hill Along Their Road to Damascus," *Harvard Crimson*, May 15, 1970.

53. Thomas C. Schelling, in an interview with the author, September 9, 2005.

54. "I think we have a very unhappy colleague-on-leave tonight," *Harvard Crimson*, May 19, 1970.

55. Ibid. Morton Halperin, who had been a member of the CFIA from 1960 to 1966, had joined Kissinger's National Security Council team in 1969. He resigned prior to this visit to Kissinger in response to the invasion of Cambodia. In his view the protests directed against the CFIA were "absurd." "Kissinger Aide Resigns in Protest to Recent 'Invasion' of Cambodia," *Harvard Crimson*, May 14, 1970. Another CFIA faculty member, Herbert Kelman, would later join his colleague Everett Mendelsohn in petitioning Kissinger to exert his influence to bring peace to Southeast Asia. "Two Professors Circulate Open Letter to Kissinger Asking End to the War," *Harvard Crimson*, March 25, 1971.

56. Center for International Affairs, Leaflets, etc., *Questions and Answers About the Center For International Affairs* [1970], p. 4. HUF.461.5004 Harvard University Archives.

57. Ibid., pp. 13–14.

58. Aiken, Lee, et al., *The Case for Abolishing the CFIA* (Cambridge, MA: Unknown typsetter, December 3, 1970). p. 1.

59. Ibid., pp. 8–14. Gordon, in his capacity as U.S. Ambassador to Brazil, did indeed support the military coup, as did his superiors in Washington.

60. Ibid., p. 26.

61. "Bomb Blasts CFIA Library; Damage Limited, None Hurt," *Harvard Crimson*, October 14, 1970.

62. "CFIA Bombing Damages Little," *Harvard Crimson*, December 7, 1970.

63. Center for International Affairs, Center for International Affairs-Clippings, "Bomb Shatters Center at Harvard," *Boston Herald Traveler*, October 14, 1970. HUF.461.5400 Harvard University Archives.

64. "Professors React to Bomb With Sadness, Not Anger," *Harvard Crimson*, October 15, 1970.

65. Center for International Affairs, Center for International Affairs-Clippings, *Harvard University Library Notes*, No. 101, 29 October 1970, p. 1. HUF.461.5400 Harvard University Archives.

66. "CFIA Bombing Damages Little," *Harvard Crimson*, December 7, 1970.

67. Center for International Affairs, Center for International Affairs-Clippings, *Press Release*, October 14, 1970. HUF.461.5400 Harvard University Archives.

227

68. "The CFIA Incident," *Harvard Crimson*, April 19, 1972. In addition, attempts to disrupt the 1971 visiting committee meeting in March 1971 were foiled by the movement of the meeting to a secret location in Boston. "Bowie's Secrecy Fools Protesters," *Harvard Crimson*, March 6, 1971.

69. Samuel P. Huntington, in an interview with the author, May 19, 2006.

70. Arthur MacEwan, in an interview with the author, March 22, 2007. Despite his sympathy for the protest movement, MacEwan did not support the more egregious excesses of the Left. Reflecting on the period, he notes that "I resent tremendously people like the Weathermen….I think they did a tremendous amount to undermine the Left and undermine the anti-war effort."

71. Center for International Affairs, Center for International Affairs-Clippings, "Protesters Ransack Harvard Center," *Boston Globe*, April 19, 1972. HUF.461.5400 Harvard University Archives.

72. Center for International Affairs, *Twelfth Annual Report* (1970), p. 4.

## Nine The Challenges and Intellectual Trends of the Second Decade

1. Center for International Affairs, *Tenth Annual Report* (1968), p. 1.

2. Ibid., p. 2.

3. Ibid., p. 3.

4. Ibid., p. 3. The Center's move to the new facilities that would become the John F. Kennedy School of Government never materialized.

5. Center for International Affairs, *Eleventh Annual Report* (1969), p. 2.

6. Ibid., p. 4.

7. Center for International Affairs, *Twelfth Annual Report* (1970), p. 2. A 1979 Ford Foundation report later confirmed the fears Bowie and Vernon had articulated a decade before and acknowledged that by the late 1960s funding for programs in international studies had been significantly reduced. As the report observed, "In the late 1960s, university administrators feared that the termination of our funding of international studies would have devastating consequences for their programs," although the foundation concluded that in the final analysis "international studies show a tenacious survival in many places and some administrators may have been too panicky." Magat, Richard, *The Ford Foundation at Work: Philanthropic Choices, Methods, and Styles* (New York: Plenum Press, 1979). p. 105. It is perhaps ironic that this precipitous reduction of funding for international programs at the Ford Foundation took place when its president was McGeorge Bundy, a role he filled from 1966 to 1979. The role Bundy played in the Johnson administration during the Vietnam War and the criticism he attracted may have figured in the

NOTES

decision to distance the Ford Foundation from international studies during his
tenure.

8. Kissinger's faculty position was held in reserve for four years, until in February
   1971 the Government Department voted to close his position and hire a replacement. "Government Dept. Terminates Kissinger's Extended Leave," *Harvard
   Crimson*, February 6, 1973.

9. Center for International Affairs, *Fourteenth Annual Report* (1972), p. 1.

10. Ibid., p. 5.

11. Arthur MacEwan, in an interview with the author, March 22, 2007.

12. Bowie had also served during the Truman administration.

13. Paul Doty, in an interview with the author, August 8, 2006.

14. Center for International Affairs, Harvard University, *Annual Report: 1975–76*
    (1976). p. 7.

15. Ibid.

16. Guagliardo, Mara Allison, *No More Ivory Tower: Harvard's Center for International Affairs
    1958–1991*, (A.B. Thesis, Cambridge, MA: Harvard Universtity, 1996). p. 97.

17. Ibid.

18. Center for International Affairs, *Fifteenth Annual Report* (1973), p. 1.

19. Ibid.

20. Ibid., p. 3.

21. Ibid., p. 4.

22. Lipset, Seymour Martin, *Political Man: The Social Bases of Politics* (Baltimore, MD:
    The Johns Hopkins University Press, 1981).

23. Altbach, Philip G., and Lipset, Seymour Martin, *Students in Revolt* (New York:
    Houghton Mifflin Company, 1969).

24. Center for International Affairs, *1973–74 Annual Report* (1974), p. 15.

25. Center for International Affairs, *Fourteenth Annual Report* (1972), p. 22.

26. Center for International Affairs, *Fifteenth Annual Report* (1973), p. 24. The project
    concluded in 1975 when Lipset left Harvard to become the Caroline S. G.
    Munro Professor of Political Science and Sociology at Stanford University.

27. Nye, Joseph S., *Peace in Parts: Integration and Conflict in Regional Organization*
    (Boston: Little, Brown, 1971).

28. Kaiser, Karl, "Transnational Politics: Toward a Theory of Multinational Politics,"
    *International Organization* XXV, no. 4 (1971). p. 797.

29. Kaiser, Karl, "Transnational Relations as a Threat to the Democratic Process,"
    *International Organization* XXV, no. 3 (1971). p. 706. This article, based on an
    earlier essay, was featured in an *IO* volume edited by Nye and Keohane and dedi-
    cated to transnational relations.

229

30. Center for International Affairs, *Twelfth Annual Report* (1970), p. 34.

31. Keohane, Robert O., and Nye, Joseph S., eds., *Transnational Relations and World Politics* (Cambridge, MA: Harvard University Press, 1973).

32. Joseph S. Nye, Jr., in an interview with the author, June 7, 2006.

33. Keohane and Nye, eds., *Transnational Relations and World Politics*, p. xii.

34. Ibid., pp. 379–80.

35. Center for International Affairs, *Fourteenth Annual Report* (1972), pp. 23–25.

36. Center for International Affairs, *Fifteenth Annual Report* (1973), p. 25.

37. Center for International Affairs, *1973–74 Annual Report* (1974), p. 11.

38. Ibid., pp. 11–12.

39. Center for International Affairs, Harvard University, *1974–75 Annual Report* (1975). p. 10.

40. Crozier, Michel J., Huntington, Samuel P. and Watanuki, Joji, *The Crisis of Democracy: Report on the Governability of Democracies to the Trilateral Commission* (New York: New York University Press, 1975). p. 9.

41. Keohane, Robert O. and Nye, Joseph S., *Power and Interdependence: World Politics in Transition* (Boston, MA: Little, Brown and Company, 1977). p. 5.

42. Ibid., pp. 23–25.

43. Center for International Affairs, *1975–76 Annual Report* (1976), p. 12.

44. Program for Science and International Affairs, Harvard University, *First Annual Report, 1973–74* (1974). p. 2.

45. Program for Science and International Affairs, Harvard University, *Fourth Annual Report, 1976–77* (1977). p. 2.

46. Center for Science and International Affairs, Harvard University, *1978–1979 Annual Report* (1979). p. 1.

47. Raymond Vernon resigned as Center Director in January 1978, and in the absence of his replacement, Samuel Huntington, Brown facilitated the transition.

48. Center for International Affairs, Harvard University, *Annual Report: 1977–78* (1978). p. 6.

49. Ibid., pp. 8–9.

50. Ibid., p. 9.

51. Center for International Affairs, Harvard University, *Annual Report: 1976–77* (1977). p. 15.

52. This endeavor culminated in the Program on International Conflict Analysis and Resolution (PICAR), which played a remarkable role in facilitating dialogue among Israelis and Palestinians, some of whom would later be instrumental in brokering the 1993 Oslo Accords. Additional projects were undertaken in Sri Lanka, Northern Ireland, Colombia, and Cyprus.

53. Klitgaard, Robert E., *Harvard International: A Report on Some International Activities at the University*, Summer 1979 May 26, p. 5. HUA 979.45 Harvard University Archives.

54. Ibid., p. 7.

55. Ibid.

56. Ibid., p. 25.

57. Ibid., p. 26.

58. Ibid., p. 152.

59. Ibid., p. 153.

60. Ibid., pp. 153–54.

61. Ibid., p. 100.

62. Ibid.

63. Ibid., p. 154.

64. Ibid., p. 145.

65. Ibid., p. 146.

66. Ibid., pp. 103–04.

67. Ibid., p. 156.

68. Ibid., p. 157.

69. Ibid., pp. 157–58.

70. Ibid., p. 159.

71. Ibid.

72. Ibid.

73. Ibid., p. 161.

74. Ibid., p. 163.

75. The Center for International Affairs, Harvard University, *Three Decades: A Report on the Past and Future Development of the Center for International Affairs, 1958–1980* (1980). p. 1.

76. Ibid., p. 7.

77. Ibid., p. 45.

78. Ibid., p. 38.

79. Ibid., pp. 37–40.

80. Ibid., p. 54.

81. Center for International Affairs, Harvard University, *Biennial Report: 1980–82* (1982). p. 10. These two "annexes" were located at 61 Kirkland Street and 9 Kirkland Place.

82. Center for International Affairs, Report from Benjamin Brown to Derek Bok, August 31, 1978, p. 2, CFIA Director Files, Samuel Huntington, 1976–1998, Box 1, Harvard University Depository.

83. Center for International Affairs, *Biennial Report* (1982), p. 10.

84. Ibid., p. 107, and Center for International Affairs, *The First Five Years* (1963), p. 46.

85. Center for International Affairs, Harvard University, *Annual Report: 1983–84* (1984).

86. Center for International Affairs, Report from Benjamin Brown to Derek Bok, August 31, 1978, p. 9, CFIA Director Files, Samuel Huntington, 1976–1998, Box 1, Harvard University Depository.

87. Ibid., pp. 10–11.

88. Ibid., p. 13.

# Bibliography

## Unpublished Material

### Harvard University Archives

Center for International Affairs, CFIA Joint Arms Control Seminar, UAV.462.1142.3.

Center for International Affairs, CFIA Joint Arms Control Seminar, UAV.462.1142.5.

Center for International Affairs, Center for International Affairs–Clippings, HUF.461.5400.

Center for International Affairs, Development Advisory Service, Correspondence and Papers, 1969–1970, UAV 462.1117.5.

Center for International Affairs, Leaflets, etc., HUF.461.5004.

Center for International Affairs, *The Program of the Center for International Affairs* 1958, HUF.461.5158.

Committee on International and Regional Studies, Minutes 1946, UAIII.10.202.A.

Center for International Affairs, *The Program of the Center for International Affairs* Revised Draft [1958?].

Committee on International and Regional Studies, Correspondence and Records, 1948–1955, UA III.10.202.10.

Development Advisory Service, Administrative and Project Records, 1958–1974, UAV 462.5095.6.

Faculty of Arts and Sciences Dean, Letters, 1957–58, UAIII.5.55.26.

Faculty Committee on Behavioral Sciences, Correspondence and Memoranda, UAI.10.545.7.

John King Fairbank Papers.

Harvard Institute for International Development, Project and Research Records, 1960–1980, UAV 462.5010.

Harvard University, Faculty of Arts and Sciences, Report on International Studies at Harvard Submitted to the Ford Foundation, UAIII 29.60.

Klitgaard, Robert E., *Harvard International: A Report on Some International Activities at the University*, Summer 1979 May 26, HUA 979.45.

### Harvard University Depository

Center for International Affairs History Pre–1970, Harvard University Depository.

Center for International Affairs, CFIA Director Files, Samuel Huntington, 1976–1998.

## MIT Institute Archives and Special Collections

Papers of Bernard Taub Feld, 1943–1990, MC 167.

Papers of Max Millikan, MC 188.

## John F. Kennedy Presidential Library

Roger Hilsman Papers.

Kissinger Series, National Security Files, Papers of President Kennedy.

McGeorge Bundy Correspondence, National Security Files,
    Papers of President Kennedy.

Papers of Arthur M. Schlesinger, Jr.

James C. Thomson Papers.

## Interviews and Correspondence

Robert Richardson Bowie, September 10, 2005.

Jorge I. Domínguez, June 22, 2006.

Paul Doty, August 8, 2006.

John Kenneth Galbraith, April 19, 2003.

Morton H. Halperin, March 19, 2006.

Samuel P. Huntington, May 19, 2006.

Karl Kaiser, April 19, 2006.

Carl Kaysen, March 15, 2006.

Arthur MacEwan, March 22, 2007.

Joseph S. Nye, Jr., June 7, 2006.

Gustav Papanek, May 5, 2006.

Dwight Perkins, August 7, 2006.

Thomas C. Schelling, September 9, 2005.

Zbigniew Brzezinski, email correspondence, May 1, 2003.

Stanley Hoffmann, email correspondence, September 19, 2006.

Alex Inkeles, email correspondence, June 21, 2006.

## Theses and Dissertations

Gilboa, Eytan, "The Scholar and the Foreign Policy-Maker in the United States," Unpublished Ph.D. Dissertation, Harvard University, Cambridge, MA, May 1974. Harvard University Archives.

Guagliardo, Mara Allison, "No More Ivory Tower: Harvard's Center for International Affairs 1958–1991," A.B. Thesis, Cambridge, MA: Harvard University, 1996.

## Public Documents

External Research Staff, U.S. Department of State, *The Scholar and the Policy Maker: A Series of Talks Given at the Plenary Session of the Association for Asian Studies* (Washington, D.C.: U.S. Department of State, 1964).

U.S. Congress, Senate Committee on Foreign Relations, *United States Foreign Policy: Ideology and Foreign Affairs (The Principal Ideological Conflicts, Variations Thereon, Their Manifestations, and Their Present and Potential Impact on the Foreign Policy of the United States)* (Washington, D.C.: U.S. Government Printing Office, 1960).

———. *Hearings Before the Committee on Foreign Relations on the Formulation and Administration of United States Foreign Policy, 87th Congress, First Session, Part 2* (Washington, D.C.: U.S. Government Printing Office, 1961).

U.S. Congress, Senate Committee on Government Operations, Subcommittee on Government Research, *Federal Support of International Social Research and Behavioral Research* (Washington, D.C.: U.S. Government Printing Office, 1967).

U.S. Congress, House Committee on Foreign Affairs, Subcommittee on International Organizations and Movements, *Behavioral Sciences and the National Security; Part IX, Winning the Cold War: The U.S. Ideological Offensive* (Washington, D.C.: U.S. Government Printing Office, 1965).

## Newspapers

*Harvard Crimson*

*New York Times*

## Books

Altbach, Philip G., and Seymour Martin Lipset, *Students in Revolt* (New York: Houghton Mifflin Company, 1969).

*The Behavioral Sciences at Harvard: Report by a Faculty Committee, June 1954* (Cambridge, MA: Harvard University, 1954).

Berman, Edward H., *The Influence of the Carnegie, Ford, and Rockefeller Foundations on American Foreign Policy: The Ideology of Philanthropy* (Albany, NY: State University of New York Press, 1983).

Blackmer, Donald L.M., *The MIT Center for International Studies: The Founding Years, 1951–1969* (Cambridge, MA: MIT Center for International Studies, 2002).

Brennan, Donald G., ed., *Arms Control, Disarmament, and National Security* (New York: George Braziller, 1961).

Brzezinski, Zbigniew K., *The Soviet Bloc: Unity and Conflict* (Cambridge, MA: Harvard University Press, 1960).

Cardozier, V.R., *Colleges and Universities in World War II* (Westport, CT: Praeger, 1993).

Chomsky, Noam, *American Power and the New Mandarins* (New York: New Press, 2002).

*Communist China 1955–1959: Policy Documents with Analysis* (Cambridge, MA: Harvard University Press, 1962).

Crozier, Michel J., Samuel P. Huntington, and Joji Watanuki, *The Crisis of Democracy: Report on the Governability of Democracies to the Trilateral Commission* (New York: New York University Press, 1975).

Engerman, David C. et al., eds., *Modernization, Development, and the Global Cold War* (Amherst and Boston: University of Massachusetts Press, 2003).

Erler, Fritz, *Democracy in Germany* (Cambridge, MA: Harvard University Press, 1965).

Ernst, John, *Forging a Fateful Alliance: Michigan State University and the Vietnam War* (East Lansing, MI: Michigan State University Press, 1998).

Gelfand, Lawrence E., *The Inquiry: American Preparations for Peace, 1917–1919* (New Haven, CT: Yale University Press, 1963).

Gilman, Nils, *Mandarins of the Future: Modernization Theory in Cold War America* (Baltimore, MD: Johns Hopkins University Press, 2003).

Hoffmann, Stanley, et al., *In Search of France* (Cambridge, MA: Harvard University Press, 1963).

Horowitz, Irving Louis, ed., *The Rise and Fall of Project Camelot: Studies in the Relationship between Social Science and Practical Politics* (Cambridge, MA: The MIT Press, 1967)

Huntington, Samuel P., *Political Order in Changing Societies* (New Haven, CT: Yale University Press, 1968).

Huntington, Samuel P., and Joseph S. Nye, eds., *Global Dilemmas* (Lanham, MD: University Press of America and the Center for International Affairs, 1985).

Isaacson, Walter, *Kissinger: A Biography* (New York: Simon & Schuster, 1992).

Inkeles, Alex, and David H. Smith, *Becoming Modern: Individual Change in Six Developing Countries* (Cambridge, MA: Harvard University Press, 1974).

Keohane, Robert O., and Joseph S. Nye, eds., *Transnational Relations and World Politics* (Cambridge, MA: Harvard University Press, 1973).

———. *Power and Interdependence: World Politics in Transition* (Boston: Little, Brown, 1977).

Kissinger, Henry A., *Nuclear Weapons and Foreign Policy* (New York: Harper & Bros. for the Council on Foreign Relations, 1957).

———. *The Necessity for Choice: Prospects of American Foreign Policy* (London: Chatto and Windus, 1960).

Knock, Thomas J., *To End All Wars: Woodrow Wilson and the Quest for a New World Order* (Princeton, NJ: Princeton University Press, 1995).

Langer, William L., *In and Out of the Ivory Tower: The Autobiography of William L. Langer* (New York: Neale Watson Academic Publications, Inc., 1977).

236

Latham, Michael E., *Modernization as Ideology: American Social Science and "Nation Building" in the Kennedy Era* (Chapel Hill: The University of North Carolina Press, 2000).

Levine, Robert, *Still the Arms Debate* (Brookfield, VT: Dartmouth Publishing Company, 1990).

Lipset, Seymour Martin, *Political Man: The Social Bases of Politics* (Baltimore, MD: Johns Hopkins University Press, 1981).

Lyons, Gene, *The Uneasy Partnership: Social Science Research and the Federal Government in the Twentieth Century* (New York: Russell Sage Foundation, 1969).

Lyons, Gene, ed., *The Role of Ideas in American Foreign Policy* (Hanover, NH: University Press of New England, 1971).

Magat, Richard, *The Ford Foundation at Work: Philanthropic Choices, Methods, and Styles* (New York: Plenum Press, 1979).

Mason, Edward S., *Foreign Aid and Foreign Policy* (New York: Harper & Row, 1964).

————. *The Harvard Institute for International Development and its Antecedents* (University Press of America, 1986).

McCaughey, Robert A., *International Studies and Academic Enterprise: A Chapter in the Enclosure of American Learning* (New York: Columbia University Press, 1984).

Morris, Charles R., *Iron Destinies, Lost Opportunities: The Arms Race Between the U.S.A. and the U.S.S.R., 1945–1987* (New York: Harper & Row, 1960).

Newhouse, John, *Cold Dawn: The Story of SALT* (Washington, D.C.: Pergamon-Brassey's, 1989).

Nye, Joseph S., *Peace in Parts: Integration and Conflict in Regional Organization* (Boston: Little, Brown, 1971).

Rieff, Philip, ed., *On Intellectuals: Theoretical Studies, Case Studies* (Garden City, NY: Doubleday and Company, Inc., 1969).

Rosenau, James N., *International Studies and the Social Sciences: Problems, Priorities and Prospects in the United States* (Beverly Hills, CA: Sage Publications, 1973).

Schelling, Thomas C., and Morton H. Halperin, *Strategy and Arms Control* (New York: The Twentieth Century Fund, 1961).

Scigliano, Robert, and Guy H. Fox, *Technical Assistance in Vietnam: The Michigan State University Experience* (New York: Frederick A. Praeger Publishers, 1965).

Seaborg, Glenn T., with Benjamin S. Loeb, *Stemming the Tide: Arms Control in the Johnson Years* (Lexington, MA: Lexington Books, 1987).

Sims, Jennifer E., *Icarus Restrained: An Intellectual History of Nuclear Arms Control, 1945–1960* (Boulder, CO: Westview Press, Inc., 1990).

Vernon, Raymond, *Sovereignty at Bay: The Multinational Spread of U.S. Enterprises* (New York: Basic Books, Inc., 1971).

237

## Articles, Pamphlets, and Periodicals

Aiken, Lee, et al., *The Case for Abolishing the CFIA* (Cambridge, MA: Unknown typsetter, December 3, 1970).

Bowie, Robert R., "The North Atlantic Nations: Tasks for the 1960s: A Report to the Secretary of State, August 1960 by Robert R. Bowie," in *Nuclear History Program: Occasional Paper* 7, (College Park, MD: Center for International Security Studies at Maryland School of Public Affairs, University of Maryland, 1991).

Center for International Affairs, Harvard University, *Annual Reports*, 1960–83

*Daedalus* ("Special Issue: Arms Control") 89, no. 4 (Fall 1960).

Huntington, Samuel P., "The Bases of Accommodation," *Foreign Affairs* 46 (July 1968).

————.Center for International Affairs, Harvard University, *Three Decades: A Report on the Past and Future Development of the Center for International Affairs, 1958–1980* (1980).

Leuchtenburg, William E., "The Historian and the Public Realm," *The American Historical Review* 97, no. 1 (February 1992).

Kaiser, Karl, "Transnational Relations as a Threat to the Democratic Process," *International Organization* XXV, no. 3 (1971).

————. "Transnational Politics: Toward a Theory of Multinational Politics," *International Organization* XXV, no. 4 (1971).

McFadzean, Andrew, "The Bigger Picture: Biography and/or History? Robert Bowie," *Australasian Journal of American Studies* 22, no. 2 (December 2003).

Morgenthau, Hans, Review of *Nuclear Weapons and Foreign Policy*, by Henry A. Kissinger. *The American Political Science Review* 52, no. 3 (September 1958).

Program for Science and International Affairs, Harvard University, *Annual Reports*, 1977–1979.

Putnam, Robert D., "Samuel P. Huntington: An Appreciation," *PS: Political Science and Politics* 19, no. 4, (Autumn 1986).

*Report of the President of Harvard College and Reports of Departments, 1957–1958*, Official Register of Harvard University, Volume LVI, No. 22, August 31, 1959.

*Report of the President of Harvard College and Reports of Departments, 1960–1961*, Official Register of Harvard University, Volume LIX, No. 26, August 31, 1962.

Russian Research Center, Harvard University, *Five Year Report and Current Projects* (May, 1953).

Schelling, Thomas C., "What Went Wrong with Arms Control?" *Foreign Affairs*, 64 (Winter 1985/86).

*Underdeveloping the World: Harvard and Imperialism* (n.p., n.d.).

# Index

academia-government relationship, 3, 4, 121–26

ACDA. *See* Arms Control and Disarmament Agency, U.S. (ACDA)

Adenauer, Konrad, 131

Africa, 49, 97–98, 118

Agency for International Development, U.S. (USAID), 93, 101, 107, 158, 159

Aćimović, Ljubivoje, 50

Almeida, Candido Mendes de, 99

Altbach, Philip G., 163

antiballistic missile systems, 86

Anti-Ballistic Missile Treaty, 89

apartheid, 171

Arab-Israeli conflict, 171–72

Argentina, 103

arms control, 35, 42, 65–90, 169

"Cambridge Approach," 79–87

and Eisenhower adminstration, 210

emerging principles, 76–78

as legitimate field of study, 72

*Arms Control, Disarmament, and National Security,* 77

Arms Control and Disarmament Agency, U.S. (ACDA), 68, 85, 159

Armstrong, Hamilton Fish, 126

Asia, 118

defense and nuclear weapons in, 68–69

research on, 98

Association for Asian Studies, 123, 124

Atlantic Community, 59–60

relations with developing world, 119

research projects, 24

"Atoms for Peace" speech, 210

Bano, Begum Gulzar, 50

Bator, Francis M., 147

Bauer, Walter, 198

*Becoming Modern: Individual Change in Six Developing Countries,* 97

behavioral sciences

assessing Harvard's strengths, 10

at Harvard in 1954, 5–7

research, 132

*Behavioral Sciences at Harvard, The,* 5, 12

Belfer Center for Science and International Affairs, 87

Bell, Daniel, 164

Bell, David, 112

*Berkeley Student Revolt, The,* 163

Berman, Edward H., 4

Bloomfield, Lincoln, 80, 81

Bloomfield, Richard, 48

bombing, 150–51

Bowie, Robert

and arms control, 73

and Atlantic community, 59, 119–20

atmosphere of CFIA, 42

as CFIA founding director, 14–18, 205

and CFIA policy formulation, 115–16

as consultant to State Department, 116

and Development Advisory Service, 103

and Development Research Group, 94

and Fellows Program, 20–23, 38, 46–48

and foreign policy research, 117

and France research, 56

government service, 14–15, 195

Harvard-MIT Joint Arms Control Seminar, 80

and Kennedy administration, 126

meets with Eisenhower, 121

and military strategy, 66

outline of areas for research, 24–26

and policy formulation, 116

recruitment of early faculty, 34–35

reflection on CFIA, 1958–1964, 59

reflection on first two years of CFIA, 41

resigns as director, 159–60

and student protests, 153

and teaching at CFIA, 27

understanding of role and function of CFIA, 19–39

and work on Faculty Advisory Committee, 61

Bowie Report, 119–21

Bowles, Samuel, 225

Bracher, Karl Dietrich, 57

Brazil, 99

Brennan, Donald G., 72, 77

Brewster, Kingman, Jr., 198

Brown, Benjamin H., 138–39, 160

government service, 195

reflects on twentieth anniversary, 170–71

report to President Bok in 1978, 181

242